The Dog Lover's Companion to The Bay Area

5TH EDITION

Maria Goodavage

AVALON
TRAVEL

THE DOG LOVER'S COMPANION TO THE BAY AREA
THE INSIDE SCOOP ON WHERE TO TAKE YOUR DOG

Published by
Avalon Travel Publishing
1400 65th Street, Suite 250
Emeryville, CA 94608, USA

Avalon Travel Publishing
An Imprint of
AVALON Avalon Publishing Group, Inc.

Printing History
1st edition—1996
5th edition—April 2005
5 4 3 2 1

ISBN: 1-56691-694-1
ISSN: 1078-8921

Editor and Series Manager: Kathryn Ettinger
Acquisitions Editor: Rebecca K. Browning
Copy Editor: Karen Gaynor Bleske
Designer: Jacob Goolkasian
Graphics Coordinator: Tabitha Lahr
Production Coordinator: Tabitha Lahr
Map Editor: Kevin Anglin
Cartographers: Mike Morgenfeld, Kat Kalamaras
Indexer: Greg Jewett

Cover and Interior Illustrations by Phil Frank

Printed in the United States by Malloy

ABOUT THE AUTHOR

© Laura Altair

Maria Goodavage and Jake the Yellow-Lab-Sort-of-Dog have traveled throughout the Bay Area to check out some of the most dog-friendly parks, beaches, lodgings, and restaurants in the world. As part of their research, they've ridden on ferries, cable cars, and steam trains. They've visited drive-in movies, kitschy tourist attractions, and dog-friendly wineries. They've eaten at restaurants where dogs are treated almost like people (except they never get the bill). They've stayed at the best hotels, the worst motels, and everything in between. Jake's favorite saying: "You're not really gonna leave the house without me, are ya?" (This is usually accompanied by all his extra folds of neck skin drooping forward into his face, his floppy ears hanging especially low, his tail sagging dejectedly, and his big brown eyes looking remarkably tearful.)

Since Jake is a dog without a driver's license (his furry feet don't reach the pedals), he relies on Maria, former longtime *USA Today* correspondent, to be his chauffeur. Maria is well qualified. She started chauffeuring dogs in 1989, when her intrepid Airedale, Joe, joined her during some of her travels for the newspaper. Joe and Maria sniffed out enough dog-friendly places that they came out with their first book, *The Dog Lover's Companion to the Bay Area,* shortly thereafter. *The Dog Lover's Companion to California* was born next. (Each book is now in its fifth edition!)

After 13 years of traveling with Maria, Joe recently left for Dog Heaven, where all the cats are slow and no one tells you not to eat horse manure. Jake says he's proud to be following in Joe's pawsteps.

Jake lives near the beach in San Francisco with Maria, her husband, and their daughter.

To get more information or offer a suggestion about dog-friendly travel in California, visit Maria's website, www.caldogtravel.com.

CONTENTS

BAY AREA COUNTIES

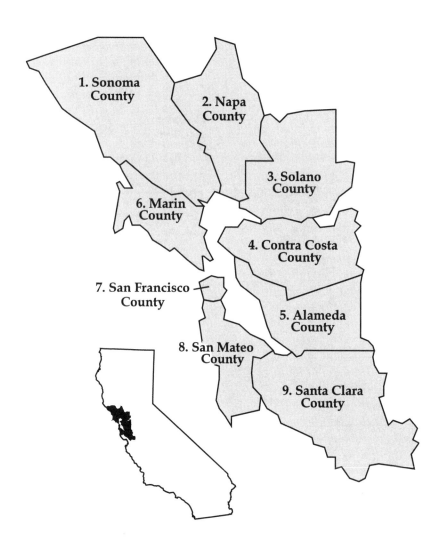

1. Sonoma County
2. Napa County
3. Solano County
4. Contra Costa County
5. Alameda County
6. Marin County
7. San Francisco County
8. San Mateo County
9. Santa Clara County

MAPS

Introduction

Now, Charley is a mind-reading dog. There have been many trips in his lifetime, and often he has to be left at home. He knows we are going long before the suitcases come out, and he paces and worries and whines and goes into a state of mild hysteria, old as he is.

John Steinbeck, *Travels with Charley*

There was a time when dogs could go just about anywhere they pleased. Well-dressed dogs with embarrassing names attended afternoon teas, while their less-kempt counterparts sauntered into saloons without anyone's blinking a bloodshot eye.

No one thought it strange to see a pug-nosed little snoochum-woochums of a dog snuggled on his mistress's lap on a long train journey. Equally accepted were dogs prancing through fine hotels, dogs at dining establishments, and dogs in almost any park they cared to visit.

But then there came a time (a period perhaps best referred to as the Doggy Dark Ages) when dogs came to be seen as beasts not fit for hotels, restaurants, or even many parks. The world was getting more crowded, patience growing thinner, there was only so much room, and dangit—four-legged varmints weren't going to be sharing it. They were just *dogs* after all—animals who eat from bowls on the floor and lick their heinies at unfortunate moments. Dogs were for the house, the backyard, sidewalks (with canines being "curbed"), and some tolerant parks. So we got used to leaving our dogs behind when we took off for an afternoon, or for a road trip. It hurt, oh, how it hurt, but what could you do?

Many of us know that guilt too well. The guilt that stabs at you as you push your dog's struggling body back inside the house and tug the door shut can be so painful that sometimes you just can't look back. Even a trip to the grocery store can become a heart-wrenching tale of woe. The most recent survey by the American Animal Hospital Association shows that the vast majority of us feel guilty when leaving pets at home. Thirty-nine percent of pet people call to talk to their pets when they're away. I've tried that, but it always made me feel even worse.

Joe, the Airedale terrier who inspired not only this book but the entire *Dog Lover's Companion* series, was born with an unparalleled gift for knowing how to make people feel guilty—and not your ordinary, run-of-the-mill guilt where you smart for a couple of hours after seeing your dog's moping eyes follow your car as you speed away. It's that deep-in-the-gut-for-days guilt, where the sight of that pouting snout, those drooping ears, and that tail lowered to half-mast hangs with you until you return home.

John Steinbeck's blue poodle, Charley, was a master of powerful pleas that were carefully designed to allow him to accompany his people on trips. Eventually, his hard work paid off and he won himself a seat in Steinbeck's brand-new truck/house on their epic journey across America. They sought and found the heart of this country in their adventures across 34 states.

Joe's guilt-inducing expertise won him a spot in my rusty, beat-up, hiccupping pickup truck in our sporadic little journeys around the Bay Area, and later, California. We sought and found thousands of dog-friendly places in our adventures and misadventures.

Joe and I were frequently joined by two other experts in the field of rating parks and sniffing out good dog attractions. Nisha, our old-lady springer spaniel, insisted on standing in the back of the truck, under the camper top, madly wagging her tail for hours on end as we drove and drove and drove. She was a real asset to have around when it came to checking out beaches, lakes, rivers, and ponds—any area with water. (Joe hated to get his paws wet, so he couldn't be impartial in his rating of watery attractions.)

Bill, a big, lovable galoot of a dog, was my other original canine researcher. I found him partway through my travels. He was trembling in the middle of a Northern California road, with a big chain tight around his neck. He'd evidently broken loose, because the last link of the thick chain was mauled. I came to find out that his owner beat him regularly. Bill went back to San Francisco with me that afternoon. During the months when I was looking for the perfect home for him (oh, and did he ever get the perfect home!), he became one of the friendliest, most outgoing dogs I've ever had the pleasure to meet. His presence during my journeys was invaluable. He lifted my spirits when I was tired, and his 85 pounds of muscle kept away bad spirits when we visited questionable areas.

Time moves on. All journeys have to end someday. Bill is the only remaining dog from the original crew. Gregarious, loveable Nisha departed for Dog Heaven years ago. There, she can chew rocks and chase sticks to her heart's content.

And Joe, my most wonderful furry friend and constant traveling buddy for 13 years, joined her after the last edition of this book came out. He is dearly missed, but his legacy—that of helping other dogs lead better lives by sniffing out places they're allowed to go with their humans—lives on. I'm pretty sure that now he's chasing—and finally catching—cats (in Dog Heaven, in case you didn't know, all cats are slow), and eating all the horse manure he wants. And he *always* gets to go for rides in the car.

Before I choke up, I'd like to introduce you to a dog you'll be seeing plenty of throughout this book. His name is Jake, and we figure he's about 97 percent yellow Lab, leaving 3 percent for hound or Great Dane or some other big thing with short fur. When he was about six months old, we were asked to foster him for a week. That was well over a year ago. (We hear this happens when you foster a dog.)

Jake now weighs in at Bill's weight—85 pounds—and is one of the sweetest, most noodley dogs I've ever met. When we're home, he can usually be found reposing on the couch (despite our best attempts to keep him off it, the couch is now referred to as "Jake's couch"), jowls sprawled over the windowsill (which is half chewed away from his younger days, a very attractive sight), big brown eyes staring off into the distance as if longing for another road trip.

We've had some terrific trips together so far. Since traveling with a giant furry termite is a bad idea, I waited until his penchant for chewing furniture, windowsills, and floorboards had disappeared. Then we hit the road, enjoying dog-friendly lodgings, restaurants, and parks around the Bay Area.

As a water dog, he's wonderful at checking out liquidy attractions, from wading pools at dog parks to ponds, lakes, and beaches. Fortunately, I never have to worry about him going after ducks, per his breed's instinct. For some reason, when swimming ducks see him dogpaddling, they make a beeline right for him. This gives Jake the creeps, and he swims away, with the ducks fast on his tail. It's a sight that would make a duck hunter cry.

On a similar note, he's always glad when we visit a dog park that has a separate section for small dogs. Tiny dogs become giants with Jake, yapping a couple of times while giving him the chase. He tucks his tail between his legs and runs away, glancing nervously behind him to make sure he's escaped before relaxing enough to be his big doggy self again.

You'll be meeting Jake throughout this edition, and Joe is still a significant part of the book, too. I think you'll find them, together with Nisha and Bill, excellent representatives of the myriad dogs in the Bay Area.

Jake and I are happy to announce that the fifth edition of the book finds the Doggy Dark Ages further behind us than ever. Dog travel is scorching hot. Everyone's getting in on it. For many reasons, dogs have become a real part of our families, and businesses have seen the golden opportunities.

Pet-travel agencies are starting to pop up. A pet-centered airline that transports dogs alongside their humans (Companion Air; www.companionair .com) is getting off the ground, with hopes business will soon take off. Iams pet food is producing handy little "Travel Meals" for "pets on the run" (www .travelmeals.com). Taxis that cater to pets and their people (such as San Diego's popular PETCAB Pet Taxi Service; www.petcabtaxi.com) are also starting to appear.

The hospitality industry, which has been lagging for a few years, is opening doors to dogs as never before. Motel 6, the first chain to allow dogs, has eliminated its policy of allowing only small dogs, and now most of its motel managers give the thumbs-up to any size good dog. Many upscale chains have taken the dog-friendly policy a step further. Loews has its "Loews Loves Pets" program. Kimpton hotels all welcome dogs and most provide them some sort of VIP package. And most recently, Starwood Hotels, one of the leading hotel companies in the world, started its Starwood LTD (Love That Dog) program in its Sheraton, Westin, and W hotels in the United States and Canada.

"Dog owners are a market niche that's been underserved by the travel industry," a Starwood press release announced. And Barry Sternlicht, Starwood's chairman and CEO, has lofty goals for Starwood. "We intend to become the most dog-friendly hotel company in the land, and not just allow dogs to stay, but actually pamper and spoil them," says Barry, who has two dogs of his own.

Many other lodgings, from the humblest cabins to the most regal luxury suites and chichi vacation rentals, are now allowing dog guests. "If we have a house that doesn't permit dogs, they're just not going to do very well," a Sonoma County vacation rental agent told me.

The vacation industry is truly going to the dogs. And the Bay Area is rife with dog-friendly destinations.

We've tried to find the very best of everything you can do with your dog in the Bay Area, so you'll never again have to face the prospect of shutting the door on your dog's nose. This book is crammed to the breaking point with descriptions of hundreds of dog-friendly parks, restaurants with outdoor tables, and lodgings. The book also describes dozens of unusual adventures you and your dog can share. You can ride on steam trains, ferries, and surreys. You can sip chardonnay at a winery where dogs are adored, attend a San Francisco Giants game, march in pet parades, and shop at high-fashion stores.

The fifth edition of this book is the most fun-packed yet. We've added countless new places to go with your dog, many of them discovered through readers whose dogs insist on writing to tell us about their favorite new park, cool eatery, or pooch-loving hotel. We're so grateful to these dogs that, whenever possible, we acknowledge them under the new listing. (See the imprint page for easy ways to get in touch with us with your hot dog tips. Or you can go to my website, www.caldogtravel.com, and click on the "contact" button.)

Bay Area dogs are lucky dogs indeed: Since the fourth edition, a couple of dozen more dog parks have come to life! Dog parks are a huge trend, one that shows no signs of slowing. It doesn't make up for the great state beaches that have banned dogs since the last edition (yes, it's true—that snowy plover is at it again, keeping dogs leashed at our once leash-free federally run beaches and entirely off certain state beaches), but these parks do put a wag in many a dog's tail.

The dog parks run the gamut from very basic (often just bones city governments provided to appease their dog-bearing constituents) to gorgeous, perfectly manicured, custom-designed doggy playgrounds. The prize for best-designed dog park goes to the new $300,000 Drigon Dog Park in Union City. (See the Union City section in the Alameda County chapter.) You've got to see it to believe it. It's worth the trip.

A traveling dog's life has changed significantly from the days when John Steinbeck and Charley traversed the country together. Dogs have less freedom, but ironically, more choices.

And you can pretty much rest assured that no one will look askance when he or she realizes that your traveling companion is none other than the furry beast at your side. "Used to be odd when someone wanted a room to stay in with their dog," says a rural innkeeper. "Now it doesn't even make us blink."

The Paws Scale

At some point, we've got to face the facts: Humans and dogs have different tastes. We like eating oranges and smelling lilacs and covering our bodies with soft clothes. They like eating roadkill and smelling each other's unmentionables and covering their bodies with horse manure.

The parks, beaches, and recreation areas in this book are rated with a dog in mind. Maybe your favorite park has lush gardens, a duck pond, a few acres of perfectly manicured lawns, and sweeping views of a nearby skyline. But unless your dog can run leash-free, swim in the pond, and roll in the grass, that park doesn't deserve a very high rating.

The very lowest rating you'll come across in this book is the fire hydrant symbol 🔥. This means the park is merely "worth a squat." Visit one of these parks only if your dog just can't hold it any longer. These parks have virtually no other redeeming qualities for canines.

Beyond that, the paws scale starts at one paw 🐾 and goes up to four paws 🐾🐾🐾🐾. A one-paw park isn't a dog's idea of a great time. Maybe it's a tiny park with few trees and too many kids running around. Or perhaps it's a magnificent-for-people park that bans dogs from every inch of land except paved roads and a few campsites. Four-paw parks, on the other hand, are places your dog will drag you to visit. Some of these areas come as close to dog heaven as you can imagine. Many have lakes for swimming or zillions of acres for hiking. Some are small, fenced-in areas where leash-free dogs can tear around without danger of running into the road.

This book is *not* a comprehensive guide to all of the parks in the Bay Area. If I included every single park, it would be ridiculously unportable. Instead, I tried to find the best, largest, and most convenient parks—and especially parks that allow dogs off leash. Some counties have so many wonderful parks that I had to make some tough choices in deciding which to include and which to leave out. Other counties have such a limited supply of parks that, for the sake of dogs living and visiting there, I ended up listing parks that wouldn't otherwise be worth mentioning.

If you're an astute, long-time reader of these books, you may notice some changes in paw ratings in this edition. Because of the big increase in the number of dog parks, I've had to revise the criteria for their paws scale. Initially, almost anything off-leash qualified for four paws—or three at the least. But with so many parks now, I have the luxury of truly looking at their amenities and sizes and not just their leash-free nature. In addition, some beaches have had paw changes. That's because so many beaches now ban dogs that Jake and I consider most dog-friendly beaches worthy of three or four paws. A final note: There are no longer half-paw ratings as in past editions.

I've provided specific directions to the major parks and parks near highways. Other parks are listed by their cross streets. I highly recommend checking an Internet map site such as Mapquest.com or picking up detailed street maps from the AAA—California State Automobile Association (maps are free for members)—before you and your dog set out on your adventures.

He, She, It

In this book, whether neutered, spayed, or au naturel, dogs are never referred to as "it." They are either "he" or "she." I alternate pronouns so no dog reading this book will feel left out.

To Leash or Not to Leash...

This is not a question that plagues dogs' minds. Ask just about any normal, red-blooded American dog whether she'd prefer to visit a park and be on leash or off, and she'll say, "Arf!" No question about it, most dogs would give their canine teeth to frolic about without a cumbersome leash.

Whenever you see the running dog symbol 🐕 in this book, you'll know that under certain circumstances, your dog can run around in leash-free bliss. Fortunately, the Bay Area is home to dozens of such parks. The rest of the parks demand leashes. I wish I could write about the parks where dogs get away with being scofflaws. Unfortunately, those would be the first parks the animal control patrols would hit. I don't advocate breaking the law, but if you're going to, please follow your conscience and use common sense.

Also, just because dogs are permitted off leash in certain areas doesn't necessarily mean you should let your dog run free. In large tracts of wild land, unless you're sure your dog will come back when you call or will never stray more than a few yards from your side, you should probably keep her leashed. An otherwise docile homebody can turn into a savage hunter if the right prey is near. Or your curious dog could perturb a rattlesnake or dig up a rodent whose fleas carry bubonic plague. In pursuit of a strange scent, your dog could easily get lost in an unfamiliar area. (Some forest rangers recommend having your dog wear a bright orange collar, vest, or backpack when out in the wilderness.)

There's No Business Like Dog Business

There's nothing appealing about bending down with a plastic bag or a piece of newspaper on a chilly morning and grabbing the steaming remnants of what your dog ate for dinner the night before. It's disgusting. Worse yet, you have to hang onto it until you can find a trash can. And how about when the newspaper doesn't endure before you can dispose of it? Yuck! It's enough to make

you wish your dog could wear diapers. But as gross as it can be to scoop the poop, it's worse to step in it. It's really bad if a child falls in it, or—*gasp!*—starts eating it. And have you ever walked into a park where few people clean up after their dogs? The stench could make a hog want to hibernate.

Unscooped poop is one of a dog's worst enemies. Public policies banning dogs from parks are enacted because of it. And not all poop woes are outside. A dog-loving concierge at an upscale hotel told us that a guest came up to her and said there was some dirt beside the elevator. The concierge sent someone to clean it up. The dirt turned out to be dog poop. The hotel, which used to be one of the most elegant dog-friendly hotels around (it even had a Pampered Pet Program), now bans dogs. (There were other reasons, including a new boss, but the poop was the last straw.)

Just be responsible and clean up after your dog everywhere you go. (And obviously, if there's even a remote chance he'll relieve himself inside, don't even bring him into hotels or stores that permit dogs!) Anytime you take your dog out, stuff plastic bags in your jacket, purse, car, pants pockets—anywhere you might be able to pull one out when needed. Or, if plastic isn't your bag, newspapers will do the trick. If it makes it more palatable, bring along a paper bag, too, and put the used newspaper or plastic bag in it. That way you don't have to walk around with dripping paper or a plastic bag whose contents are visible to the world. If you don't enjoy the squishy sensation, try one of those cardboard or plastic bag pooper-scoopers sold at pet stores. If you don't feel like bending down, buy a long-handled scooper. There's a scooper for every taste.

This is the only lecture you'll get on scooping in this entire book. To help keep parks alive, I should harp on it in every park description, but that would take another 100 pages—and you'd start to ignore it anyway. And, if I mentioned it in some park listings but not others, it might imply that you don't have to clean up after your dog in the parks where it's not mentioned.

A final note: Don't pretend not to see your dog while he's doing his bit. Don't pretend to look for it without success. And don't fake scooping it up when you're really just covering it with sand. I know these tricks because I've been guilty of them myself—but no more. I've seen the light. I've been saved. I've been delivered from the depths of dog-doo depravity.

Etiquette Rex: The Well-Mannered Mutt

While cleaning up after your dog is your responsibility, a dog in a public place has his own responsibilities. Of course, it really boils down to your responsibility again, but the burden of action is on your dog. Etiquette for restaurants and hotels is covered in other sections of this chapter. What follows are some fundamental rules of dog etiquette. I'll go through it quickly, but if your dog's a slow reader, he can read it again: no vicious dogs; no jumping on people; no incessant barking; no leg lifts on surfboards, backpacks, human legs, or any other personal objects you'll find hanging around beaches and parks; dogs should come when they're called; dogs should stay on command.

Joe Dog managed to violate all but the first of these rules at one point or another. (Jake has followed in his pawsteps to an amazing extent, considering he never even met Joe.) Do your best to remedy any problems. It takes patience, and it's not always easy. For instance, there was a time during Joe's youth when he seemed to think that human legs were tree trunks. Rather than pretending I didn't know the beast, I strongly reprimanded him, apologized to the victim from the depths of my heart, and offered money for dry cleaning. Joe learned his lesson-many dry-cleaning bills later.

Safety First

A few essentials will keep your traveling dog happy and healthy.

Heat: If you must leave your dog alone in the car for a few minutes, do so only if it's cool out and if you can park in the shade. *Never, ever, ever* leave a dog in a car with the windows rolled up all the way. Even if it seems cool, the sun's heat passing through the window can kill a dog in a matter of minutes. Roll down the window enough so your dog gets air, but also so there's no danger of your dog's getting out or someone breaking in. Make sure your dog has plenty of water.

You also have to watch out for heat exposure when your car is in motion. Certain cars, such as hatchbacks, can make a dog in the backseat extra hot, even while you feel okay in the driver's seat.

Try to time your vacation so you don't visit a place when it's extremely warm. Dogs and heat don't get along, especially if the dog isn't used to heat. The opposite is also true. If your dog lives in a hot climate and you take him to a freezing place, it may not be a healthy shift. Check with your vet if you have any doubts. Spring and fall are usually the best times to travel.

Water: Water your dog frequently. Dogs on the road may drink even more than they do at home. Take regular water breaks, or bring a heavy bowl (the thick clay ones do nicely) and set it on the floor so your dog always has access to water. I use a nonspill bowl, which comes in really handy on curvy roads. When hiking, be sure to carry enough for you *and* a thirsty dog.

Rest Stops: Stop and unwater your dog. There's nothing more miserable than being stuck in a car when you can't find a rest stop. No matter how tightly you cross your legs and try to think of the desert, you're certain you'll burst within the next minute...so imagine how a dog feels when the urge strikes, and he can't tell you the problem. There are plenty of rest stops along the major California freeways. I've also included many parks close to freeways for dogs who need a good stretch with their bathroom break.

How frequently you stop depends on your dog's bladder. If your dog is constantly running out the doggy door at home to relieve himself, you may want to stop every hour. Others can go significantly longer without being uncomfortable. Watch for any signs of restlessness and gauge it for yourself.

Car Safety: Even the experts differ on how a dog should travel in a car. Some suggest doggy safety belts, available at pet-supply stores. Others firmly believe in keeping a dog kenneled. They say it's safer for the dog if there's an accident, and it's safer for the driver because there's no dog underfoot. Still others say you should just let your dog hang out without straps and boxes. They believe that if there's an accident, at least the dog isn't trapped in a cage. They say that dogs enjoy this more, anyway.

I'm a follower of the last school of thought. Jake loves sticking his snout out of the windows to smell the world go by. The danger is that if the car kicks up a pebble or angers a bee, his nose and eyes could be injured. So far, he's been okay, as has every other dog who has explored the Golden State with us, but I've seen dogs who needed to be treated for bee stings to the nose because of this practice. If in doubt, try opening the window just enough so your dog can't stick out much snout.

Whatever travel style you choose, your pet will be more comfortable if he has his own blanket with him. A veterinarian acquaintance brings a faux-sheepskin blanket for his dogs. At night in the hotel, the sheepskin doubles as the dog's bed.

Planes: Air travel is even more controversial. Personally, unless my dogs can fly with me in the passenger section (which very tiny dogs are sometimes allowed to do), I'd rather find a way to drive the distance or leave them at home with a friend. I've heard too many horror stories of dogs suffocating in what was supposed to be a pressurized cargo section, dying of heat exposure, or ending up in Miami while their people go to Seattle. There's just something unappealing about the idea of a dog's flying in the cargo hold, as if he's nothing more than a piece of luggage. Of course, many dogs survive just fine, but I'm not willing to take the chance. (That said, an airline called Companion Air is hoping to be the first to offer a way for humans and any size dog to be together during plane travel—and not in the cargo section! It's still in the planning stages, but you can visit the website at www.companionair.com for updates.)

If you need to transport your dog by plane, try to fly nonstop, and make sure you schedule takeoff and arrival times when the temperature is below 80°F (but not bitterly cold in winter). You'll want to consult the airline about regulations, required certificates, and fees. Be sure to check with your vet to make sure your pooch is healthy enough to fly.

The question of tranquilizing a dog for a plane journey is very controversial. Some vets think it's insane to give a dog a sedative before flying. They say a dog will be calmer and less fearful without a disorienting drug. Others think it's crazy not to afford your dog the little relaxation he might not otherwise get without a tranquilizer. Discuss the issue with your vet, who will take into account the trip length and your dog's personality.

Many websites deal with air-bound pooches. I highly recommend checking them out for further info on safe air travel with your dog. (Most of the web pages have long and cumbersome names, so you're best off searching for keywords such as "Traveling Airlines Pets."

The Ultimate Doggy Bag

Your dog can't pack his own bags, and even if he could, he'd probably fill them with dog biscuits and chew toys. It's important to stash some of those in your dog's vacation kit, but here are other handy items to bring along: bowls, bedding, a brush, towels (for those muddy days), a first-aid kit, pooper-scoopers, water, food, prescription drugs, tags, treats, toys, and—of course—this book.

Make sure your dog is wearing his license, identification tag, and rabies tag. Bringing along your dog's up-to-date vaccination records is a good idea, too. If you should find yourself at a park or campground that requires the actual rabies certificate, you'll be set. In addition, you may unexpectedly end up needing to leave your dog in a doggy day care for a few hours so you can go somewhere you just can't bring your dog. A record of his shots is imperative. (You'll also have to get him a kennel-cough shot if boarding is a possibility.)

It's a good idea to snap a disposable ID on your dog's collar, too, showing a cell phone number or the name, address, and phone number either of where you'll be vacationing, or of a friend who'll be home to field calls. That way, if your dog should get lost, at least the finder won't be calling your empty house. Paper key-chain tags you buy at hardware stores offer a cheap way to change your dog's contact info as often as needed when on vacation. Dog-book author and pet columnist Gina Spadafori advises always listing a local number on the tag. "You'd be surprised how many people don't want to make a long-distance phone call," she writes in her book *Dogs for Dummies*.

Some people think dogs should drink only water brought from home, so their bodies don't have to get used to too many new things. I've never had a problem giving my dogs tap water from other parts of the state, nor has anyone else I know. Most vets think your dog will be fine drinking tap water in most U.S. cities.

"Think of it this way," says Pete Beeman, a longtime San Francisco veterinarian. "Your dog's probably going to eat poop if he can get hold of some, and even that's probably not going to harm him. I really don't think that drinking

water that's okay for people is going to be bad for dogs." (Jake can attest to the poop part. But let's not talk about that.)

Bone Appétit

In some European countries, dogs enter restaurants and dine alongside their folks as if they were people, too. (Or at least they sit and watch and drool while their people dine.) Not so in the United States. Rightly or wrongly, dogs are considered a health threat here. But many health inspectors I've spoken with say they see no reason why clean, well-behaved dogs shouldn't be permitted inside a restaurant. "Aesthetically, it may not appeal to Americans," an environmental specialist with the state Department of Health told me. "But the truth is, there's no harm in this practice."

Ernest Hemingway made an expatriate of his dog, Black Dog (aka Blackie), partly because of America's restrictive views on dogs in dining establishments. In "The Christmas Gift," a story published in *Look* magazine in 1954, he describes how he made the decision to take Black Dog to Cuba, rather than leave him behind in Ketchum, Idaho.

> This was a town where a man was once not regarded as respectable unless he was accompanied by his dog. But a reform movement had set in, led by several local religionists, and gambling had been abolished and there was even a movement on foot to forbid a dog from entering a public eating place with his master. Blackie had always

tugged me by the trouser leg as we passed a combination gambling and eating place called the Alpine where they served the finest sizzling steak in the West. Blackie wanted me to order the giant sizzling steak and it was difficult to pass the Alpine.... We decided to make a command decision and take Blackie to Cuba.

Fortunately, you don't have to take your dog to a foreign country to eat together at a restaurant. The Bay Area is full of restaurants with outdoor tables, and hundreds of them welcome dogs to join their people for an alfresco experience. The law on outdoor dining is somewhat vague, and each county has different versions of it. In general, as long as your dog doesn't go inside a restaurant (even to get to outdoor tables in the back) and isn't near the food preparation areas, it's probably legal. The decision is then up to the restaurant proprietor.

The restaurants listed in this book have given us permission to tout them as dog-friendly eateries. But keep in mind that rules can change and restaurants can close, so I highly recommend phoning before you set your stomach on a particular kind of cuisine. Since some restaurants close during colder months, phoning ahead is a doubly wise thing to do. (Of course, you can assume that where there's snow or ultracold temperatures, the outdoor tables will move indoors for a while each year.) If you can't call first, be sure to ask the manager of the restaurant for permission before you sit down with your sidekick. Remember, it's the restaurant proprietor, not you, who will be in trouble if someone complains to the health department.

Some basic rules of restaurant etiquette: Dogs shouldn't beg from other diners, no matter how delicious their steaks look. They should not attempt to get their snouts (or their entire bodies) up on the table. They should be clean, quiet, and as unobtrusive as possible. If your dog leaves a good impression with the management and other customers, it will help pave the way for all the other dogs who want to dine alongside their best friends in the future.

A Room at the Inn

Good dogs make great hotel guests. They don't steal towels, and they don't get drunk and keep the neighbors up all night. The Bay Area is full of lodgings whose owners welcome dogs. This book lists dog-friendly accommodations of all types, from motels to bed-and-breakfast inns to elegant hotels—but the basic dog etiquette rules are the same everywhere.

Dogs should never be left alone in your room. Leaving a dog alone in a strange place invites serious trouble. Scared, nervous dogs may tear apart drapes, carpeting, and furniture. They may even injure themselves. They might also bark nonstop and scare the daylights out of the housekeeper. Just don't do it.

DIVERSION

Ch-Ch-Chains: An increasing number of stores permit pooches these days, including many within chains such as Borders, Saks Fifth Avenue, REI, Nordstrom, Big Dogs Sportwear, and Restoration Hardware. Not all stores within these chains welcome dogs, but most do. If your dog is longing to do more than just window shop, she'll likely be in luck if one of these stores is on your shopping list.

Only bring a house-trained dog to a lodging. How would you like a house-guest to go to the bathroom in the middle of your bedroom?

Make sure your pooch is flea-free. Otherwise, future guests will be itching to leave.

It helps to bring your dog's bed or blanket along for the night. Your dog will feel more at home and won't be tempted to jump on the hotel bed. If your dog sleeps on the bed with you at home (as 47 percent do, according to the American Animal Hospital Association survey), bring a sheet and put it on top of the bed so the hotel's bedspread won't get furry or dirty.

Don't wash your dog in the hotel tub. "It's very yucky," I was told by one motel manager who has seen so many furry tubs that she's thinking about banning dogs.

Likewise, refrain from using the ice bucket as a water or food bowl. Bring your own bowls, or stay in a hotel that provides them, as many of the nicer ones do these days.

After a few days in a hotel, some dogs come to think of it as home. They get territorial. When another hotel guest walks by, it's "Bark! Bark!" When the housekeeper knocks, it's "Bark! Snarl! Bark! Gnash!" Keep your dog quiet, or you'll both find yourselves looking for a new home away from home.

For some strange reason, many lodgings prefer small dogs as guests. All I can say is, "Yip! Yap!" It's really ridiculous. Large dogs are often much calmer and quieter than their tiny, high-energy cousins.

If you're in a location where you can't find a hotel that will accept you and your big brute (a growing rarity these days), it's time to try a sell job. Let the manager know how good and quiet your dog is (if he is). Promise he won't eat the bathtub or run around and shake all over the hotel. Offer a deposit or sign a waiver, even if they're not required for small dogs. It helps if your sweet, soppy-eyed dog is at your side to convince the decision-maker.

I've sneaked dogs into hotels, but I don't recommend it. The lodging might have a good reason for its rules. Besides, you always feel as if you're going to be caught and thrown out on your hindquarters. You race in and out of your room with your dog as if ducking sniper fire. It's better to avoid feeling like a criminal and move on to a more dog-friendly location. With the numbers of lodgings that welcome dogs these days, you won't have to go far.

The lodgings described in this book are for dogs who obey all the rules. I list a range of rates for each lodging, from the least expensive room during low season to the priciest room during high season. Most of the rooms are doubles, so there's not usually a huge variation. But when a room price gets into the thousands of dollars, you know we're looking at royal suites.

Many lodgings charge extra for your dog. If you see "Dogs are $10 (or whatever amount) extra," that means $10 extra per night. Some charge a fee for the length of a dog's stay, and others ask for a deposit. These details are also noted in the lodging description. A few places still ask for nothing more than your dog's promise that she'll be on her best behavior. So, if no extra charge is mentioned in a listing, it means your dog can stay with you for free.

Natural Troubles

Chances are your adventuring will go without a hitch, but you should always be prepared to deal with trouble. Make sure you know the basics of animal first aid before you embark on a long journey with your dog.

The more common woes—ticks, foxtails, poison oak, and skunks—can make life with a traveling dog a somewhat trying experience. Ticks are hard to avoid in many parts of Northern California. They can carry Lyme disease, so you should always check yourself and your dog all over after a day in tick country. Don't forget to check ears and between the toes. If you see a tick, just pull it straight out with tweezers, not with your bare hands.

The tiny deer ticks that carry Lyme disease are difficult to find. Consult your veterinarian if your dog is lethargic for a few days, has a fever, loses her appetite, or becomes lame. These symptoms could indicate Lyme disease. Some vets recommend a new vaccine that is supposed to prevent the onset of the disease.

Foxtails—those arrow-shaped pieces of dry grass that attach to your socks, your sweater, and your dog—are an everyday annoyance. In certain cases, they can also be lethal. They may stick in your dog's eyes, nose, ears, or mouth and work their way in. Check every nook and cranny of your dog after a walk if you've been anywhere near dry grass. Despite my constant effort to find these things in Joe's curly tan fur, I missed several and they beat a path through his foot and into his leg. Be vigilant.

Poison oak is also a common California menace. Get familiar with it through a friend who knows nature or through a guided nature walk. Dogs don't generally have reactions to poison oak, but they can easily pass its oils on to people. If you think your dog has made contact with some poison oak, avoid petting her until you can get home and bathe her (preferably with rubber gloves). If you do pet her before you can wash her, don't touch your eyes and be sure to wash your hands immediately.

If your dog loses a contest with a skunk (and she *always* will), rinse her eyes first with plain warm water and then forget the old tomato-juice remedy. All that does is make a dog itchy—and if she starts out white, she can turn a creepy shade of orange.

I've had the fortune of being handed the best-ever recipe for de-skunking by Jamie Ray, an expert in the field. She's the founder of the San Francisco Rescued Orphan Mammal Program (SF ROMP), an urban wildlife rescue group. And it just so happens that some of the urban wildlife her group rescues is black and white and furry and occasionally whiffy, if you get my drift.

I phoned her one day after Jake had a much-too-close encounter of the skunky kind. The fumes were so bad I could barely breathe. Tomato juice wasn't an option, as it had never worked for our other dogs. I figured if anyone could help, Jamie could. And did she ever. Jake was left with barely any eau d'skunk, and you had to get very close to smell it. On two subsequent occasions, the recipe also worked magic.

I suggest you write down the recipe and keep it handy. You may also want to keep an extra bottle or two of hydrogen peroxide around so you'll always be ready. The other ingredients are in just about any household.

Make a mixture with the ratio of one cup hydrogen peroxide, two tablespoons of baking soda, and one tablespoon of dishwashing soap—Dawn works best. (For Jake, we multiplied this recipe times six, since he is so big and was so stinky.) Stir, and apply it all over your dog. Don't hold back. Use plenty, being careful to keep it away from the eyes. Rub it in, wait a couple of minutes,

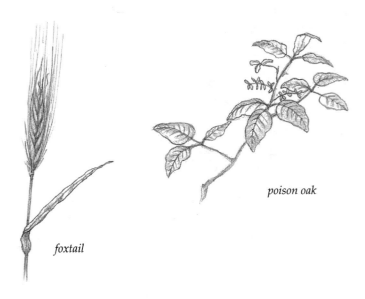

poison oak

foxtail

and rinse. You may need to do it again to really eradicate the stink. Rinse well. I've followed up each de-skunking with some gentle dog shampoo.

(If you ever use this recipe, you might want to consider sending a small thank-you to SF ROMP, which always needs donations. You can find info on SF ROMP at www.sfwildlifeservices.org.)

Ruffing It Together

Whenever we went camping, Joe insisted on sleeping in the tent. He sprawled out and wouldn't budge. At the first hint of dawn, he'd tiptoe outside (sometimes right through the bug screen) as if he'd been standing vigil all night. He tried not to look shamefaced, but under all that curly hair lurked an embarrassed grin.

Actually, Joe might have had the right idea. Some outdoor experts say it's dangerous to leave even a tethered dog outside your tent at night. The dog can escape or become a late dinner for some hungry creature.

All state parks require dogs to be kept in a tent or vehicle at night. Some county parks follow suit. Other policies are more lenient. Use good judgment.

If you're camping with your dog, chances are you're also hiking with him. Even if you're not hiking for long, watch out for your dog's paws, especially the paws of those who are fair of foot. Rough terrain can cause a dog's pads to become raw and painful, making it almost impossible for him to walk. Several types of dog boots are available for such feet. It's easier to carry the booties than to carry your dog home.

Be sure to bring plenty of water for you and your pooch. Stop frequently to wet your whistles. Some veterinarians warn against letting your dog drink out of a stream because of the chance of ingesting giardia and other internal parasites, but it's not always easy to stop a thirsty dog.

A Dog in Need

If you don't have a dog but could provide a good home for one, I'd like to make a plea on behalf of all the unwanted dogs who will be euthanized tomorrow—and the day after that and the day after that. Animal shelters and humane organizations are overflowing with dogs who would devote their lives to being your best buddy, your faithful traveling companion, and a dedicated listener to all your tales of bliss and woe.

Need a nudge? Remember the oft-quoted words of Samuel Butler:

> "The great pleasure of a dog is that you may make a fool of yourself with him and not only will he not scold you, but he will make a fool of himself, too."

Keep in Touch

Our readers mean everything to us. We explore the Bay Area so you and your dogs can spend true quality time together. Your input to this book is very important. In the last few years, we've heard from many wonderful dogs and their people about new dog-friendly places or old dog-friendly places we didn't know about. If you have any suggestions or insights to offer, please contact us using the information listed in the front of this book, or via my website, www.caldogtravel.com.

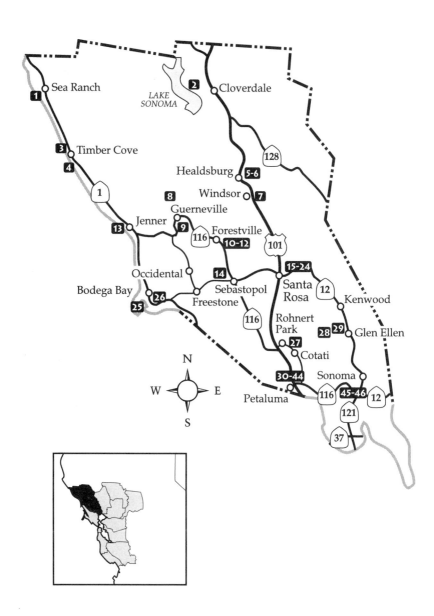

Sea Ranch

LAKE SONOMA

Cloverdale

Timber Cove

Healdsburg

Windsor

Guerneville

Jenner

Forestville

Occidental

Bodega Bay

Sebastopol

Freestone

Santa Rosa

Kenwood

Rohnert Park

Glen Ellen

Cotati

Sonoma

Petaluma

N

W   E

S

CHAPTER 1
Sonoma County

The horticulturist Luther Burbank, who made his home in Santa Rosa and Sebastopol from 1875 to 1926, called Sonoma County "the chosen spot of all the Earth as far as nature is concerned." Practically anything will grow in Sonoma County. It's the Bay Area capital for trees, flowers, and vegetables, as well as goats, sheep, cattle, chickens, pigs, and probably a few farm animals that are just now being invented.

Unfortunately, dogs and farm animals don't mix. Some Sonoma sheep ranchers have been known to impose the ultimate penalty on loose dogs that they see near their livestock: They shoot them. They're not acting under the law of the Wild West, either. It's a county ordinance that dogs harassing livestock in unincorporated areas or on private property may be shot by the property owner.

But fear not. Sonoma County has many enchanting places where the only shot your dog will experience is a shot of adrenaline when he lays eyes on the stunning scenery and some mesmerizing, dog-friendly hangouts. The off-leash doggy areas in Sonoma County are increasing every year. Oh joy of joys! It's hard to find a Sonoma County dog whose tail isn't wagging a little faster these days.

PICK OF THE LITTER—SONOMA COUNTY

BIGGEST AND BEST DOG PARK
Rocky Memorial Dog Park, Petaluma (page 47)

BEST BEACH
Sonoma Coast State Beaches, Jenner (page 32)

MOST DOG-FRIENDLY PLACE TO EAT
Garden Court Cafe, Glen Ellen (page 42)

MOST BEAUTIFUL OCEANFRONT HOUSE
Robinsong, rented through Sea Ranch Vacation Homes, Sea Ranch (page 23)

MOST DOG-FRIENDLY PLACES TO STAY
Creekside Inn and Resort, Guerneville (page 28)
Fern Grove Cottages, Guerneville (pages 28–29)
Larissa's House, rented through Russian River Vacation Homes, Guerneville (page 30)
Sheraton Sonoma County, Petaluma (page 49)

BEST SECLUDED INN
Stone Grove Inn, Sonoma (page 51)

MOST DOG-FRIENDLY WINE TASTING
The Wine Room, Kenwood (page 26)

Sea Ranch

PARKS, BEACHES, AND RECREATION AREAS

◼ Sea Ranch Beach Trails

🐾🐾🐾 (See Sonoma County map on page 20)

Sea Ranch is a private development, but seven public foot trails cross the property leading to the beach, which is also public property. The smooth, wide dirt trails are managed by Sonoma County Regional Parks, and they offer incomparable solitary walks through unspoiled grassy hills.

All the trails are clearly marked on Highway 1. Each trailhead has restrooms and a box where you are asked to deposit $4 for parking. No motorcycles, bicycles, or horses are allowed. Keep your dog on leash.

Here are the distances to the beach, listing trails from north to south: Salal Trail, .6 mile; Bluff-Top Trail, 3.5 miles; Walk-On Beach Trail, .4 mile; Shell Beach Trail, .6 mile; Stengel Beach Trail, .2 mile; Pebble Beach Trail, .3 mile; Black Point Trail, .3 mile. 707/785-2377.

PLACES TO STAY

Sea Ranch Vacation Homes: The Sea Ranch Vacation Homes rental agency offers 14 beautiful, dog-friendly homes for rent in the glorious oceanfront community of Sea Ranch. Some homes are almost on the water, some are set in wooded areas. All are attractive, but our favorite is Robinsong, a stellar example of how a seaside home can live up to its landscape. The fireplace flanked by smartly cushioned "window seats" is worth the price of admission. You will love reading there, and your dog will adore snoozing on a blanket beside you. The look of the interior is clean and crisp, yet amazingly cozy. The spacious kitchen, which boasts an island, is set up for the chef in you.

Rates for the Robinsong are $240 nightly (there's a two-night minimum) and $1,440 for the week. It's one of the more expensive dog-friendly homes, but if you have it in your budget, it's worth it. Rates for the variety of dog-friendly homes are $130–240. Weekly rates are $780–1440. Dogs are $10 extra nightly. For reservations and information, call 707/884-4235; www .searanchrentals.com.

Cloverdale

PARKS, BEACHES, AND RECREATION AREAS

🐾 Lake Sonoma Recreation Area

🐾🐾🐾 (See Sonoma County map on page 20)

This is the only recreation site in the nine counties of the Bay Area run by the U.S. Army Corps of Engineers, and it's too bad. The Corps has a liberal attitude toward dogs, and this park is beautifully developed and managed, not to mention clean. It's also free. You must keep your dog on a six-foot leash, and he's not allowed on the swimming beach at the north end, but rangers told us there's no rule against dogs swimming anywhere else.

If you're the type who doesn't clean up after your dog, here's a warning: Change your act, or stay far from here. Rangers have been known to charge a cleanup fee for owners who ignore the deposits of their dogs.

A large lawn with picnic tables, some shaded, is at the visitor center. You can rent a boat from the private concession on the lake, which allows leashed dogs on all boats. Follow signs from the visitor center. To reserve a boat, call 707/433-2200. Waterskiing and camping are also popular here.

For a good dog hike, pick up a map at the visitor center and drive west on Dry Creek Road to the trailheads, which have their own parking lots. There are 40 miles of trails. Here are two of our favorites: There's a bit of shade at the Gray Pine Flat Trailhead. This smooth foot trail goes down to the lake through an unusual forest of foothill pines, madrone, manzanita, and blooming desert brush. The buzz of motorboats on the lake blends with the hammering of wood-peckers. You get a good view of the lake fairly quickly. If you'd prefer less of a climb back to the trailhead, take the Little Flat Trail, which starts lower down.

Horses are allowed on these trails, but bikes aren't—a plus for your dog's safety. Unfortunately, it gets bone-dry here in summer, and poison oak is common.

Camping is available at 113 sites at Liberty Glen Campground and several primitive boat-in sites on the lake. None of these sites has water. (Campers at Liberty Glen can stock up nearby.) Rates are $10–14. For reservations (advised in summer), phone 877/444-6777.

Take U.S. 101 to the Canyon Road exit. Go west to Dry Creek Road and turn right into the entrance. Take a right at the only fork. 707/433-9483.

PLACES TO STAY

Lake Sonoma Recreation Area: See the Lake Sonoma Recreation Area, above, for camping information.

Timber Cove

PARKS, BEACHES, AND RECREATION AREAS

3 Salt Point State Park

🐾🐾🐾 (See Sonoma County map on page 20)

Dogs are allowed only on South Gerstle Cove Beach—south of the rocky tidepool area, which is an underwater reserve—and in the Gerstle Cove, Woodside, and Fisk Mill Cove picnic areas and campsites. Gerstle Cove picnic area is right above the section of the beach where dogs are allowed, so that's your best bet. The surf is usually gentle here, but if in doubt, you can call for an ocean-conditions recording at 707/847-3222. As far as walking around, dogs get to do it only on paved roads. They must be leashed everywhere.

The parking fee is $6. Dogs are allowed at all campsites here except the walk-in and group sites. The park has about 30 tents in the upland part of the park. East of Highway 1 are 80 family sites. Sites are $15–20 per night. Call 800/444-7275 for reservations.

The park is about five miles north of Timber Cove and six miles south of Stewarts Point, off Highway 1. For park info, call 707/847-3221.

4 Stillwater Cove Regional Park

🐾🐾🐾 (See Sonoma County map on page 20)

This is a tiny but delightful beach at the foot of spectacular pine-covered cliffs. Park in the small lot beside Highway 1, leash your dog, and walk down. There is a larger picnic area above the highway, where a $4 day-use fee is charged. From here, you have to cross the highway to get to the cove. Look both ways!

There are 23 campsites, available on a first-come, first-served basis. If you want to make a reservation, they're available through park headquarters. Sites are $17 per night. The turnout is about one mile north of Fort Ross State Park (where dogs are banned). 707/847-3245.

PLACES TO STAY

Salt Point State Park: See Salt Point State Park, above, for camping information.

Stillwater Cove Regional Park: See Stillwater Cove Regional Park, above, for camping information.

Healdsburg

PARKS, BEACHES, AND RECREATION AREAS

5 Villa Chanticleer Dog Park

🐾🐾🐾🐾🦴 (See Sonoma County map on page 20)

This 1.5-acre fenced dog park is a great place to take your dog whether you live here or you're just visiting. It's within a beautiful oak grove setting, so it's easy on the eyes, plus there's plenty of shade. Lucky dogs who come here have it all: trees, enough room to romp, and the smells of nature. It has all the good dog-park amenities, including benches and water. The ground cover is wood chips, which adds to the woodsy feeling here, but Jake thinks each wood chip is a delicacy and is content to plop himself down and gnaw away until an interesting dog or errant tennis ball catches his eye.

The park is set within the larger Villa Chanticleer Park, which has buildings and backdrops that are popular for weddings. Be sure your dog is on leash if you explore beyond the dog area: You don't want your dog interfering with any nuptials. The address is 1248 Chanticleer Way.

6 Badger Park Dog Park

🐾🐾🐾🦴 (See Sonoma County map on page 20)

If only this park were bigger than a quarter acre we could give it an extra paw. It's a lovely little fenced park, with one gorgeous large oak that people tend to congregate under. The ground is grassy, which dog paws appreciate. The park is set within Badger Park, which is at 750 Heron Drive. 707/431-3384.

DIVERSION

Merlot Over and Play Dead: I didn't make up this pun. (Mine are usually worse.) It's the name of a wine made by a Healdsburg vintner who owns the Mutt Lynch Winery. Other "doggone good wines," as Brenda Lynch calls them, are Canis Major and Portrait of a Mutt.

Sonoma County wineries are going to the dogs. Two have their own lines of dog-labeled wines. Many allow well-behaved dogs in their tasting rooms and at their picnic areas. Below is a sampling of some of Sonoma's more dog-friendly wineries, listed by area. Phone the individual wineries for hours, prices, and dog-friendly specifics.

GUERNEVILLE:
Korbel Champagne Cellars, 13250 River Road; 707/824-7000.

HEALDSBURG:
Foppiano Vineyards, 12707 Old Redwood Highway; 707/433-7272.
Lambert Bridge Winery, 4085 West Dry Creek Road; 707/431-9600.
Mutt Lynch Winery, 1960 Dry Creek Road; 707/942-6180. Open by appointment only. Dog-labeled wines abound.

KENWOOD:
The Wine Room, 9575 Sonoma Highway; 707/833-6131. Dogs get dog treats at this multiwinery co-op tasting room. A new wine line, The Family Dog, has rolled out its first label, Barney. The dog wine line is seeking more dogs for its labels.

SANTA ROSA:
De Loach Vineyards, 1791 Olivet Road; 707/526-9111.
Martini and Prati Winery, 2191 Laguna Road; 707/823-2404.

SONOMA:
Sebastiani Vineyards and Winery, 389 4th Street East; 707/933-3230. Visiting dogs get to drink fresh water from the outside dog bowls. Leashes are available, lest you forget yours.

WINDSOR:
Martinelli Vineyards and Winery, 3360 River Road; 707/525-0570.

PLACES TO EAT

Costeaux French Bakery: Stroll around Healdsburg's good-looking town square, with its old buildings and benches for shady rest stops, and then drop in here for dinner or a wonderful pastry snack at an outdoor table. The bakery sells delicious homemade dog bones, should your dog inquire. 417 Healds-burg Avenue; 707/433-1913.

Oakville Grocery: This gourmet grocer is the home of a terrific alfresco café where dogs are welcome. The outdoor café features a wood-burning fireplace, which makes for cozy evenings. Jake loves sniffing the rotisserie chicken, and the pizzas are to drool for. Wine is big here, too, but dogs should stick with water, which is plentiful: There's always a doggy bowl here for thirsty pooches. 124 Matheson Street; 707/433-3200.

PLACES TO STAY

Best Western Dry Creek Inn: Rates are $69–129. Dogs are $20 extra. 198 Dry Creek Road 95448; 707/433-0300.

Windsor

Until 1992, Windsor wasn't anything but an unincorporated county area. Then it became a town, thanks to the "d" word (development). In 1997, it spawned its very first park, and with that park came a fenced-in dog park. Dogs think Windsor's movers and shakers are very smart people, indeed.

PARKS, BEACHES, AND RECREATION AREAS

7 Pleasant Oak Park

🐾🐾🐕 (See Sonoma County map on page 20)

This is a fine example of how a fenced-in dog park can become a decent place, despite a rather austere start. In the park's early days, it was little more than a dirt lot surrounded by a very high fence with double gates. But now it's really something to wag about. It has water, grass, and enough trees to cast a cooling shade in the summer. Dogs from miles around come to socialize. Their humans have been known to follow suit. The park is at Old Redwood Highway and Pleasant Avenue. 707/838-1260.

Guerneville

PARKS, BEACHES, AND RECREATION AREAS

8 Armstrong Redwoods State Reserve

🐾🐾 (See Sonoma County map on page 20)

As is usual in state parks, you can take a dog only on paved roads and into picnic areas. But here you can give your dog and yourself an exceptional treat. The picnic grounds are a cool, hushed redwood cathedral. You can walk on Armstrong Woods Road, which winds along Fife Creek (usually lush, but dry in the heart of summer) all the way to the top of McCray Mountain, about three miles.

The drive is fairly terrifying, so you may prefer to walk anyway. Hikers, bicycles, and autos all share the road, so be very careful. Your dog must be leashed everywhere in the park. From Guerneville, go about 2.5 miles north on Armstrong Woods Road. The day-use fee is $6, but if you park out front you can walk in for free. 707/869-2015 or 707/865-2391.

⑨ Vacation Beach

 (See Sonoma County map on page 20)

Vacation Beach is not really a beach, but an access point where the Russian River is dammed by two roads across it. It's one of several public spots where you and your dog used to be able to legally jump into the drink, but leashes seem to be the law here now. It's still fun. People and pooches picnic, swim, put in canoes, and cool their feet and paws in the cool river.

From Highway 116 between Guerneville and Monte Rio, turn south at the unmarked road where you see Old Cazadero Road veering north. You can park at the approaches to the dams but not on the crossing itself. 707/869-9000.

PLACES TO STAY

Creekside Inn and Resort: Dogs get to stay at three of several cottages and rooms at this fun inn near the Russian River. Bird dogs enjoy lounging in the Quail Cottage, a small, bright cottage with a fireplace. The Deck House, another poochy haven, is a little larger, with a sunny deck. The sweet one-bedroom Apple House is separated from the inn by a very old apple tree.

The real apple of your dog's eyes will be the Dog Days Package. You and your dog will each get a tasty treat (gourmet chocolate for you, liver goody for your dog, and aren't you glad it's not vice-versa?) You'll also receive a coupon for a little doggy gift and discounts on a grooming for your dog and a massage for you. The package entails staying a few nights, but it ends up being less expensive than doing a night-by-night tally. Other packages, such as the popular Gay Honeymoon package, are also available.

The inn's land is dotted with several large redwoods. The property spans three acres, and dogs are welcome to cruise around on leash. Human guests may hang out in the inn's main dining room and lounge, both of which have fireplaces. Humans can also swim in the pool here. Dogs have to be content to do the dog paddle in the Russian River, not too far away.

Rates are $105–165. Weekly rates are available. If you'd like to stay in a larger house, you can also rent the Summer Crossing, a small vacation home here. It goes for $285 nightly and sleeps up to four. 16180 Neeley Road, P.O. Box 2185 95446; 707/869-3623 or 800/776-6586; www.creeksideinn.com.

Fern Grove Cottages: Sleep in one of 20 charming cabins under 200-

foot redwoods here! The friendly owners, Mike and Margaret Kennett, will even point you and your pooch toward their favorite (secret) dog hike, which includes a dip in a pristine creek. It's a dog's idea of a perfect vacation.

The Kennetts welcome good pooches. "We've had some great dogs stay here," says Margaret, who doles out biscuits at check-in and provides old blankets for your dog's sleeping pleasure.

The cottages are simple, but cozy, with tasteful decor. Most have fireplaces, and some have kitchens. A delicious continental breakfast comes with your stay. The homemade granola and scones are divine. Rates are $89–209. Dogs are $15 extra. 16650 Highway 116 95446; 707/869-8105; www.ferngrove.com.

Fifes Guest Ranch: The cottages on this 15-acre redwood-festooned property will melt your heart if you like older abodes. These were built in 1905, and they still have the charm of their day, updated with a simple, light, airy decor. They're super comfy, too. Dogs think they're the cat's meow, but truth be told, they really like walking around the ranch better. The meadows, the trees, the river, all speak to a dog's soul.

If you like camping, you can pitch your tent at one of 85 tents-only sites, some of which are along the river. Camping rates are $19–50 for one-tent sites. Cottages are $65–305. Dogs are $25 for the length of their stay while camping or in the cottages.

The ranch hosts many events throughout the year. Recent events included a food and wine fest; the LeatherSIR and Leatherboy outdoor-themed weekend (the event tied up many guests); and Liquid, a pool party for women. 16467 Highway 116, P.O. Box 45 95446; 707/869-0656 or 800/734-3371; www.fifes.com.

Highlands Resort: If your dog has never been to a bar, ask to stay in the Highland's studio: The large room not only has a cozy fireplace and love seat, but it has its own wet bar. Teetotaling dogs might prefer the five larger cabins that allow dogs. The cabins have fireplaces, and some have kitchenettes, but no bar.

The Highlands, known as "a straight-friendly gay resort," is set on three wooded acres (which dogs can explore on leash) and has the feel of a country retreat. It has a swimming pool and outdoor hot tub—both clothing-optional. In the resort's brochure there's a bird's-eye–view picture of a fellow standing in the hot tub, with just a bit of bun showing. Joe Dog blushed and came back for another look. The owner asked us to mention that people with diverse lifestyles feel right at home here.

Rates are $85–135. Dogs are $25 extra for the length of their stay. 14000 Woodland Drive 95446; 707/869-0333; www.highlandsresort.com.

Russian River Getaways: If you and your dog want a home away from home while you vacation in the Russian River area, you've hit the jackpot. Russian River Getaways has about 50 beautiful dog-friendly homes for rent on a nightly or weekly basis. The homes are generally quite upscale, but the prices are fairly down to earth. (An aside that will put a smile on your dog's snout: Only six of the 56 homes rented through Russian River Getaways don't permit dogs. "We tell them that if they don't allow dogs, they're not going to do such good business," says an employee. "They really can't compete.")

Most of the homes are very attractive, with wonderfully creative touches. Just the names of some of the homes make you and your dog friend want to check them out: Bellagio, Bohemian Rhapsody, Jujube, The Bird Cage/La Cage aux Folles, the Luv Shack, and the Grand Prix (please don't pronounce the "x." You'll embarrass your dog.) are not your typical vacation home rental names. If you're looking to drop some dollars, check out Grandma's House (let's just say this must be some grandma with a billiard table in her 31-foot living room and a hot tub in her gazebo) and the River Queen, a fabulous manse on the river.

Rates for the homes range $175–975 nightly. Weekly rates are $1,050–5,850. For a brochure describing the homes, write Russian River Getaways at 14075 Mill Street, P.O. Box 1673 95446, or phone 707/869-4560 or 800/433-6673. The best way to check out the rentals is at www.rrgetaways.com.

Russian River Vacation Homes: Spend your Russian River–area vacation in your own charming private house. This is an ideal way to vacation with your pooch. Russian River Vacation Homes offers two dozen beautiful, quaint houses for pets and their people. From a one-bedroom rustic log cabin on the river to a three-bedroom riverside home complete with hot tub, you and your holiday hound will find the home of your dreams.

One of Joe's favorites was Larissa's House, a sweet one-bedroom home with a flowery, fenced-in yard on the river. Larissa, the owner, lives next door and adores dogs. In fact, you pretty much have to have a dog to stay here. It's so doggone dog-friendly that the shower is designed so that you and your dog can shower at the same time. (Joe was shy, so he didn't care for this arrangement.) If Larissa has time, she'll make sure your pooch has a welcoming bag of treats when she arrives. Dogs fall instantly in love when they meet Larissa, and the love-fest often continues year-round, because she sends them (note: *them,* not *you*) Christmas cards.

Rates are $145–535. Weekly rates are $700–2,400. For a brochure describing all the dog-friendly properties, write Russian River Vacation Homes at 14080 Mill Street 95446; 707/869-9030, 800/310-0804 (California only), or 800/997-3312 (nationwide); www.riverhomes.com.

Forestville

This beautiful town's motto is: "Where wine country meets the redwoods." This is Russian River country, and dogs love sniffing around some terrific beaches here. Be sure to visit the historic community's little "downtown." It's an eclectic charmer.

PARKS, BEACHES, AND RECREATION AREAS

If you have a dog who likes splashing in water, prepare for a very happy pooch: Forestville is home to three county beaches that permit leashed dogs. They're all Russian River havens, with good river access, old black walnut forests, German ivy, and lots of birds. Dogs need to be leashed, but there's plenty to enjoy, even tethered together. Since this pretty much describes all three river access locales, below we'll just list the pertinent info for each.

🔟 Steelhead Beach

🐾🐾🐾 (See Sonoma County map on page 20)

At 50 acres, with lots of picnic areas and flat grassy territory, this is the largest and most developed of the three county beach access areas in Forestville. If you drive in, you pay $4. Walk in and it's free. For info on the park's natural features, see the introduction to the Parks section, above. The park is at 9000 River Road. 707/565-2041.

🔟🔟 Forestville River Access/Mom's Beach

🐾🐾🐾 (See Sonoma County map on page 20)

It's 10-acres of on-leash fun here. This is a totally undeveloped area, at 10584 River Drive, off River Road. For info on the park's natural features, see the introduction to the Parks section, above. 707/565-2041.

1️⃣2️⃣ Sunset Beach

🐾🐾🐾 (See Sonoma County map on page 20)

This is a wild and lovely river access location, with about 10 acres to explore with your leashed dog. For info on the park's natural features, see the introduction to the Parks section, above. 11057 Sunset Drive. 707/565-2041.

Jenner

PARKS, BEACHES, AND RECREATION AREAS

⓲⓳ Sonoma Coast State Beaches

🐾🐾🐾🐾 (See Sonoma County map on page 20)

A string of beautiful, clean beaches runs south from Jenner to Bodega Bay, and you can't go wrong from Goat Rock Beach south to Salmon Creek Beach: Gorgeous bluff views, stretches of brown sand, gnarled rocks, and grassy dunes welcome you. Always keep an eye on the surf and a leash on your dog.

Dogs are not allowed on any of the trails that run on the bluffs above the beaches, on Bodega Head, in the Willow Creek area east of Bridgehaven, or in the seal rookery upriver from Goat Rock Beach. (Watch for the warning sign.) No camping is permitted on any of the beaches, except Bodega Dunes and Wright's Beach, which have campgrounds. These two also charge a $6 day-use fee. Day use of all other beaches is free. 707/875-3483.

The Bodega Dunes Campground has 99 developed sites, and Wright's Beach Campground has 27 developed sites. Sites are $20 at Bodega, and $30 at Wright's. Reservations are highly recommended. Call 800/444-7275. For general beach info, call 707/875-3483.

PLACES TO EAT

Seagull Deli: Don't look up when you eat at the outdoor tables here! Hah. It's an old joke, apparently, based on the deli's name. You and your dog can dine on creamy clam chowder while overlooking the mouth of the Russian River from one of the picnic tables. It's a tasty way to spend part of a crisp autumn afternoon. 10439 North Coast Highway (Highway 1); 707/865-2594.

PLACES TO STAY

Jenner Inn: This area is a black hole for cell phones, and only a few of the rooms and cottages have phones, and none have TVs, so this is a great place to visit if you really want to get away from it all. (That said, they're considering getting high-speed Internet access in the main inn.)

There's so much relaxing to be done here that you'll scarcely notice that you're not doing anything. The early-20th-century rooms and cottages are comfy and furnished with antiques. Some have fireplaces, some have kitchens, some have river views. The Russian River is just a bone's throw away, and it's a fairly quick walk to the ocean, should you want to see big water. The best part of staying here with a dog is the big three-acre meadow in the back: Pooches are welcome to trot around off leash! You won't need to worry about finding a local dog park if you stay here.

Rates are $138–188. A wonderful vacation home is available for $288. Highway 1, Box 69 95450; 707/865-2377; www.jennerinn.com.

Sonoma Coast State Beaches: See Sonoma Coast State Beaches, above, for camping information.

Occidental

If you become an accidental Occidental tourist, you and your leashed pooch can enjoy a stroll through this historic landmark town, with its interesting assortment of shops and galleries. If you want to spend the night, here's a dog-friendly lodging.

PLACES TO STAY

Negri's Occidental Hotel: This is a very basic, although decent, motel. It's close to the village, and there's a pool, should you feel like doing the dog paddle. (Your dog needs to stay dry here.) Rates are $59–139. Dogs are $8.70 extra. 3610 Bohemian Highway 95465; 707/874-3623 or 877/867-6084; www.occidentalhotel.com.

Sebastopol

Dogs enjoy sniffing out this sweet semirural community. It's got oodles of little Farm Trails farms (see the Sniff Out the Farm Trail Diversion), should you be drooling for some fresh produce. (Some sell meat, too, should that interest your dog.)

PARKS, BEACHES, AND RECREATION AREAS

🐾 Ragle Ranch Regional Park

😺😺😺 (See Sonoma County map on page 20)

While some of this 156-acre park is developed with sports fields and courts, much of it is devoted to being its good old natural self. A lovely nature trail will take you and your leashed dog to Atascadero Creek. Hang onto that leash, because this is a primo bird-watching area. Boy dogs love the oak grove that shades this area.

It costs $5 to park inside the park. From Highway 12, drive north on Ragle Road. The park will be on your left in several blocks. 707/565-2041.

PLACES TO EAT

Pasta Bella: The linguine with tomatoes is to drool for. Jake likes the bowl of water provided for thirsty dogs. 796 Gravenstein Highway South; 707/824-8191.

DIVERSION

Sniff Out the Farm Trail: This area is replete with fun little farms, selling everything from apples to wine to Christmas trees to meat and cheese. Well-behaved leashed dogs are often invited to join you at the many different farms that are part of the **Sonoma County Farm Trails.** Phone ahead to make sure it's OK. You can get a Farm Trails map and booklet with descriptions and phone numbers by contacting Sonoma County Farm Trails, P.O. Box 6032, Santa Rosa, CA 95406; 800/207-9464; or from the local Chamber of Commerce, P.O. Box 178, Sebastopol, CA 95473; 707/823-3032. Better yet, check out www.farmtrails.org.

Santa Rosa

PARKS, BEACHES, AND RECREATION AREAS

This sprawling city has gone to the dogs in the last few years, and dogs and their people couldn't be happier. It used to be that if you wanted to give your pooch a little off-leash exercise, you'd go out of town or sneak out to a park at night and hope no one was watching. But now the city has five very attractive off-leash dog parks and four parks that aren't fenced and have limited off-leash hours. That sound you hear is the sound of tails thumping. Hard. (Children's tails aren't wagging quite as quickly: Kids under 10 aren't allowed in any of the dog parks—not even on leash.)

For the most part, the dog parks are wonderful. And if you don't mind getting up early, the parks with limited off-leash hours offer even more room and more doggy-heaven scents. Dogs who visit these parks are allowed to run off leash 6–8 A.M. every day. The hours are strictly enforced, so be sure to wind your watch. Dogs have to be under voice control, nonaggressive, spayed or neutered, and more than four months old. As always, be sure to scoop the poop. The highest fine for poop lawbreakers could buy you a round-trip ticket to Hawaii, and then some: up to $500.

We like the philosophy of the parks department people here. In a nutshell, if there's a rough part of a park where people are afraid to go, they put in a dog park because they believe "it brings positive activities into the parks. It makes it much safer and more comfortable for kids and others," according to Bill Montgomery, the department's now-retired deputy director. We hope other communities look to Santa Rosa as an example of how to incorporate dogs into the park scene so that it makes life better for everyone.

🐾 DeTurk Round Barn Park

🐾🐾🐾🐾 (See Sonoma County map on page 20)

This is one of the more interesting parks to peruse with your pooch. It's a smallish park in the historic westside district of town, and it's home to a wonderful rare round barn that was built in the 1870s. Dogs have to be leashed to explore around the barn area.

What dogs like best about this park is a relatively small (9,000 square feet) dog park where they can throw their leashes to the wind. It's fenced with attractive white wood and has some young trees working to become shade trees. The dog park is actually called Maverick Park, in honor of a valuable member of the K-9 Corps of the Sonoma County Sheriff's Department who was killed in the line of duty in Santa Rosa. We won't forget you, Maverick.

The park is at Donahue and 8th Streets. 707/543-3292 or 707/539-5979.

🐾 Doyle Park

🐾🐾🐾🐾🐾 (See Sonoma County map on page 20)

Doyle Park is a very stately place to take a pooch. A little stone bridge takes you over a stream and into the park's main entry area. The trees here have an elegant, deep-rooted look. The grass is like a cool, plush green carpet. At Doyle, even the squirrels don't look squirrelly.

Dogs think it's all grand. But what they think is even better is the fact that they can run around all this splendor without a leash 6–8 A.M., thanks to a great program run by the city. Dogs who can't make these hours don't have to mope around on leash, though: Doyle Park is graced not only with the off-leash program, but it has its very own fenced doggy park. It's not as riveting as the rest of the park, but it's got water and some trees, and it's a very safe place to take even an escape artist. Unlike Rincon Park's dog run, Doyle's dog run doesn't close during the winter rains.

In addition to the rules mentioned in the beginning of this section, there's one that's a little tough if you're a parent of a dog and a youngish child: No children under 10 years old are allowed in the dog run, whether accompanied by a parent or not. The park users devised this rule, which was apparently meant to protect kids from getting mowed over by herds of dogs, and also to protect herds of dogs from lawsuits.

For the main entrance, take Sonoma Avenue to Doyle Park Drive and turn south, driving a few hundred feet over insufferable speed bumps to the parking area. The dog run will be way over to the left. To park closer to the dog run, take Sonoma Avenue to Hoen Avenue and turn south. The parking lot is on the right, and the dog run is on the other side of the ball field. 707/543-3292 or 707/539-5979.

17 Franklin Park

😊😊🐾 (See Sonoma County map on page 20)

Franklin is the smallest of the four parks that allow dogs off leash 6–8 A.M. It's green and slopey, with enough trees to make any boy dog happy. Be careful, because it's not as safe from traffic as some of the other parks (though it's not exactly Indy 500 territory around here).

The park is at Franklin Avenue and Gay Street. 707/543-3292 or 707/539-5979.

18 Galvin Community Park

😊😊😊🐾 (See Sonoma County map on page 20)

Yahoo! This is yet another addition to Santa Rosa's growing legion of dog parks. The fenced dog park is where your pooch can run free here. It's about three-quarters of an acre. Amenities include benches for your tired tush and water for your thirsty pooch. The ground cover is mostly wood chips. And it smells so good when it's first brought in. Sometimes it can be a little hard to tell the poop from the wood chips, but you get used to it. Jake always poops in the grass, which is easy to see, but so hard to clean up. (This is more than you needed to know about Jake.)

The park is at Yulupa Avenue and Bennett Valley Road. 707/543-3292 or 707/539-5979.

19 Hood Mountain Regional Park

😊😊😊 (See Sonoma County map on page 20)

Dogs and people love the trails in this 1,450-acre park, but the hiking isn't a walk in the park, so to speak. You'll end up going up, up, up if you expect to get to any of the best spots here. From Gunsight Rock, you can see the Golden Gate Bridge on a clear day.

To get to the only entrance, from Highway 12 turn east on Los Alamos Road—not Adobe Canyon Road, which leads only to Sugarloaf Ridge State Park, where dogs aren't allowed on trails. (If a sign appears at the Los Alamos Road turnoff saying that the park is closed, believe it: The park is subject to closures when there's danger of mudslides or fire.) The road is long, winding, steep, and narrow for the last two miles. It's not for nervous drivers or carsick pooches, but it's a beautiful four-mile drive, with a good close-up of Hood Mountain's bare rock outcropping "hood."

A machine in the parking lot will ask you to pay $4. Call to make sure the park is open before driving here. A final note: Watch out for ticks. They're rampant. 707/565-2041.

20 Northwest Community Park

😻😻😻🐾 (See Sonoma County map on page 20)

The fenced dog park within Northwest Park has doubled in size since its inception, and is once again up and running—and so are the neighborhood dogs. (No, smarty, the dogs haven't actually doubled in size.)

The dog area is now an acre and has two sections, grass, some shade, and at press time water and benches were about to go in. The dog park is just northwest of Northwest Park's soccer fields. The park is on Marlow Road, behind Comstock Junior High School, north of Guerneville Road. 707/543-3292 or 707/539-5979.

21 Rincon Valley Community Park

😻😻😻😻🐾 (See Sonoma County map on page 20)

The fenced dog park here is one of the more attractive dog parks in these parts. That's mostly because it has grass. Real grass. Not just a few green sprigs fighting their way through the tough dirt, but good ol' carpety grass. That's not because the dogs here pussyfoot around. In fact, dogs are so happy to be here that they tear around with great gusto. We're not exactly sure why there's so much grass, but we do know that the dog run closes during the rainy winter months, so that could have something to do with it.

A few trees grace the dog-run area, and the views of the surrounding hills make it seem as if it's in the middle of the countryside. As of this writing, it's actually on the edge of the countryside.

The dogs who come to Rincon's dog run are a friendly lot, running to the fence and sniffing all newcomers, tails wagging exuberantly. The people who come here are much the same, except they chat rather than sniff. An interesting rule: No little kiddies under 10 allowed, even if they're with their parents. A parks department spokesman says the park users made up the rule. So apparently if you've got a kid and a dog, you'll have to hire a sitter to bring your dog here. Boo!

But now here's something to cheer about: The dog park includes a little wading pond! This puts some big wag in a water dog's tail. There's also a separate section for large and small dogs. The park is on Montecito Boulevard, west of Calistoga Road. Don't forget that it's closed during the rainy months. 707/543-3292 or 707/539-5979.

22 Southwest Community Park

😻😻😻🐾 (See Sonoma County map on page 20)

If your dog doesn't need a park in the hoity-toitiest part of town, this is a mighty convenient and friendly place to take him. First of all, it's relatively close to the freeway, so it's easy to get to if you're on the road. But better than that, it's big and green, with neatly paved paths that meander by cascading willows. It's also far enough from the road that the traffic danger is minimal. Why care about traffic? Because your dog can be off leash here 6–8 A.M., thanks to a program that's got dogs at its very heart.

From U.S. 101, take the Hearn Avenue exit and drive west for nearly a mile. The park is on the left, across from Westland Drive. 707/543-3292 or 707/539-5979.

23 Spring Lake Regional Park

🐾🐾🐾 (See Sonoma County map on page 20)

In winter, this county park doesn't offer dogs much more than a leashed trot around the lake. But in summer, it's leafy and full of the sounds of kids yelling and thumping oars. It's more fun here for people than dogs, who must be leashed. This is a good spot for a picnic, blading, working out on a parcourse fitness trail, a boat ride, or human swimming (no dogs allowed in the swim area). The path around the lake is paved for skaters, strollers, and bicyclists, and there are short dirt paths off into the open oak and brush woods. You can fish from the banks, where they're cleared of tules and willows.

The parking fee is $4 in winter, $5 in summer; the large lot has some shady spots. Campsites are $17, plus $1 extra for a dog. Most of the 30 sites are reservable, and a few are first-come, first-served. For reservations phone 707/565-2267. Dogs must have proof of a rabies vaccination. The campground is open daily May 1–September 30, weekends and holidays the rest of the year.

From Highway 12, on the Farmer's Lane section in Santa Rosa, turn east on Hoen Avenue. Take Hoen four stoplights to Newanga Avenue. Turn left on Newanga, which goes straight to the entrance. 707/539-8092.

24 Youth Community Park

🐾🐾🐾🐾 🐕 (See Sonoma County map on page 20)

If you like oak trees, come here. Big oaks hang out all over the park. Some really big, really old oaks even have their own fences, so no one can do leg lifts or initial carving on their trunks.

The main attraction for dogs is the big green meadowy lawn area. Pooches love rolling on it and cantering over it. Your dog can be off leash here 6–8 A.M. thanks to a dog-friendly program.

A word of warning: Skateboarders abound here. A little skateboard area is in front of the park, and kids love skateboarding around the parking lot, too. Some dogs don't even notice them; others get nervous about the sound of board crashing on pavement.

The park is in the far west reaches of the city, on the west side of Fulton Road, about a quarter of a mile south of Piner Road. 707/543-3292.

PLACES TO EAT

Flying Goat Coffee: Want to justify eating a doughnut from this fun Railroad Square eatery? You can get organic ones here! Dine with your dog at the four umbrella-topped tables outside. There's usually a bowl of water out here, too. (For your dog, not your feet.) 10 4th Street; 707/575-1202.

Juice Shack: In the summer, come here with your hot pooch and cool off with a creamy smoothie or a fresh organic juice. In cooler months, you can enjoy hot juices here. Hmm. I'd rather go for the hot soup served here, or the wrap sandwiches. Dine with your dog at the outdoor area under the big pine tree. Thirsty dogs will get water on request. 1810 Mendocino Avenue; 707/528-6131.

PLACES TO STAY

Best Western Garden Inn: Dogs should be under 50 pounds to stay here. Rates are $72–185. Dogs are $15 extra. 1500 Santa Rosa Avenue 95404; 707/546-4031.

Los Robles Lodge: Rates are $60–129. Dogs are $15 extra. 1985 Cleveland Avenue 95401; 707/545-6330 or 800/255-6330; www.losrobleslodge.com.

Spring Lake Regional Park: See Spring Lake Regional Park, above, for camping information.

Vineyard Lodge: Rates at this former TraveLodge are $55–89. Dogs are $20 extra. 1815 Santa Rosa Avenue 95407; 707/542-3472.

Bodega Bay

PARKS, BEACHES, AND RECREATION AREAS

25 Westside Regional Park

(See Sonoma County map on page 20)

This is an undistinguished but handy park and campground built on landfill right on the water, with picnic tables and barbecues. Spud Point Marina, just to the north, also allows leashed dogs.

The fee for day use is $4 most of the year, and $5 Memorial Day to Labor Day. There are 47 campsites, costing $17, plus $1 for each dog. It's first-come, first-served. The park is on Westshore Road, a westward turn off Highway 1 in town. Phone 707/875-3540 for more info, or 707/565-2267 for camping reservations.

26 Doran Beach Regional Park

(See Sonoma County map on page 20)

This Sonoma County regional park offers leashed dogs access to marshland full of egrets, herons, and deer, as well as to the Pinnacle Gulch Trail. The plain but serviceable beach has almost no surf (which is great for dog swims), and there are picnic tables near the beach.

The fee for day use is $4 most of the year, and $5 Memorial Day to Labor Day. Campsites are $17 plus $1 for each dog. The campground, which has 134 sites, is on a first-come, first-served basis. The park is on Highway 1, one mile south of Bodega Bay. Phone 707/875-3540 for more info, or 707/565-2267 for camping reservations.

PLACES TO EAT

The Boat House: This restaurant in downtown Bodega Bay will allow you to sit with your dog as you eat fish-and-chips, oysters, and calamari at one of the six unshaded tables on its patio. If fish isn't your dog's wish, he can order a burger. 1445 Highway 1; 707/875-3495.

The Dog House: The name of the restaurant says it all. But if you need more, here are the words of one of the servers: "Dogs are treated better than people here." The Dog House is indeed a very dog-friendly place to dine. The food is unpretentious (hot dogs, burgers, etc.), and the servers love seeing a dog come to one of the eight outdoor tables. They often offer a bowl of water before the pooch even gets a chance to peruse the menu. 537 Highway 1; 707/875-2441.

Lucas Wharf: Your dog's nose will flare and drip with excitement as you dine at the outdoor tables here. That's partly because of the tasty deli specials, but it's mostly because your dog will be getting high on sea smells at this place right on the water. Speaking of water, the folks here love dogs and will provide your pooch with water, should she need to wet her whistle. 595 Highway 1; 707/875-3522.

PLACES TO STAY

Bodega Bay RV Park: If you have an RV and want to stay in this wonderful area, park 'er here. The managers will point you to some nearby property where you can run your good dog without a leash. Rates are $25–39. 2000 Highway 1 94923; 707/875-3701 or 800/201-6864.

Doran Beach Regional Park: See Doran Beach Regional Park, above, for camping information.

Westside Regional Park: See Westside Regional Park, above, for camping information.

Rohnert Park

PARKS, BEACHES, AND RECREATION AREAS

27 Crane Creek Regional Park

🐾🐾🐾 (See Sonoma County map on page 20)

For years, this 128-acre patch of grazing land in the middle of nowhere has been undeveloped open space for your dog's pleasure. Recent improvements include an upgraded parking lot, the addition of picnic tables, and the widening of 2.6 miles of hiking trails. Unfortunately, the leash law is enforced here, and a sign tells you why: "Dogs Caught in Livestock May Be Shot." Carry water; you may get thirsty just trying to find the place in your car.

From Rohnert Park, drive east on the Rohnert Park Expressway to Petaluma Hill Road. Turn south on Petaluma Hill Road to Roberts Road, and go east for two miles on Roberts Road. You'll find the park shortly after Roberts turns into Pressley Road. A machine is there to collect a $4 parking fee from you. 707/565-2041 or 707/823-7262.

PLACES TO STAY

Best Western Rohnert Park: This hotel is right next door to a huge veterinary center that is nationally renowned for its neurology department. If you find yourself taking your dog there, stay here. The manager, Johnny, loves dogs and brings his own pooch to work with him. According to Baron, a quesadilla-loving German shorthaired pointer who wrote to me, Johnny and the staff bent over backward making his stay as comfortable as possible when Baron was getting MRIs next door. Rates are $95–105. 6500 Redwood Drive 94928; 707/584-7435.

Glen Ellen

PARKS, BEACHES, AND RECREATION AREAS

28 Jack London State Historic Park

🐾🐾🐾 (See Sonoma County map on page 20)

The extensive backcountry trails here are off-limits to dogs, but the parts of historic interest are not. You're free to take your leashed dog the half mile to Wolf House, visiting Jack London's grave en route, and around the stone house containing the museum of Londoniana (open 10 A.M.–5 P.M., no pets inside). The trail is paved and smooth up to the museum, but then it becomes dirt and narrow.

Oaks, pines, laurels, and madrones cast dappled light, and the ups and downs are gentle. Signs warn of poison oak and rattlesnakes. The ruins of the huge stone lodge that was London's dream Wolf House are impressive and sad. A fire of unknown origin destroyed it in 1913. London planned to rebuild it, but he died three years later.

Dogs are also allowed in the picnic areas by the parking lot and the museum. From Highway 12, follow signs to the park. Turn west on Arnold Drive, then west again on London Ranch Road. The fee is $6 for day use. 707/938-5216.

29 Sonoma Valley Regional Park/ Elizabeth Anne Perrone Dog Park

😊😊😊😊🐾 (See Sonoma County map on page 20)

This large, welcoming park has a paved, level trail that winds alongside a branch of Sonoma Creek. Better yet for dogs who like to roll, it sports many dirt trails that head off into the oak woodlands above. Varied grasses, wildflowers, madrones, and moss-hung oaks make this a scenic walk. Dogs like to chew some of the grasses, roll on the wildflowers (don't let them do this!), and do leg lifts on the madrones and oaks. They may enjoy the park even more than you. If you start at the park entrance off Highway 12 and walk westward across the park to Glen Ellen for about a mile, you'll end up at Sonoma Creek and the old mill, with its huge working waterwheel.

Dogs need to be on leash for all that fun. But the big fenced dog park within the park is an exception. The Elizabeth Anne Perrone Dog Park is only about an acre, but it feels like more. It's totally landscaped, with grass and trees. "A dog lover's paradise," as reader Robin Domer and her furry children, Max and Oliver, wrote us. Pooper-scoopers, poop bags, and fresh water are supplied. As if this weren't enough, the super-dog-friendly Garden Court Cafe is right across the street.

The park is just south of Glen Ellen between Arnold Drive and Highway 12. The entrance is off Highway 12. The parking fee is $4. 707/539-8092.

PLACES TO EAT

Garden Court Cafe: This sweet café, right across the street from the leash-free Elizabeth Anne Perrone Dog Park (see above), is just as dog-friendly as the park! Dogs may join you on the patio (open only on weekends), where they can drink from dog water bowls and even choose from a few items on a dog menu. Jake likes the Blue Plate Special, a kind of egg scramble with burger, zucchini, and garlic. (His dog breath is rather interesting after such a meal.) If your dog hankers for something Italian, try the "Babaloo" pizza, which is a biscuit crust topped with ketchup, jack cheese, and fresh herbs. It's good-looking enough that you might be tempted to share it with your dog, but the human food here is tasty, too, and your dog will like you better if you order your own. If your dog doesn't feel like paying for one of these dishes, he can get a free house-made pooch biscuit. (Far from a consolation prize, judging by the blissful expression on Jake's face.) 13875 Highway 12; 707/935-1565.

Cotati

PLACES TO EAT

Johnny's Java: This coffeehouse is home to tasty baked goods. Dine with doggy at the four umbrella-topped tables on the patio. 8492 Gravenstein Highway; 707/794-0168.

Petaluma

Petaluma is a captivating Sunday afternoon stroll, with its tree-lined streets and pocket parks for your dog's pleasure. Victorian buildings, old feed mills, and a riverfront that remains mostly original, but not dilapidated, complete the charming picture. And let's not forget an added canine bonus: Depending on the wind direction, you can often smell fresh cow manure wafting in from the surrounding hills. Dogs thrive on this.

Best of all, dogs get to run leashless during set (if early) hours in a whopping 13 parks, and all day at their very own pooch park! No wonder they call this place PET-aluma.

PARKS, BEACHES, AND RECREATION AREAS

Dogs who live in Petaluma are lucky dogs indeed. A few years back, the enlightened Parks and Recreation Department decided that dogs needed places to run off leash and gave dogs who are under voice control the OK to be leash-free in a dozen parks during certain hours. Most of those hours have increased since then, but you should still watch your off-leash hours like a hawk—the fine for a first offense is up to $100! Better to invest that money in a good watch.

Dogs also have their very own park, called Rocky Memorial Dog Park. It's one of the largest dog parks in the state. Dogs are singing its praises ("Howl-elujah!").

30 Arroyo Park

🐾🐾🐾🐕 (See Sonoma County map on page 20)

Most of Arroyo Park is very well groomed, with golf course–like green grass and a perfectly paved walking path running through its three acres. However, it seems many dogs prefer the seedier side of the park—the weedier, uncut area on the right as you face the park. We hope that area remains like this for dogs who like to walk a little on the wild side.

Dogs are allowed off leash here 6–11 A.M. weekdays and 6–8 A.M. weekends, and 8–10 P.M. every night. It's just a bone's throw from Wiseman Airport Park (listed below), though, which is a much safer place to run a dog, since you can get farther from the road. The park is at Garfield and Village East Drives. 707/778-4380.

31 Bond Park

🐾🐾🐾🐕 (See Sonoma County map on page 20)

It's green here, so green that Joe couldn't help but run out of the car and throw himself down on the grass and start wriggling and writhing in ecstasy. I thought for sure he'd found something odious to roll in, but underneath him was just clean, green grass. He rolled for about 10 minutes, got up, and heaved himself down in another spot, rolling and groaning and making the children in the playground giggle. The park is pleasant, with some shade from medium-sized trees. With six acres, it's a good size for dogs. And it's set in a quiet area, on Banff Way just south of Maria Drive, so traffic is minimal. Dogs are allowed off leash here 6–11 A.M. weekdays and 6–8 A.M. weekends, and 8–10 P.M. every night. 707/778-4380.

32 Del Oro Park

🐾🐾🐾🐕 (See Sonoma County map on page 20)

Del Oro is very suburban. It's got a nice little play area for kids. It's got green grass. It's surrounded by not-too-old suburban homes. It's got soccer goal posts. When we last visited, there were even two old Suburban sport utility vehicles parked in front.

Something not terribly suburban, a fire hydrant in one of the grassy areas, is probably the most coveted part of the park—at least for boy dogs. Well-behaved pooches can be off leash here 6–11 A.M. weekdays and 6–8 A.M. weekends, and 8–10 P.M. every night. The park is at Sartori Drive and Del Oro Circle. 707/778-4380.

33 Glenbrook Park

🐾🐾🐕 (See Sonoma County map on page 20)

Who'd believe it? When we last visited, a great blue heron landed in this narrow park, which is surrounded by newish homes. This was a wonderful sight, because the land around here looks as if it's still in shock from all the development of the past decade.

The park is nearly four acres and is much longer than it is wide. It's directly across the street from Sunrise Park (listed below), but it's a little quieter and more attractive, with some medium-sized trees here and there. Its off-leash hours are generous on the hind end: 6–10 A.M. and 6–10 P.M. daily. The park is at Maria Drive and Sunrise Parkway. 707/778-4380.

34 Helen Putnam Regional Park

🐾🐾🐾 (See Sonoma County map on page 20)

This 216-acre county regional park is, and will remain, a minimally developed stretch of converted cow pasture with oak trees. A wide paved trail shared by hikers and bicyclists runs between the main entrance and the Victoria housing development (to enter from that end, go to the end of Oxford Court). Dogs must be leashed. There's no shade from the scrub oaks, and it can get mighty windy. The paved trail has gentle ups and downs. Some other dirt trails give you steeper hill climbs. About a quarter of a mile in from the main entrance is an old cattle pond good for a dog swim (if the dog stays on a leash—quite a feat).

Parking is $4. Next to the lot is a kids' playground and a picnic gazebo, set by a creek that's only a gully in summer. Drive south on Western Avenue and turn left on Chileno Valley Road. After a half mile, you'll see the turnoff to the park. 707/565-2041.

35 Lucchesi Park

😻 😻 😻 🐕 (See Sonoma County map on page 20)

This is a well-kept, popular city park with a postmodern community center that impresses people but doesn't stir dogs much. Dogs prefer strolling through empty sports fields, picnicking at shaded tables, lounging under the weepy willows, watching ducks and the spewing fountain at the large pond, and trotting along the paved paths here. No dog swimming is allowed in the pond. It's a rule that makes it impossible to take Jake Dog near the pond, because he can't contain his excitement at the idea of being in the water. We've met other water dogs with the same affliction here.

Dogs are allowed off leash here 6–11 A.M. weekdays and 6–8 A.M. weekends, and 8–10 P.M. every night. Be sure to keep dogs away from the ducks and geese who like to lounge beside their pond, because feathers should not fly as a result of the city's kindly off-leash allowances. The park is at North McDowell Boulevard and Madison Street. 707/778-4386.

36 McNear Park

😻 😻 😻 🐕 (See Sonoma County map on page 20)

McNear is an attractive seven-acre park, with green, green grass, plenty of shade, picnic tables, and a playground. But the part of the park dogs like best is the enclosed athletic field, where they're allowed to romp off leash 6–11 A.M. weekdays and 6–8 A.M. weekends, and 8–10 P.M. every night. The field is usually green and almost entirely fenced, but there are a couple of spots where a clever escape artist could slip out, so heads up. It's at F and 9th Streets. 707/778-4380.

37 Oak Hill Park

😻 😻 😻 😻 🐕 (See Sonoma County map on page 20)

Dogs love running up and down the gently rolling hills on this five-acre park set in the midst of beautiful old Victorian homes near downtown Petaluma. Oak Hill Park is hilly and oaky (surprise!), qualities dogs enjoy. Some good-sized oaks make their home in various parts of the park, and dogs appreciate their shade-giving arms.

Dogs are permitted to run off leash on the east side of the creek from Sunnyslope to Westridge Drive 6 A.M.–10 P.M. Monday–Friday. That's a lotta hours. But wait, that's not all! They can also visit the park off leash 6–11 A.M. and 5–10 P.M. on weekends. These are magnificent hours. The park is at Howard and Oak Streets. 707/778-4380.

38 Petaluma Adobe State Historic Park

 (See Sonoma County map on page 20)

Leashed dogs are welcome here, if they behave well around goats and such, and if you avoid the farm animal courtyard. From the parking lot, walk across a wooden bridge over a wide, willow-lined creek (dry in summer) to the house, built in 1836 as headquarters for General Mariano Vallejo's 66,600-acre Rancho Petaluma. Clustered around the house are tempting displays of animal hides, saddles, and tallow makings, as well as sheep, chickens, and a donkey. Dogs must use their best manners. If you see them starting to think of lamb chops for dinner, make sure you hang on hard to that leash.

The park is southeast of Petaluma at Adobe Road and Casa Grande Road. From U.S. 101, you'll see an exit sign for the Petaluma Adobe. Admission is $2 for adults. 707/762-4871.

39 Petaluma City Hall Lawn

(See Sonoma County map on page 20)

If you have business to conduct at city hall, your dog can conduct his own kind of business outside. (Unlike your business, your dog's will have to be scooped.)

The west lawn area permits off-leash dogs 6–8 A.M. every day, with evening hours 8–10 P.M. August–October, and 6–10 P.M. November–July. Petaluma City Hall is at 11 English Street. 707/778-4380.

40 Prince Park

(See Sonoma County map on page 20)

Dogs are permitted off leash at this attractive 20-acre park during longer hours than they are at most other parks in the city, and they think this is just swell. On a recent visit, a springer-shepherd mix was running around drooling and panting and smiling like a dog in love. His person said when he comes here, he's ecstatic. "Willie loves the grass and the trees. I love the hours for off leash, and I love its safety from traffic," she said. (The park is set back quite far from street traffic.) Off-leash hours are rather confusing at first glance, but they're actually quite simple at second glance: 6 A.M.–3 P.M. weekdays September–May, 6–8 A.M. weekdays June–August, 6–8 A.M. weekends, and 8–10 P.M. every night. The park is across East Washington Street from the airport, just a little north of the airport sign. 707/778-4380.

41 Rocky Memorial Dog Park

🐾🐾🐾🐾🐕 (See Sonoma County map on page 20)

The scenery isn't great, and the land has nary a tree on it, but it's one of the biggest dog parks we've ever encountered. And size does matter, at least when it comes to fenced dog parks.

This flat nine-acre piece of land is the best thing that's happened to Petaluma's dogs since the park system began allowing them off leash at certain parks during limited hours a few years back. Dogs enjoy the smell that can pervade the land; it's beside a marshy area next to the Petaluma River. Fortunately, it's well fenced so dogs can't chase the marsh birds or roll in the marsh muck. The fencing keeps the dogs from escaping to all areas but the parking lot, which leads to the park entrance, which eventually leads a busy road. So if you have a pooch who's prone to running away, be aware the place is safe, but it isn't foolproof.

Because it's so barren here, it can really roast on hot days. Be sure to bring water. A sign at the entrance says "No dogs in heat," and I thought it was nice of them to be so concerned about the temperature for dog walking. It took me a few seconds and an eye roll from my husband to realize the sign's true intent.

On our first visit, Joe searched in vain for something to lift a leg on. He found only some garbage cans and a few big weeds, and they were right next to the parking lot. The next visit he just succumbed to the lack of leg-lift targets and took to relieving his bladder like a girl dog. But not, of course, until looking around to make sure no one was watching.

Rocky Park was named after a big-hearted police dog who died at the too-young age of 10 during a narcotics search. It was kidney failure that got him, not the wrong end of a dealer's pistol. Rocky had helped seize a few million dollars of narcotics in his career, but his greatest act came in 1992 when he saved the life of his beloved handler one night. A felon had escaped and the officer chased him to a creek, where the felon got the upper hand and was holding the officer's head underwater. The officer managed to hit a remote control button that opened the windows of the patrol car and released Rocky, who'd seen his friend in trouble. Rocky bolted to the creek and got the upper paw. He saved his friend and helped bag the bad guy. "It was the beginning of the era of Rocky," said Officer Jeff Hasty, a dog handler with the Petaluma Police Department. A bust of Rocky now graces the front lobby of the police department.

This is an easy park to visit if you're on U.S. 101 and your pooch is hankering to stretch his gams. Take the Highway 116 east (*not* west)/Lakeville exit and follow the street just over a half mile to Casa Grande Road, where you'll take a sharp right. Drive a few hundred feet past ugly storage bins and trucks and you'll soon hit the entrance to the park. Unlike most of the other city parks with off-leash times, this one has great hours: 6 A.M.–10 P.M. 707/778-4380.

42 Sunrise Park

 (See Sonoma County map on page 20)

If you're a real estate developer, there's a chance you might enjoy this park. It's very, very narrow, squeezed like an old tube of toothpaste by cookie-cutter condos and townhouses. It's too close to traffic. It's not terribly attractive. But in its defense, it does have decent grassy areas and fun (for dogs) weedy patches. Another plus: Dogs can be off leash 6–10 A.M. and 6–10 P.M. daily. Those are some pretty long hours for a pretty slim park. It's at Marina Drive and Sunrise Parkway. 707/778-4380.

43 Westridge Open Space

(See Sonoma County map on page 20)

Dogs get to peruse the east side of this three-acre park off leash 6–10 A.M. and 6–10 P.M. daily. The park is long and narrow, with plenty of medium-sized trees, which turn a warm red in autumn. When we visited, a fluffy black cat teased Joe from the middle of the road. Another kitty was there when we recently sniffed out the park with Jake. Cat-chasers, exercise caution when off leash. The park is on Westridge Drive, near its intersection with Westridge Place. 707/778-4380.

44 Wiseman Airport Park

(See Sonoma County map on page 20)

Plenty of pooches visit this park, and for good reason. Wiseman is 32 acres of well-kept playing fields, uncut grass, many shade trees, and comfortably wide walking paths. It's also a good place to watch little planes land and take off, because of its proximity to the airport. (They don't call it Airport Park for nothing.) Best of all, dogs can run off leash in the athletic fields during these hours: 6–11 A.M. weekdays and 6–8 A.M. weekends, and 8–10 P.M. every night. The best access is at St. Augustine Circle. 707/778-4380.

PLACES TO EAT

Apple Box: A store of antiques and housewares, this charmer also serves good desserts, teas, and coffee. There are 10 tables outside, right by the river. It's real olfactory bliss for your dog. 224 B Street; 707/762-5222.

Aram's Cafe: Dine on really good Mediterranean and Armenian food at the five outdoor tables. Aram's is in downtown Petaluma. 131 Kentucky Street; 707/765-9775.

Dempseys Restaurant and Brewery: There's always a dog water bowl here, and it's kept filled to the brim. The menu here is terrific. Jake drools over our neighbors' chicken and chops. (Fortunately not right over it.) Thank you to John Flynn and his dogs for sniffing this place out for us. 50 East Washington Street; 707/765-9694.

PLACES TO STAY

Motel 6: Rates are $44–70 for the first adult, $3 for the second. 1368 North McDowell Boulevard 94954; 707/765-0333.

San Francisco North KOA: This is Jake's kind of camping. Upon arrival at this family camping resort, dogs get a little treat attached to a card that lists the doggy rules. The 60-acre campground is more attractive than most KOAs we've visited. The setting is rural, and there are trees everywhere. Like other KOAs, the campsites are drive-up and pretty doggone close to each other, but it's still a fun place to pitch a tent, especially if you like hot showers and cool pools as part of your camping experience. Better yet, try one of the cute log "Kamping Kabins." They're cozy, with a bunk bed and a queen bed. (You provide the bedding.)

Adding to its rural charm, this KOA even has a pen that houses several goats. Visit in the spring to see some adorable furry kids.

The managers here ask that you walk your dog on leash, either on camping roads or the designated field (which has poop bags!). The rule here, as it is at many KOAs, is no pit bulls. Rates are $29–47 for camping. Kamping Kabins are $49–69. 20 Rainsville Road 94952; 707/763-1492 or 800/992-2267; www .sanfranciscokoa.com.

Sheraton Sonoma County: Dogs are welcome to stay at this attractive hotel, as long as they weigh no more than 80 pounds. They're so welcome, in fact, that they'll get use of a big dog bed and doggy bowls. "We like to make their stay nice, too," says a hotelier. The hotel has a heated outdoor pool and a hot tub for the humans in your crew. It's close to a popular jogging trail that permits pooches on leashes. Dogs must stay in first-floor rooms, and they mustn't smoke. (The entire hotel is nonsmoking.) Rates are $129–269. 745 Baywood Drive 94954; 707/283-2888.

Sonoma

Downtown Sonoma is a treat for people, and until the last few years, dogs had been banned from all the good spots—most city parks, Sonoma plaza, and the state historic park. But there's finally something to wag about: a new park just two blocks from the plaza.

PARKS, BEACHES, AND RECREATION AREAS

45 Ernest Holman Dog Park

🐾🐾🐾🐕 (See Sonoma County map on page 20)

Ernest was a good dog. So good that his person, Sue Holman, donated enough money for a dog park in his name. (Most of my human friends don't even have such formal-sounding names.) Opened in 1999, Ernest Holman Dog Park is a welcome addition to downtown Sonoma. It's small—a little under an acre—and the turf can be mushy in the wet season, but it's incredibly popular. Happy dogs of every ilk tear around this fenced area. When they need to catch their doggy breaths, they repose in the shade of the park's enormous redwood trees. People enjoy sitting on benches and chatting with other dog folks while watching their panting pooches. (There's water for when they—the dogs, not the people—need to wet their whistles.)

The park is two blocks north of the plaza, on 1st Street West, next to the police station. It's part of the Field of Dreams sporting field complex. 707/938-3681.

Maxwell Farms Regional Park

🐾🐾 (See Sonoma County map on page 20)

This park offers playing fields, picnic tables, a generous kids' playground, smooth paths, and a large undeveloped area where paths follow Sonoma Creek under huge laurels wound with wild grapevines. The creek is dry in summer, but leashed dogs like to sniff it anyway.

The entrance is off Verano Avenue, west of Highway 12. The day-use fee is $2. 707/565-2041.

PLACES TO EAT

Coffee Garden: This is a peaceful haven for dogs and their people. The magnificent garden patio has a fountain that fascinates some dogs and makes others look as if they need to head to the nearest tree fast. Actually, a big, 160-year-old fig tree is in the middle of the patio area, but leg lifts are definitely not permitted.

The café is housed in the historic Captain Salvador Vallejo Adobe, which was built in the late 1830s. A brochure you can pick up at the café explains its history and suggests carefully examining its architecture for various details. Most dogs would rather not have to closely explore the unique adobe brick construction of the walls, as suggested by the brochure, unless there happened to be a little chicken salad splattered on it.

Brandon Dog, pooch extraordinaire of Forest Service spokesman extraordinaire Matt Mathes and his wife (also extraordinaire, says Matt), loves this place. When Brandon visited recently, a guitar player was strumming out some gentle melodies. "Brandon seemed to enjoy the guitar. But he was more interested in the food," says Matt.

The food here is light and very tasty. Try the smoked salmon sandwich or the zesty Chinese chicken sandwich. There's a good espresso menu and a small selection of beers and wines. The Coffee Garden is on the Sonoma Plaza, at 415-421 1st Street West; 707/996-6645.

PLACES TO STAY

Best Western Sonoma Valley Inn: If you want to stay close to the town plaza, this hotel is just a little more than a block away. Rates are $114–354. One dog is $30 extra. Two are $45 extra. 550 2nd Street West 95476; 707/938-9200 or 800/334-5784; www.sonomavalleyinn.com.

Stone Grove Inn: Dogs think they've died and gone to Greece when they stay at this rustic, charming inn. That's because owner Charles Papanteles has a flair for decorating with the old-world Mediterranean flair of his ancestors.

But what really makes dogs say *"Opa!"* is that the inn is surrounded by acres of gorgeous meadows, pastures, and organic veggie gardens. There's plenty of room for leashed walking. ("A dog walk path is one cornfield away," we're told.) The stone cottage, where dogs are permitted (they aren't allowed in the red barn studio), is really made of stone, and it's small, private, and secluded. It had better be secluded, because it has a detached bathroom and an outdoor shower. We found this kind of fun, but if your bladder is the size of a peanut, this may not be the place for you. Bathrooms aside, the stone cottage, which is more than 100 years old, can be mighty cozy with the potbellied stove blazing.

Rates are $95–125. Dogs are $10–20 extra. The cottage is just a bone's throw from Sonoma's town square, at 240 2nd Street 95476; 707/939-8249; www.stonegrovebb.com.

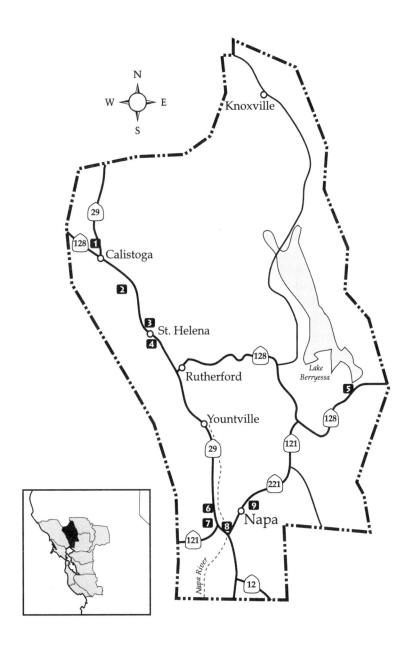

N
W   E
S

Knoxville

29

128   **1**   Calistoga

2

3   St. Helena
4

Rutherford

128

Lake
Berryessa

5

128

Yountville

29

121

221

6   **9**   Napa
7
8

121

Napa River

12

CHAPTER 2
Napa County

Napa dogs don't whine. They wine. And since there are plenty of dog-friendly restaurants here, they often wine and dine.

This is the home of California's most famous wine-making valley, and dogs get to experience some of the fringe benefits of this productive area. A few attractive wineries invite well-behaved dogs to relax and sniff around with their owners (our favorite is the Dutch Henry Winery in the Calistoga area; see the Diversions Grape Expectations for this and others), but most don't want to publicize their dog policy. When you do find a dog-friendly winery, don't let your dog do leg lifts on inappropriate items, because Bacchus will get you. And your little dog, too.

Since the book's last edition, a few more terrific inns in Napa have opened their doors to dogs, who would give this a thumbs-up if only they had opposable ones.

The county's parks come up a little on the dry side. With the county's lush, fertile, and inviting vineyards, it seems as if there's so much land that dogs would be in heaven here. Jake and I only wish the parks could follow in the

PICK OF THE LITTER—NAPA COUNTY

BEST DOG PARK
Alston Park/Canine Commons, Napa (page 64)

PRETTIEST RESTAURANT
Ristorante Tra Vigne, St. Helena (page 61)

MOST DOG-FRIENDLY RESTAURANT
Angele Restaurant, Napa (page 65)

MOST DOG-FRIENDLY PLACES TO STAY
Washington Street Lodging, Calistoga (page 59)
Napa River Inn, Napa (pages 66–67)
Napa Valley Country Cottage, Napa (page 67)

BEST FUNKY ATTRACTIONS
Old Faithful Geyser, Calistoga (page 57)
Petrified Forest, Calistoga (page 58)

BEST PLACE TO TRY SOME BUBBLY
Mumm Napa Valley, Rutherford (page 60)

pawsteps of three Calistoga lodgings that have land from 11 to 40 acres: Dogs with well-behaved humans can not only sniff around the acreage, but they can do so off leash!

Only about a dozen public parks and a few miscellaneous sites in Napa County allow dogs. The city of Napa has four parks where dogs are allowed, and all four permit them off leash in certain sections. You may incur the grapes of your dog's wrath if you don't take her to visit one of these leash-free lands next time you're in town.

Calistoga

PARKS, BEACHES, AND RECREATION AREAS

1 Pioneer Park

🐾🐾 (See Napa County map on page 52)

This is a small park, but its location so close to the heart of Calistoga makes it a great place to stop for a relaxing picnic with your leashed pooch. The two-acre park has plenty of shade trees and enough open area so your canine won't feel claustrophobic.

Going north on Foothill Boulevard, turn right on Lincoln Avenue. In two blocks, turn left on Cedar Street. The park will be on your right within a block. 707/942-2800.

2 Bothe-Napa State Park

🐾🐾 (See Napa County map on page 52)

Dogs are relegated to paved roads and campgrounds here, and it's a crime because of all the alluring trails. Hiking the asphalt can be fun, though. Joe seemed especially captivated by a man who was burning bacon over the campfire, his wife yelling that this was some vacation.

A wilderness haven this park is not, at least for you and your dog. Dogs must be leashed at all times. One of the two roads they're allowed on parallels Highway 29 and is so close you can see the drivers' eyes, often bloodshot from too much wine-tasting.

On the positive end, the roads are stunning in autumn when the leaves change color. And dogs are allowed to camp with you, on leash. Dogs are also allowed in some of the picnic areas just off the roads.

The day-use fee is $6. There are 50 campsites. Fees are $20. Call 800/444-7275 for reservations. The park is on Highway 29, halfway between St. Helena and Calistoga, just north of Bale Lane. The entrance is on the west side of the road. 3801 North St. Helena Highway (Highway 29). 707/942-4575.

PLACES TO EAT

Home Plate: Far from the tourist parking woes in town, this inexpensive, unassuming short-order restaurant makes some of the best grilled-cheese sandwiches that ever melted in a mouth. Dine at one of three big outdoor tables. If your dog is thirsty, you can get a bowl of water here. 2448 Foothill Boulevard (Highway 128); 707/942-5646.

PLACES TO STAY

Hillcrest II Bed and Breakfast: On the outside it's a good-looking, large, modern house. But on the inside, it's filled with antiques and other family heirlooms of the locally famed Tubbs family. Debbie O'Gorman, owner of Hillcrest II, is the last of the Tubbs family to live in the Napa area, and she's tastefully stocked the house with items from the family mansion, which burned down in 1964. There's even an old Steinway grand piano waiting to be played in the sitting room (which also has a fireplace).

All this is well and good with dog guests, but what they *really* adore is that the house is set on 40 acres where they're allowed to romp on terrific trails without a leash if their humans are well behaved. This is a dog's dream come true, because there just aren't leash-free stomping grounds like these in Napa County, unless you own big property. Fisherfolks and their dogs love it here, too, because there's a fishing pond on the property stocked with all kinds of fishies, including catfish and bluegill. The property is at the base of Mt. St. Helena, and the house is on a hilltop (thus the name), so the views are breathtaking.

Humans enjoy using the gorgeous 40-foot-long pool. Dogs enjoy dipping their paws in the pond. Humans can also use the kitchen and barbecue areas, which is convenient if you don't want to go out to eat every day. A delectable continental breakfast is served on weekends.

Debbie, who has two friendly dogs of her own, asks that you bring a bed for your dog, if he sleeps on the floor, or a blanket to place under him if he sleeps on human furniture. She also provides a large outdoor kennel should you want to head out for a little bit and have a dog who doesn't mind kennels. In addition—and better yet for many dogs—Debbie can sometimes pet-sit while you go out. Dogs love her and are happy in her care.

Rates are $69–175. Dogs are $10 extra. 3225 Lake County Highway 94515; 707/942-6334; www.bnbweb.com/hillcrest.

Meadowlark Country House: The simple elegance of this secluded 20-acre estate makes guests feel right at home. The house where dogs with people get to stay has a light and airy feel and attractive decor, but it's really the surrounding property that makes this place so special. Beware, though. Cats and guinea hens also make their home around the house, so if your dog is a chaser, hang on to that leash.

You and your pooch can hike on the estate's trails, past pastured horses, ancient oaks, and fields replete with wildflowers (and meadowlarks, thus the name). It's quiet here—a perfect place for a hilltop picnic with the pooch. If your dog can be trusted off leash, he can hike naked. It's "leashes optional" here, and that's a perfect match for the pool. If it's warm, the humans in your party can cool their heels (and knees and shoulders) in the beautiful swimming pool, which is surrounded by a cobblestone walk. The pool is clothing-optional, so if your dog blushes when he sees tushies, best wear your clothes. If all this isn't enough to fill your day, take a quick drive down the road and spend some time at the Petrified Forest.

Rates are $195–265. A delicious, large breakfast is included in the price. 601

DIVERSION

See Old Faithful in Your Own Backyard: You know you're in for a treat when a big sign greets you at the entry to **Old Faithful Geyser:** "Many Notable People Have Come to SEE HEAR AND LEARN the mysteries of this WONDER OF NATURE which captures the imagination. IT'S AMAZING."

And indeed, when dogs see the 350°F plume of water gushing 50 to 70 feet into the air, they generally stare for a few seconds with their mouths agape. But the sight of tourists jumping in front of the geyser for a quick photo before the eruption subsides quickly bores them. Dogs then try to wander to the snack bar and persuade the person on the other end of the leash to buy a couple of hot dogs. But even more fascinating is the scent of goat and pig in nearby pens.

If your dog is the brave sort, don't hesitate to bring him to visit Clow, the fainting goat. Clow butts her head against her fence at first, but she's only playing. After a few minutes, she was calming Joe's fears by licking him on the nose. Soon he was in love. Valentino, the Vietnamese potbellied pig who scared the heck out of Joe, is no longer here. (I hope he didn't go the way of so many of his oversized brethren.)

Old Faithful erupts every 40 minutes, and the eruptions last about two to three minutes. Picnic tables are plentiful, so bring a snack or buy one here between eruptions. A sign at the site warns that dogs aren't allowed in the geyser viewing area, but you can bring your dog—securely leashed—within a safe distance of the geyser and not get scolded or scalded.

The geyser and goats are between Highways 128 and 29 on Tubbs Lane in Calistoga and are open 9 A.M.–6 P.M. in summer, 9 A.M.–5 P.M. in winter. Admission is $8 for adults. 707/942-6463.

Petrified Forest Road 94515; 707/942-5651 or 800/942-5651; www.meadow-larkinn.com.

Napa County Fairgrounds: A far cry from the great outdoors, this flat landscape with few trees is at least a good, fair-priced campground if all the inns and motels are booked. There are 70 sites, mostly decent places to park your recreational vehicle. Some tents sites are available in a grassy area. Sites are $22–25. 1435 Oak Street 94515; for info: 707/942-5221; for reservations: 707/942-5111.

Pink Mansion: This enchanting old place is an 1875 Victorian—very picturesque and very pink. It's a frequent recipient of numerous awards for its charm and beauty.

Dogs are allowed in only one room—the Wine Suite (not the Whine Sweet,

DIVERSION

Sniff Out a Petrified Forest: You and your leashed dog can roam among trees entombed by a volcanic explosion 3.4 million years ago. During a summertime visit, Joe found out why they call it the **Petrified Forest.** The sign announced in big bold letters, "Once Towering Redwoods—Now the Rock of Ages." But Joe didn't know the true meaning of petrified until we encountered—the elves.

The Elves of Ages, that is. The ceramic kind you find on suburban lawns. They appeared everywhere Joe looked and at eye level for an Airedale. Every time he saw a new one, he backed away with his tail between his legs, checking periodically to make sure it wasn't following him.

Then came the petrifying elf. It didn't look any different from the others. But as soon as Joe laid eyes on it and its donkey companion, his tail went down. For about two minutes, he was too frightened to look at the elf, growling instead at a tree. Then, suddenly he decided enough was enough and bolted—leash and all. He was waiting by the wishing well when I finally caught up to him. He would have left the park if he could have negotiated the turnstile by himself. I couldn't help wondering how Airedales have remained so popular for frontline duty during wars.

The Petrified Forest is at 4100 Petrified Forest Road, off Highway 128. It's actually in the outskirts of Sonoma County, but its address is in Calistoga. The unpaved trail is a quarter-mile loop. Admission is $6 for adults. Dozens of tables are around the gift shop, so pack a picnic. The forest is open 9 A.M.–7 P.M. in summer, 9 A.M.–6 P.M. in winter. 707/942-6667.

as some dogs may do to stay here)—so book ahead lest another dog beats you to the phone. It has a fireplace, a private entrance that leads to the garden, and a private sitting room with an extra bed upstairs. Dogs must be of the non-barking, clean, well-behaved variety, and they need to keep off the furniture and the beds.

If you have a bird dog, think twice about staying here, since also in residence are some doves and a chicken. Water dogs will enjoy watching you splash around in the comfy heated indoor pool and adjacent hot tub, but they mustn't set paw in the water. Rates are $185. Pooches are $30 extra. 1415 Foothill Boulevard (Highway 128) 94515; 707/942-0558 or 800/238-7465; www.pinkmansion.com.

Triple S Ranch: Once a working ranch, this hidden 11-acre spread in the hills above Calistoga still retains that old ranch feel. The nine rustic yet cozy cabins have only one large room each, so they feel like bunkhouses. But each comes with a private bathroom, so you won't have to wander out to the outhouse in the middle of the night. They're pretty basic, and definitely for those with a macaroni-and-cheese budget for touring Napa, but they fill the budget bill.

What really sets dogs' tails to wagging is that if they're obedient, they get to run around the ranch's property without a leash. That's right, a leash-free doggy haven. (Watch out for foxtails.) Don't be surprised if your dog doesn't want to leave this place. You'll probably be feeling much the same yourself. It's hard to kiss all this—and a pool, and a fun restaurant (in the converted barn) with some of the best onion rings around—good-bye. The fried frog legs, on the other hand...

Rates are $85–95. 4600 Mountain Home Ranch Road 94515; 707/942-6730.

Washington Street Lodging: Relax in any of several cabins, each with its own little kitchen. You're just a couple of blocks from Calistoga's main drag here. Joan, the animal-loving owner, has cats, but she says if they don't like your pooch, or vice versa, they'll make themselves scarce. She also has a happy basset hound who will probably become your fast friend when you visit. Your stay here includes a continental breakfast and a doggy treat or two. Cabins are $90–130, and dogs are charged a $15 fee per visit. 1605 Washington Street 94515; 707/942-6968 or 877/214-3869; www.washingtonstreetlodging.com.

St. Helena

PARKS, BEACHES, AND RECREATION AREAS

🟦 Lyman Park

🐾🐾 (See Napa County map on page 52)

You'll think you're on a movie set for some old-time village scene when you and your dog wander into this small, cozy park on historic Main Street. Leashes are mandatory, but the park has a gazebo, lots of trees and benches, a flower garden, and—best of all for dogs—an antique horse/dog water fountain. The top part is for horses, the lower bowl for dogs. Horses aren't allowed here anymore, so if your dog is huge, he might as well sip from the equine bowl.

The park is nestled snugly between the police station and a funeral home, at 1400 Main Street, and is open dawn–dusk. 707/963-5706.

🟦 Baldwin Park

🐾🐾 (See Napa County map on page 52)

Baldwin Park has everything you could want in a park, except size. But what it lacks in acreage, it makes up for in dog appeal. Set off a small road, it's almost entirely fenced and full of flowering trees, oaks, and big pines. A dirt path winds through green grass from one end of the park to the other, passing by a water fountain and a conveniently placed garbage can.

DIVERSION

Grape Expectations: Dogs are welcome at so many wineries in Napa Valley these days that you may start wishing your dog could be your designated driver. (Don't try it: Dogs just don't have the opposable thumbs to operate those pesky steering wheels.)

Many of the wineries listed below allow dogs in their tasting rooms, but since health department officials aren't sure what to think about this, we're not going to point them out specifically. Most welcome dogs at their picnic areas. Some even allow pooches on vineyard tours. Phone the individual wineries for hours, prices, and dog-friendly specifics.

Here's a taste of some of Napa's most dog-friendly wineries, listed by area:

CALISTOGA:
Cuvaison, 4550 Silverado Trail North; 707/942-6266.
Dutch Henry Winery, 4310 Silverado Trail North; 707/942-5771. Winery Airedale Buggsy and her occasional city-cousin sidekick, Teddy, greet dog guests. Check out the website www.dutchhenry .com for a page dedicated to the winery pets.
Graeser Winery, 255 Petrified Forest Road; 707/942-4437. Graeser has a new line of dog-labeled wines named after various winery dogs.

RUTHERFORD:
Mumm Napa Valley, 8445 Silverado Trail North; 707/967-7700. Dogs get royal treatment, with dog treats and water. Mumm Napa Valley even has its own line of logo doggy products.
Sullivan Vineyards, 1090 Galleron Road; 707/963-9646. Open by appointment only.

ST. HELENA:
Casa Nuestra, 3451 Silverado Trail North; 707/963-5783. A most mellow winery where dogs can stare at the resident goats who have a nonvintage table wine named after them. Dogs get tasty biscuits, too.
Markham Vineyards, 2812 St. Helena Highway North; 707/963-5292.
RustRidge Winery, 2910 Lower Chiles Valley Road; 707/965-2871. Open by appointment only. Two big, friendly resident dogs welcome you and yours.
V. Sattui Winery, 1111 White Lane; 707/963-7774.

YOUNTVILLE:
Domaine Chandon, 1 California Drive; 707/944-2280.

Unfortunately, dogs must be leashed, but it's still a pleasant place to stretch all your legs after a tour through the wine country. The park is on Spring Street between Stockton Street and North Crane Avenue and is open dawn–dusk. 707/963-5706.

PLACES TO EAT

Pizzeria Tra Vigne: The little sister of the more expensive and upscale Tra Vigne Ristorante (see below), this pizzeria is just what the vet ordered if you have a pooch and a pedigreed palate but a more paltry pocketbook. Lots of families come here. The pastas, pizzas, and salads are delicious. Munch with your dog at the four tables on the patio. Got a thirsty dog? The staff will provide her a bowl of water. 1016 Main Street; 707/967-9999.

Ristorante Tra Vigne: This is one of the most attractive restaurants with some of the best food in the Bay Area. The wood-burning oven gives even the most simple pasta, pizza, and meat dishes a taste that's out of this world. Your dog can dine with you at the 20 tables in the large, gardenlike lower courtyard. (The terrace is out because you have to go through the restaurant to get there, and that's a no-no.) The two of you are sure to drool over the gourmet cuisine. Thirsty dogs get a bowl of water. 1050 Charter Oak Avenue (you'll see the restaurant from Main Street, though); 707/963-4444.

PLACES TO STAY

El Bonita Motel: This little motel provides decent lodging at fairly reasonable prices for this area. Rates are $90–229. Dogs are $5 extra. 195 Main Street 94574; 707/963-3216 or 800/541-3284; www.elbonita.com.

Lake Berryessa

PARKS, BEACHES, AND RECREATION AREAS

🐾 Lake Berryessa

🐾🐾 (See Napa County map on page 52)

Lake Berryessa, one of the largest man-made lakes in Northern California, offers 165 miles of shoreline for human and canine enjoyment. Most of the resort areas on the lake allow leashed dogs. Better yet, they allow them off leash to swim. The summer heat is stifling here, so your dog will want to take advantage of the water.

Most resorts rent fishing boats and allow dogs to go along on your angling adventure. The fishing is fantastic, especially for trout in the fall and black bass in the spring. It's cooler then, too, so you won't have to contend with so many folks riding personal watercraft, and your dog won't roast.

If you just want to hike and swim for an afternoon, explore the Smittle Creek Trail. The entrance is just north of the lake's visitor center, on Knoxville Road. The trail takes you up and down the fingers of the lake. Dogs must be leashed, except when swimming. In the future there may be much more romping room for dogs—even some off-leash areas—if plans for a 150-mile shoreline trail go through, as lobbyists are hoping it will. (See www.berryessatrails.org for more. A link will take you to a page called The Dog Owner's Vision for Lake Berryessa.)

To get to Lake Berryessa from the Rutherford area, take Highway 128 and turn left at the Lake Berryessa/Spanish Flat sign. It's a very curvy route, so take it easy if you or your dog tend toward car sickness. For more information about the lake, call the Bureau of Reclamation Visitor Information Center at 707/966-2111. For questions about lakeside businesses, call the Lake Berryessa Chamber of Commerce at 800/726-1256.

PLACES TO STAY

Here are a few places to pitch a tent, park an RV, or stay in a yurt (Spanish Flat only) on Lake Berryessa.

Rancho Monticello Resort: Stay in a tent or in your RV with your pooch. There are 56 tent sites and 20 RV sites. Rates are $24–31. Dogs are $2. The day-use fee, should you not want to camp, is $11. 707/966-2188.

Spanish Flat Resort: Camping will cost you $24–32. Dogs are $2 extra and love sniffing around the waterfront and walking on the meandering roads on leash. The very cool yurts are $45 nightly. Day-use fee is $12. 707/966-7700; www.spanishflatresort.com.

Steele Park Resort: Dogs can go only RV camping here. Rates are $32–40. Dogs are $2 extra. Day-use fee is $15. 707/966-2123 or 800/522-2123; www.steelepark.com.

Rutherford

PLACES TO EAT

Rutherford Grill: The outdoor area is *the* place to eat at this wonderful restaurant (and of course, the only place to eat with a dog). It features a wood-burning fireplace, a fountain, and several attractive umbrella-topped tables. Try the "Knife and Fork Baby Back Barbecue Ribs," one of the most requested entreés. (Fear not: If you're not of the carnivorous persuasion, the restaurant offers several tasty dishes without meat.) The only time dogs aren't allowed is when there's live music outside—usually Thursday nights. 1180 Rutherford Road, Rutherford, CA 94573; 707/963-1792.

Yountville

Unlike the Yountville town government, which bans dogs from its parks, restaurateurs here have the right idea. Several exquisite restaurants welcome dogs to their patios, which are generally shaded and very accommodating to people and their canines. The only word of warning is to avoid these restaurants when they're packed with people from the tour buses that occasionally descend upon the town. It's just too crowded for dogs, who usually get tripped on and later photographed as tourist souvenirs.

PLACES TO EAT

Compadres Mexican Bar and Grill: Tropical landscaping, intoxicating jasmine and honeysuckle, and umbrellas over tables make this one of the most pleasant restaurants for spending a few hours with your dog. Try the *pollo borracho,* a whole chicken cooked with white wine and tequila. 6539 Washington Street, at the Vintage 1870 complex; 707/944-2406.

Napa Valley Grill: California cuisine reigns here, with fresh seafood as the focal point. Several outdoor tables with oversized umbrellas keep you and your dog cool. 6795 Washington Street; 707/944-2330.

Piatti Restaurant: The atmosphere at the 10-table semienclosed patio is enchanting, and the food is just as wonderful. Choose from a couple of dozen house-made pastas, rotisserie-cooked chicken, fresh-caught fish, pizzas from a wood-burning oven, and many other delectable items. As long as it's not too crowded, your dog is welcome to dine at your side. Thirsty pooches get a bowl of water. 6480 Washington Street; 707/944-2070.

PLACES TO STAY

Vintage Inn: Dogs who get to stay here are lucky dogs indeed. This inn ("inn" is an understated description of this place) puts dogs and their people in the lap of luxury, with a perfect blend of old-world charm and new-world design. The airy, beautiful, multilevel villas have fireplaces, and many have views of nearby vineyards. Dogs swoon over the grounds, which have pools, gardens, courtyards, and even a fountain.

This is a great place to stay if you're checking out the wineries on warm days and don't want to bring your dog along. The staff here can arrange for a pet-sitter to watch your pooch so he can keep cool and comfy while you sip your way through wine country.

Rates are $215–455 and include a "California Champagne breakfast." Dogs pay a $30 fee per visit. 6541 Washington Street 94599; 707/944-1112 or 800/351-1133; www.vintageinn.com.

Napa

The city of Napa has about 40 parks. Dogs are allowed in a whopping four, each of which has an off-leash section. You'll see dogs in some of the bigger parks, such as the Lake Hennessey Recreation Area, but they're not officially sanctioned, so we can't officially mention them.

PARKS, BEACHES, AND RECREATION AREAS

6 Alston Park/Canine Commons

🐾🐾🐾🐾🦮 (See Napa County map on page 52)

With 157 acres of rolling hills surrounded by vineyards, Alston Park seems to stretch out forever. The lower part of the land used to be a prune orchard, and these prunes are just about the only trees you'll find here.

From there on up, the park is wide-open land with a lone tree here and there. Without shade, dogs and people can fry on hot summer days. But the park is magical during early summer mornings or any cooler time of year.

Miles of trails take you and your dog to places far from the road and the sound of traffic. Dogs are supposed to be off leash only in the lower, flat section of the park, known as Canine Commons. There's now a decent-sized fenced dog park there, complete with poop bags and drinking water.

From Highway 29, take Trower Avenue southwest to the end, at Dry Creek Road. The parking lot for the park is a short jog to your right on Dry Creek Road and across the street. It's open dawn–dusk. 707/257-9529.

7 Century Oaks Park

🐕🦮 (See Napa County map on page 52)

This park is a cruel hoax on canines. Dogs are restricted to a dangerous dog run—a tiny postage stamp of an area without fences, just off a busy street. And as for the park's name, which promises granddaddy oak trees, we're talking saplings here—maybe a dozen in the whole dog-run area. We don't know how many are in the rest of the park, because dogs aren't allowed there even on leash.

The dog-run area (we suggest keeping all but the most highly trained dogs on leash here) is on Brown's Valley Road, just off Westview Drive. Park on Westview Drive and walk around the corner to the dog run. The short walk to the park, with its shade and shrubs, is more enjoyable than the park itself. It's open dawn–dusk. 707/257-9529.

8 John F. Kennedy Memorial Park

🐾🐾🐾🦮 (See Napa County map on page 52)

Throw your dog's leash to the wind here and ramble along the Napa River. Dogs are allowed in the undeveloped areas near the park's boat marina. The only spot to avoid is a marshland that's more land than marsh during dry times.

Dogs enjoy chasing each other around the flat, grassy area beside the parking lot. There's also a dirt trail that runs along the river. You can take it from either side of the marina, although as of this writing, the signs designate only the south side as a dog-exercise area. The scenery isn't terrific—radio towers and construction cranes dot the horizon—but dogs without a sense of decor don't seem to mind.

Dogs like to amble by the river, which is down a fair incline from the trail. But be careful if you've got a water dog, because riders of personal watercraft and motor-boaters have been known to mow over anything in their path. There's no drinking water in the dog area and it gets mighty hot in the summer, so bring your own.

Take Highway 221 to Streblow Drive, and follow the signs past the Napa Municipal Golf Course and Napa Valley College to the boat marina/launch area. Park in the lot and look for the trail by the river. The park is open dawn–dusk. 707/257-9529.

9 Shurtleff Park

(See Napa County map on page 52)

The farther away from the road you go, the better it is in this long, narrow park. It gets shadier and thicker with large firs and eucalyptus trees. Dogs are allowed off leash as soon as you think they're safe from the road.

The park is almost entirely fenced, but there are a few escape hatches. Two are at the entrance and two others are along the side that lead you into the schoolyard of Phillips Elementary School. This isn't normally a problem, unless your dog runs into the day-care center at lunchtime, as Joe once did. A teacher escorted him out by the scruff of his neck before he could steal someone's peanut butter sandwich.

You'll find the park on Shelter Street at Shurtleff, beside Phillips Elementary School. It's open dawn–dusk. 707/257-9529.

PLACES TO EAT

Angele Restaurant: Doggies who dine at this restaurant's riverfront tables get treats and water! "We love dogs!" says a server. The food is excellent—French with a Napa Valley flair. The restaurant is just a couple of blocks from the wonderful Napa River Inn. A big thanks to the aptly named Bacchus, a personable traveling rottie, for sniffing this one out for us. 540 Main Street; 707/252-8115.

Brown's Valley Yogurt and Espresso Bar: Cool off with a cold frozen one at the outside tables shaded by a wooden awning. 3265 Brown's Valley Road; 707/252-4977.

Downtown Joe's: This microbrewery is housed in a 100-year-old landmark building on the Napa River. Dogs get to sit with you at the edge of the area with outdoor tables (not in the covered section, though), or they can stretch out beside you on the comfy lawn. Dogs get to drink water in doggy bowls while you get to sip good beers made right on the premises. The brewery even makes a red ale called Tail Waggin' Ale. Our first time here I thought Joe was foaming at the mouth with enthusiasm for the place, but I soon discovered he'd just dipped his snout into a near-empty, still-foamy glass of Tail Waggin' someone had left behind. Hungry? The food's as good as the beers. 902 Main Street; 707/258-2337.

Napa Valley Traditions: Enjoy fresh baked goods and cappuccino at four outside tables shaded by two trees and an awning. Your dog will find as much to enjoy here as you will—inside, the shop also sells dog biscuits. 1202 Main Street; 707/226-2044.

PLACES TO STAY

The Chablis Inn: Don't be fooled by the name of this place: It's not a darling wine-country bed-and-breakfast inn. It's simply a decent motel with an enticing moniker. But it's striving to be more innlike, with some rooms offering down comforters and whirlpool tubs. All rooms come with bottled water, too. The motel has a couple of features that most charming inns don't, namely a pool and cable TV. Rates are $89–235. (The high-end price is for the fancier rooms in high season.) Dogs are $10–15 extra, depending on their size. 3360 Solano Avenue 94558; 707/257-1944 or 800/443-3490; www.chablisinn.com.

The Napa Inn: If Queen Anne–style Victorians are your dog's cup of tea, sniff out this terrific 1899 bed-and-breakfast. Dogs are allowed to stay in a pretty garden guest room and a separate cottage here. Angelina's Garden Room has 12-foot-high ceilings, a whirlpool bath for two (your dog can't be one of the two), a shower for two (ditto about the dog), a fireplace, and even a private garden area. The Garden Cottage has a fireplace, minikitchen, and French doors that look out on a private flower garden. Dogs mustn't sleep on the beds in either accommodation. If the inn is really busy the innkeepers prefer small dogs, but they're open to well-behaved larger pooches at other times.

Your stay includes breakfast for two (humans) in the inn's sumptuous dining area. On cooler evenings, the humans in your party can sidle up to a fire in the relaxing parlor. Rates are $195–255. Dogs are $20 extra. 1137 Warren Street 94559; 707/257-1444 or 800/435-1144; www.napainn.com.

Napa River Inn: This dog-friendly full-service luxury hotel doesn't just permit pooches: It showers them with goodies and services.

But before I gush further, you need to know that dogs have to weigh less than 50 pounds to stay here. If your dog is on the medium-large side or larger, don't read on, because it'll break your heart.

If you're still reading, you're one of the lucky ones with a lighter dog (or else you're a sucker for punishment). You won't believe what this upscale boutique hotel offers dogs. Upon check-in, your dog gets use of a pet blanket embroidered with the inn's logo, a matching placemat, and attractive food and water bowls to put on the placemat. (If you want to buy these items, the gift shop sells them. The ones that come with your room are just loaners.) In addition, dogs get poop bags and locally made gourmet dog biscuits. As you may have guessed, unlike the aforementioned goodies, you don't have to give these items back when you're done with them. If you need a little assistance with dog duties, the bell staff here is often available to take your dog for a little walk along the inn's namesake, the Napa River. Dog-sitting can also be arranged through an outside service.

One of the three buildings that make up the inn dates from 1887. Its rooms are opulent but unpretentious, with fireplaces, claw-foot tubs, and canopy king-sized beds. Rooms at the other two lovely buildings feature nautical themes or "contemporary wine country design." Included in your stay is a delicious breakfast at any of the wonderful restaurants on the 2.5-acre property. Rates are $179–499. Dogs are $25 extra. 500 Main Street 94559; 707/251-8500 or 877/251-8500; www.napariverinn.com.

Napa Valley Country Cottage: A sweet patch of pooch paradise awaits you and the dog of your life here. This cozy cottage is surrounded by 12 acres of gardens, woods, walking paths, and open areas that are perfect for throwing a stick. Some of the acreage is fenced and gated, for that extra-secure leash-free romp. There's even a little vineyard, should you want some real wine-country ambience. A wooded area with a seasonal creek separates the cottage from the cottage-owners' house, so there's plenty of privacy.

The wood cottage itself is a very cute one-bedroom affair with a little kitchen and dining area, and a living room. (The futon in the living room folds out, should you be traveling with extra humans.) The large, sunny deck makes great setting for dining alfresco with your dog friend. The cottage is perfect for pooches: It has Italian tile floors and is well stocked with doggy treats, doggy dishes, and a pooch bed.

Rates are $950 for one week, plus a $50 cleaning fee (even for nondog people). Dogs are $50 extra for the length of their stay; two dogs will cost you $75. During slow times you can rent the cottage for four nights, for $575 plus the cleaning and dog fees. The cottage is on beautiful Mount Veeder. When you make your reservation you'll get the address. 707/226-6621; www.napavalleycasa.com.

Redwood Inn: Rates are $67–139. Dogs are $10 extra. 3380 Solano Avenue 94558; 707/257-6111 or 877/872-6272; www.napavalleyredwoodinn.net.

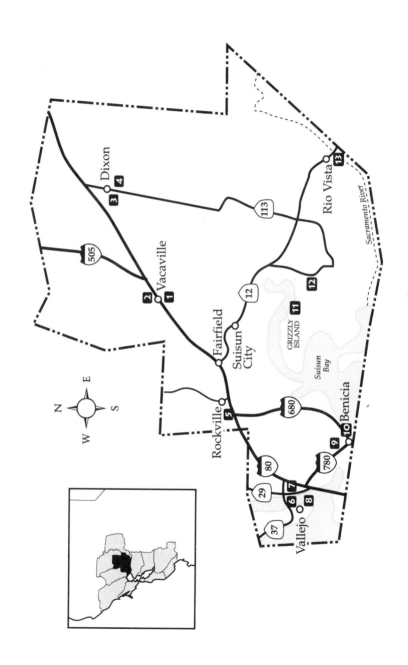

CHAPTER 3

Solano County

Solano County is slowly going to the dogs. The marvelous 2,070-acre Rush
Ranch Open Space now permits leash-free pooches on a two-mile trail with
views that are to drool for. This alone makes it absolutely worth the trip to
Solano County. So does the Grizzly Island Wildlife Area, in the thick of the
Suisun Marsh. As long as you visit when dogs can be off leash, your pooch
will think she's in heaven. It's mud heaven. Bring a towel.

Smaller leash-free areas (much smaller!) include dog parks in Vacaville and
Benicia. Two parks in Dixon allow off-leash dogs, but if your dog isn't at perfect heel when you're at the parks, leash him fast, or you could find yourself
paying a fine old fine. The county is growing so rapidly that there's a real need
for more leash-free areas.

If you find yourself at the famed Jelly Belly jelly bean factory in Fairfield,
you'll be happy to know that while you wait for the rest of your crew to take
the tour inside, you and your dog can have a decent time at the teeny little dog
"relief" area beside the parking lot. You'll find some very green grass, some
pretty ivy, poop bags, water, and a red fire hydrant ("This hydrant is here for
your dog's pleasure," a big sign says. "Not a working hydrant." If God forbid

PICK OF THE LITTER—SOLANO COUNTY

MOST TEMPTING HYDRANT
Jelly Belly dog "relief" area, Fairfield (pages 69–70)

BEST POOCH PARK FOR A BARBECUE
Phenix Community Dog Park, Benicia (pages 75–76)

BEST OFF-LEASH HIKING
Rush Ranch Open Space, Suisun City (pages 77–78)

MOST DOG-FRIENDLY PLACES TO EAT
Java Point, Benicia (page 76)
Valley Cafe, Suisun City (page 78)

the Jelly Belly factory goes up in flames, at least the firefighters won't be fooled by the doggy decor.) It's not exactly Rush Ranch, but it's better than sitting in your car the whole time watching tired, jelly bean–stuffed children having sugar-induced meltdowns on the asphalt.

Vacaville

PARKS, BEACHES, AND RECREATION AREAS

Vacaville finally has its very own dog park.

◻ Janine Jordan Park for Dogs

🐾🐾🐾🐕 (See Solano County map on page 68)

Jake gives this park three paws despite its relatively small size of two-thirds of an acre. That's because it has friendly people, grass (although not always of the green variety), shade trees, and best of all: a golden fire hydrant (most dogs probably only dream of such idols) and a doggy drinking fountain made out of a decommissioned fire hydrant. The golden hydrant is a memorial to Panto, a dearly departed Vacaville Police K-9 partner. The fountain hydrant is an homage to all dogs.

The dog park is within Lagoon Valley Regional Park. If you're going to become a park regular, you should join its organizational group, P.A.W.S. The $25 membership fee goes toward park upkeep and supplies. (From what a visitor tells us, the park looks as if it's in need of some TLC lately. It wasn't when we saw it, though. Either way, your membership dollars will be put to good use.) Plus your membership will get you into the park without having to pay the $3 entry fee for the regional park. But if you're just passing through and want to check it out, it's worth the $3. (You'll also have to sign a waiver. They're available at the kiosk, or you can download one by going to the dog park's website, www.ourdogpark.org.)

Exit I-80 at Pena Adobe Road/Lagoon Valley Regional Park. Go right at the stop sign (this is Riviera Road), and go left onto Pena Adobe. Follow the signs to Lagoon Valley Regional Park, which will be on your right. Drive .2 more miles and you'll come to the dog park. Lagoon Valley's number is 707/449-6122. The number to contact P.A.W.S. is 866/510-3681.

◻ Andrews Park

 (See Solano County map on page 68)

If you need a shopping cart, try this park first. For some reason, the creek that cuts through the west end of the park contains more shopping carts than most supermarkets.

The chunk of park to the east of the creek is graced with gentle rolling hills, picnic areas, barbecues, deciduous trees, and a lawn as green and smooth as a golf course. But dogs must be leashed.

The west side of the creek is just a shady trail that officially stops at the first overpass and can get pretty seedy if you continue.

The best parking for the east side is on School Street, near Davis Street. For the west side of the creek, park in a lot at Kendal Street, off Dobbins Street. 707/449-6122.

PLACES TO STAY

Best Western Heritage Inn: Small to medium dogs are allowed here. Don't try to pass your Saint Bernard off as a lapdog, even if he is your lapdog. Rates are $70–90. Pooches are $10–20 extra. 1420 East Monte Vista Avenue 95688; 707/448-8453.

Motel 6: If you want to shop at the famous outlet mall in Vacaville and you're traveling with someone who will watch your pooch, this is a convenient place to stay—it's about 1,000 feet from the mall. Shop 'til you drop, then drag yourself back here. Rates are $55–60 for the first adult, $6 for the second. 107 Lawrence Drive 95687; 707/447-5550.

Dixon

Although it's no more stringent than most, the pooper-scooper law in Dixon has such a formidable name that we had to pass it on. It's called the "Canine Defecation Ordinance." Yowza! It doesn't sound like anything we want to break.

Here's the good news: If your dog is super-obedient and stays really close to you (actually, he'd need to stay at your heel), he can be off leash in the parks here!

PARKS, BEACHES, AND RECREATION AREAS

3 Northwest Park

🐾🐾🐕 (See Solano County map on page 68)

If your dog will stay very close at heel without a leash, she may go leashless at this grassy, 20-acre park. Otherwise, use your leash. With these fairly stringent rules, she probably wouldn't notice her freedom anyway.

The park is on West H and North Lincoln Streets. 707/678-7000.

4 Hall Memorial Park

🐾🐾🐕 (See Solano County map on page 68)

If you have to conduct business with city government and you want your dog to conduct business, too, you couldn't have asked for a better location for a park. It's right behind City Hall.

There's not much in the way of shade here, but on cooler days this park proves a decent stroll for dogs, provided they're leashed or at very firm heel. The park also has a playground, a swimming pool, tennis courts, and picnic areas with barbecues, so it's even better for people. The park is at Hall Park Drive and East Mayes Street. 707/678-7000.

PLACES TO STAY

Best Western Inn: This is a convenient place to stay if you have to attend a packed University of California event and no rooms are available in Davis. It's just eight miles away, and a swift drive. The staff prefers to have small dogs here but doesn't always demand it. Rates are $90–100. Dogs are $10 extra. 1345 Commercial Way 95620; 707/678-1400 or 800/528-1234.

Fairfield

PARKS, BEACHES, AND RECREATION AREAS

City park ranger Teri Geiger has been longing to get a group of locals together to try to implement a fairly large dog park at one of the larger park parcels. If you're interested in her mission (if you have a dog, you should be), phone her at 707/428-7614.

5 Rockville Hills Regional Park

🐾🐾🐾 (See Solano County map on page 68)

Hike, fish, and enjoy nature in this 630-acre park filled with trees and trails. The main trail is fairly steep and takes you to the top of the park, where you'll find two small ponds for fishing. After this hike on a summer afternoon, many dogs jump in when they reach the summit. A man told me that a small beagle once disappeared for several seconds and came up with a tiny fish flailing in her mouth. Could this be just another flagrant flailing fish story?

Once you enter the park, you're safe from traffic. But dogs are supposed to be leashed anyway, since the park is officially run by the city of Fairfield, which has a strict leash law. Check out the nature trail that a local Eagle Scout troop has created. A favorite of many dogs is the Mystic Trail. The 25 miles of trails are arranged in sort of stacked loop formations, so it's easy to get lost. No brochures or trail maps are available at the entrance. Phone the number below for both, or for advice, before you visit.

For the most vigorous workout, try the main trail. It's the one that bends slightly to the left and up a steep hill as you enter from the parking lot. The park is often desolate, so use judgment about hiking alone.

Exit Highway 80 at Suisun Valley Road and drive 1.5 miles (in the opposite direction from the myriad fast-food outlets) to Rockville Road. Go left on Rockville. In about .7 mile you'll come to a small brown sign for the park. In 1,500 feet you'll find a small parking area. At press time there was no entrance fee, but by the time you read this, you may have to drop some cash into the iron ranger, so bring a few bucks. (The fee could be $3 for humans, $1 for dog.) 707/428-7614.

Vallejo

PARKS, BEACHES, AND RECREATION AREAS

Jake Dog and I are crossing our fingers that by the next edition we'll have a real dog park to describe. At press time, the city's dog people were hoping to convince the city to establish a five-acre leash-free area at Wardlow Park. Phone 707/648-4600 for updates.

🐾 River Park

🐾🐾🐾 (See Solano County map on page 68)

With goldenrod as high as an elephant's eye and a preponderance of low brush, this waterfront park looks like a huge abandoned lot. That's actually one of its charms—you don't have to worry about your dog's mowing over children in a playground or digging up a plug of green grass. The only park-like features here are a couple of benches along the Mare Island Strait.

A wide dirt path leads you toward the water and far from traffic danger. Unfortunately, the leash law is in effect here, and unless your dog is inclined to wade through several yards of mucky marsh to get to the water, he's not going to go swimming. It's still fun to walk along the water and look at the now-defunct Mare Island Naval Shipyard.

There are two entry points. If you're driving, use the south entrance on Wilson Avenue, just north of Hichborn Street, which has a small parking lot.

Otherwise, you can enter at Wilson Avenue just across the street from Sims Avenue. 707/648-4600.

7 Dan Foley Park

 (See Solano County map on page 68)

You won't often see this at Marine World–Africa USA—professional water-skiers practicing their acts over sloping jumps, then landing headfirst in the water when everything doesn't work out perfectly.

But you and your dog will be treated to this unpolished spectacle if you visit this park on the right day. The park is directly across Lake Chabot from Marine World, so you get to witness a good chunk of the goings-on there. Since dogs aren't allowed at Marine World, this is an ideal place to walk them if your kids are spending a few hours with more exotic animals. You still get to hear the sound of jazz bands and the roar of amazed crowds.

Dan Foley Park is so well maintained we initially were afraid it was a golf course. Willows and pines on rolling hills provide cooling shade, and there's usually a breeze from the lake. Leashed dogs are invited everywhere but the water. Even humans aren't supposed to swim in it. Picnic tables are right across from the water-ski practice area, so if your dog wants entertainment with his sandwich, this is the place.

The park is on Camino Alto North just east of Tuolumne Street. There is a $3 parking fee, $4 for nonresidents. 707/648-4600.

8 The Wharf

(See Solano County map on page 68)

This is the place for hip Vallejo dogs, and it's not even an official park. The paved path along the Mare Island Strait looks toward the old Mare Island Naval Shipyard on the other side of the strait, providing a real nautical atmosphere.

It's also the perfect place to take your dog while you're waiting for your ship to come in, since this is where the Vallejo–San Francisco ferry stops.

There's a substantial strip of grass beside the path where dogs like to take frequent breaks. Here, they can socialize without getting under joggers' sneakers. Leashes are a must.

The wharf area covers almost the entire length of Mare Island Way, starting around the Vallejo Yacht Club. Your best bet is to park at the public parking area of the ferry terminal. 707/648-4600.

PLACES TO EAT

Sardine Can: Get a view of the strait while you eat some of the freshest seafood available. Dogs get great treatment here, including a big bowl of water. Dine at the two outdoor tables. It's at 0 (as in zero) Harbor Way; 707/553-9492.

DIVERSION

Seize the Bay from Vallejo: Lucky dogs! You get to take a ferry ride to San Francisco on the **Blue and Gold Fleet.** Fares are $9.50 one-way for adults. Additional destinations are available through San Francisco. The ferry terminal is at 495 Mare Island Way in Vallejo. Phone 415/705-8200 for schedules and more information, or 415/705-5555 for tickets; www.blueandgoldfleet.com.

PLACES TO STAY

Holiday Inn: While the kids are busy turning upside-down at unnerving speeds at the nearby Six Flags Marine World, you and your small dog (the only pooches allowed) can curl up, read a book, and enjoy the peace. Rates are $109–149. Dogs are charged a $25 fee per visit. 1000 Fairgrounds Drive 94590; 707/644-1200.

Motel 6: This one's a mere two blocks from Six Flags Marine World. Rates are $40–56 for the first adult, $6 for the second. 458 Fairgrounds Drive 94589; 707/642-7781.

Quality Inn: Rates are $59–79. Dogs are $10 extra. 44 Admiral Callaghan Lane 94591; 707/643-1061.

Ramada Inn: Rates are $68–150. Dogs are charged a $50 fee per visit. 1000 Admiral Callaghan Lane 94591; 707/643-2700.

Benicia

PARKS, BEACHES, AND RECREATION AREAS

◪ Phenix Community Dog Park

😊😊😊😊🐕 (See Solano County map on page 68)

Phenix Community Dog Park, named after a brave retired police dog, is a swell place for dogs. It's got a little more than an acre of grassy leash-free running room, and it's fenced, with water, picnic tables (which little dogs love to dodge under during chase games), poop bags, and small trees that are growing into shade-givers.

And here's a first—this pooch park comes with its own barbecue grills! And you can use them! Of course, you have to be prepared to fend off burger-minded dogs, but if you don't mind, the park people don't mind either. I love this happy, relaxed attitude. Some dog parks I've visited won't even let you bring in a graham cracker for fear you'll be mauled. Those are generally the same parks that ban children. The attitude at Phenix toward children: "You have to allow kids. Kids need to have these friendly interactions with dogs," says Gretchen Burgess, who was behind the park's founding. I like this woman's attitude.

The park is in the northwest corner of the 50-acre Benicia Community Park. Enter the parking lot at Rose and Kearny Drives and drive to the far west end. Then just follow the wide asphalt path with the painted paw prints (I love it!) to the dog park. Keep in mind that the rest of the park prohibits dogs, so don't let your dog talk you into visiting anywhere but the pooch park. If you enter the park elsewhere, the paw prints will still lead to Phenix. 707/746-4285.

🔟 Point Benicia Fishing Pier Area

🐾 🐾 (See Solano County map on page 68)

Park and fish at this big drive-on pier at the end of 1st Street that juts into the Carquinez Strait. It's a popular spot among local anglers. If you're not up for fishing, bring a lunch from a nearby restaurant and park yourself on one of the benches near the old train station. You'll be amazed at the numbers of gulls vying for your crusts.

Dogs enjoy the smells of the strait. While the pier itself isn't conducive to dog exercise, there's an area of undeveloped land nearby where they can cut loose as much as their leashes will allow.

This area also happens to be along the Waterfront Trail that winds through the city. The trail is a fun walk for you and your leashed dog, but make sure that when the trail passes through city parks, you and your dog take a detour.

The pier is at the southern end of 1st Street, just past A Street. 707/746-4285.

PLACES TO EAT

Java Point: You and the dog of your choice are sure to enjoy the soups, sandwiches, bagels, and jammin' good java served here. This would be a terrific place to bring the pooch even if the food was just so-so. The folks here bring pooches organic dog treats and a fresh bowl of water. Dine with your smiling dog at the umbrella-topped patio. 366 1st Street; 707/745-1449.

Pacifica Pizza: Choose from a large selection of pizzas to eat at tables shaded by umbrellas. 915 1st Street; 707/746-1790.

PLACES TO STAY

Best Western Heritage Inn: Rates are $89–120. Dogs pay a $25 fee for the length of their stay. 1955 East 2nd Street 94510; 707/746-0401.

Suisun City

PARKS, BEACHES, AND RECREATION AREAS

🐾 Grizzly Island Wildlife Area

🐾🐾🐾🐾🐾 (See Solano County map on page 68)

This is what dogs have been praying for since they started living in cities: 8,600 acres of wide-open land where they can run—leashless—among the sort of wildlife you see only in PBS specials.

This sprawling wetland, in the heart of the Suisun Marsh, is home to an amazing array of fauna, including tule elk, river otters, waterfowl of every type, jackrabbits, white pelicans, and peregrine falcons.

Of course, walking in marshy areas has its pros and cons. But you don't have to get muddy feet here; the landscapes are as varied as the animal life. Dry upland fields are plentiful. You can also canoe down a slough with your steady dog or hike on dozens of dirt trails. Many folks bring dogs here to train them for hunting, which brings us to the unfortunate subject of the park's schedule.

Because of hunting and bird-nesting seasons, Grizzly Island Wildlife Area is closed during fairly large chunks of the year. Be sure to phone first!

If your dog helps you hunt for ducks or pheasant, she's allowed to join you during some of the hunting seasons. Department of Fish and Game staff also occasionally open small sections to people during the off-season, but it's unpredictable from one year to another when and if they'll do it. Even when the park is open, certain sections may be off-limits to dogs. Check with staff when you come in.

To get to the Grizzly Island Wildlife Area, exit I-80 at Highway 12 heading toward Rio Vista. Turn onto Grizzly Island Road at the stoplight for the Sunset Shopping Center. Drive 10 miles, past farms, sloughs, and marshes, until you get to the headquarters. You'll have to check in here and pay a $2.50 fee unless you have a hunting or fishing license. Then continue driving to the parking lot nearest the area that you want to explore (staff can advise you). Don't forget your binoculars. 707/425-3828.

🐾 Rush Ranch Open Space

🐾🐾🐾🐾🐾 (See Solano County map on page 68)

From freshwater and saltwater marshes to rolling grass-covered hills and meadowlike pastures, this 2,070-acre open-space parcel is home to some wonderfully diverse landscapes.

The to-wag-for news for dogs is that they're allowed to be off-leash on one of the three trails here if they're under voice control. (They're not allowed to even set paw on the other two.) Suisun Hill Trail is a big hit among canines. The two-mile trail takes you into hills with killer 360-degree views of the

Suisun Marsh and the hills and mountains to the north. Rangers tell us that on a clear day, you can see the Sierra Nevada.

Cattle are in these here hills, so if your dog is a chaser, or a herder with an uncontrollable urge to do his job, keep him leashed. (Cattle dogs have been known to try to herd bevies of bovines. The cattle don't think this is cute. Neither do Rush Ranch rangers.) Plenty of wildlife is here, too. If in doubt, leash. (Bikes and horses aren't allowed, so those are two fewer distractions to worry about.)

This is a special place, run by the Solano Land Trust. If you'd like to help support the educational and interpretive activities of the Rush Ranch Educational Council, or if you want more information, phone 707/432-0150. For details on Rush Ranch's history, flora and fauna, and other park info, see www.rushranch.org.

From Highway 12, exit at Grizzly Island Road and drive south for a couple of miles. To get to the trail, park near the entrance sign and cross Grizzly Island Road to the gate. Walk to the left and follow the trail markers.

PLACES TO EAT

Valley Cafe: Your dog will have a hard time forgiving you if you're on your way to Lake Berryessa and you don't stop at this cute eatery. That's because the owner loves dogs and makes 'em feel right at home. Next to the register is a jar of pooch treats that calls dogs from far and wide. If you cock your head just right, you can almost hear it in the breeze. "Oh dogggggyyyyy! Come eat us!!!! We're really yummmmmyyyyyy!!" Dogs also can wet their whistles with bowls of fresh water here. By the way, humans enjoy the café/diner cuisine. The BLT on grainy artisan bread is to drool for. Dine with your dog at the seven umbrella-covered tables outside. 4171 Suisun Valley Road; 707/864-2507.

Rio Vista

Humphrey the humpback whale visited this Delta town, and so should your dog. For now, this is a real, dusty Old West town—not one of those cute villages loaded with boutiques and "shoppes." It's refreshing to find a town with more bait shops than banks. However, in the name of "progress," Rio Vista is slowly becoming home to some major housing developments and all the shopping centers and other unsightly amenities that go with them. Get here now, and take some photos on the old streets with your smiling dog. In a few years, they could be collector's items.

Rio Vista isn't bursting with dog amenities. In fact, it's really appropriate to visit with your dog only if you're on a fishing holiday. Then you and your pooch can slip your boat into the water and take off on the Delta for a few

DIVERSION

Hire a Houseboat: There's nothing like cruising around the Delta in your very own house. Your dog can feel right at home, and nothing makes her happier than having you home all the time. Just remember that, as on land, you have to walk your dog—only you have to dock to do it. Call the Rio Vista Chamber of Commerce at 707/374-2700 for information on houseboat rentals in the Delta.

hours. Come back with your catch and eat dinner at the county park as the sun goes down on another Delta day.

PARKS, BEACHES, AND RECREATION AREAS

13 Sandy Beach County Park

(See Solano County map on page 68)

Take your dog to the very back of the park, and he can run around off leash and even do the dog paddle in the Sacramento River! It's not a huge area, but it's all you'll need to show your dog a good time. The closer day-use section is completely off-limits to dogs, so be sure you end up in the right area.

Your dog has another chance of getting wet if he follows you into the showers at the campground. Dogs are allowed at the campground. It's not terribly scenic and can get mighty dry at times, but hey, it's a place to stay on the river. There are 42 sites. Fees are $14–21 a night. Dogs are $1 extra. Half the sites are first-come, first-served. Reservations are recommended during summer.

Take Highway 12 all the way to Rio Vista; follow Main Street to 2nd Street, and go right. When the street bears left and becomes Beach Drive, the park is within a quarter mile. Bring proof of a rabies vaccination. 707/374-2097.

PLACES TO EAT

Shelby's Drive-In: Shelby's has got every kind of fast food you could ever want and several picnic tables for your feast. The staff will bring your dog water if he needs to wet his snout. 650 Highway 12; 707/374-2020.

PLACES TO STAY

Sandy Beach County Park: See Sandy Beach County Park, above, for camping information.

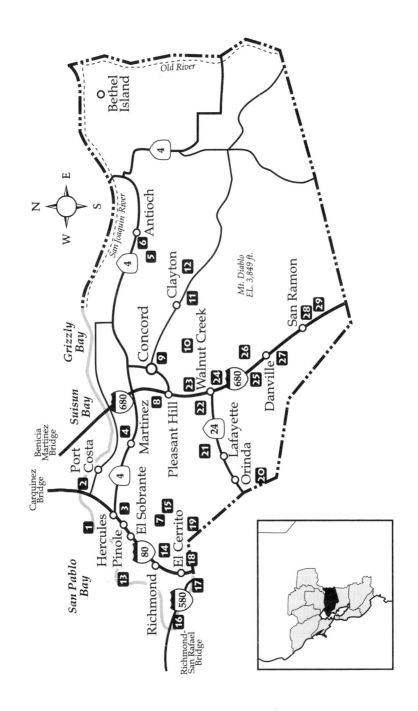

CHAPTER 4

Contra Costa County

Although much of Contra Costa County is considered a sleepy bedroom community for San Francisco, it's a rip-roaring frontierland of fun for dogs. From the renowned off-leash dog haven of the Point Isabel Regional Shoreline to the leash-free inland nirvanas of the East Bay Regional Park District (such as the Morgan Territory, in Clayton), this county enables every dog to have her day, day after day. (For more on the wonders of the East Bay Regional Park District, see the introduction to the Alameda County chapter.)

For dogs who like long hikes through highly diverse lands, 10 long regional trails lace Lafayette, Walnut Creek, and the other urban areas of the Diablo Valley. There are 60 miles of trails in all, linking a dozen towns and many beautiful parklands. Dogs must be leashed, but with all the horses and bikes that can visit here, it's a sensible rule.

The Briones to Diablo Regional Trail is one of the more popular trails. It's about 12 miles long and it snakes through some terrific parkland, including the off-leash wonderlands of the Acalanes Ridge Open Space Recreation Area and the Shell Ridge Open Space Recreation Area (both described in the Walnut Creek section). The trail, which is part paved/part dirt, starts at

PICK OF THE LITTER—CONTRA COSTA COUNTY

BEST OFF-LEASH HIKING
Sobrante Ridge Regional Preserve, El Sobrante (pages 82–83)

Black Diamond Mines Regional Preserve,
Antioch (pages 85–86)

Morgan Territory Regional Preserve, Clayton (page 89)

Briones Regional Park, Lafayette (pages 96–97)

Las Trampas Regional Wilderness, Danville (page 99)

BEST DOG PARK
The Paw Patch, Concord (page 88)

BEST OFF-LEASH BEACH
Point Isabel Regional Shoreline, Richmond (pages 93–94)

BEST CHURCH
**First Presbyterian Church of Richmond car church
services,** Pinole (page 84)

Briones Regional Park's Lafayette Ridge Staging Area, on Pleasant Hill Road just north of Highway 24.

The Contra Costa Canal Regional Trail is a good one for dogs who like to look at water but not set foot in it. We love this 12-mile trail that follows the off-limits canal. For information and a trail map of all 10 regional trails, call 510/635-0135.

Dogs who like more civilized settings will be happy to know that since this book's last edition, eight dog parks have sprouted up around the county. If it seems a little breezier around here lately, it could be from all the wagging tails.

El Sobrante

PARKS, BEACHES, AND RECREATION AREAS

🏷 Sobrante Ridge Regional Preserve

🐾🐾🐾🐾 🐕 (See Contra Costa County map on page 80)

Dogs love visiting this quiet preserve, but Sobrante Ridge hasn't always been a place where animals smile. In the 1970s, the property belonged to Cutter Laboratories, which raised horses and cattle and used their blood to produce various vaccines. That breeze you may feel while visiting is just an equine and bovine sigh of relief that Cutter is outta here.

These days, Sobrante is a happy place, full of deer, coyotes, salamanders, and oodles of birds. Unless your dog is under perfect voice control, it's a good idea to use a leash here. From the Coach Way entrance, follow the dirt trail branching back to the left 100 feet from the entrance. This is the Sobrante Ridge Trail, which will take you through grass, dwarf manzanita, oaks, and coyote brush, up a half mile to views of both Mt. Tam and the top of Mt. Diablo. Branch off on the short loop, Broken Oaks Trail, for a picnic at one of the tables under cool oaks.

This 277-acre preserve is the habitat of the extremely rare Alameda manzanita. So that your dog knows what to watch out for, this manzanita is a gnarled, red-barked shrub that may have sprays of urn-shaped blossoms or clusters of red berries, depending on the time of year. The manzanitas cling to the hillsides. Don't let your boy dog do anything the manzanitas wouldn't want him to do.

From I-80 in Richmond, exit at San Pablo Dam Road and drive south to Castro Ranch Road. Turn left on Castro Ranch, then left at Conestoga Way, going into the Carriage Hills housing development. Take another left on Carriage Drive and a right on Coach Way. Park at the end of Coach and walk into the preserve. 510/635-0135 or 510/223-7840.

Port Costa

Port Costa is a sleepy, picturesque town of Victorian cottages. In the 19th century, it was a booming wheat export dock. Of course, if your dog remembers Frank Norris's book *The Octopus,* he already knows this.

PARKS, BEACHES, AND RECREATION AREAS

2 Carquinez Strait Regional Shoreline

🐾🐾🐾🐾🐾 (See Contra Costa County map on page 80)

This regional shoreline, run by East Bay Regional Parks, lies just east of Crockett. From the Bull Valley Staging Area, on Carquinez Scenic Drive, you can choose one of two leash-free hillside trails. The Carquinez Overlook Loop, to the right, gives better views of Port Costa, the Carquinez Bridge, and Benicia. We once surprised a deer here sleeping in the shade of a clump of eucalyptus.

The eastern part of the park, east of Port Costa, is contiguous with Martinez Regional Shoreline. But beware: You can't get there from here. (Carquinez Scenic Drive is closed at a spot between Port Costa and Martinez. You must turn south on twisty McEwen Road to Highway 4 instead.)

To get to the Carquinez Strait Regional Shoreline from I-80, exit at Crockett and drive east on Pomona Street through town. Pomona turns into Carquinez Scenic Drive, from which you'll see the staging area. 510/635-0135 or 925/228-0112.

Pinole

PARKS, BEACHES, AND RECREATION AREAS

🖪 Pinole Valley Park

🐾🐾🐾🐕 (See Contra Costa County map on page 80)

This city park is fortunate enough to be contiguous with Sobrante Ridge Regional Preserve (see the El Sobrante section). The paved bike path off to the right past the children's playground leads to Alhambra Creek—a good plunge for your dog if he can negotiate the banks wearing a leash. The path then becomes a fire trail and ambles through brush, oaks, and nicely varied deciduous trees. This trail is quite wild and litter-free. It ends at an outlet on Alhambra Road.

And joy of joys! There's now a dog park within the park, between the baseball field and the barbecue pits. It's about an acre, with grass, benches, poop bags, and water. It's fun to mix a little off-leash romp with a leashed walk around the rest of the attractive park.

The entrance to the main park is at Pinole Valley Road and Simas Avenue. 510/724-9002.

DIVERSION

Drive Your Pooch to the Pulpit: Want to take your dog to church? If you don't think he's ready to pray in a pew, you can bring him along to attend a service in the comfort of your car. Since 1975, the **First Presbyterian Church of Richmond** has offered a drive-in service in a shopping mall parking lot. Held at 8:30 A.M. every Sunday outside the Appian 80 shopping center in Pinole, the ceremony attracts a few dozen worshippers every week.

Pastors David and Ruth Sandberg transmit the service over shortwave radio from a mobile pulpit, complete with a sermon and choral music. Church elders bring communion around to each car on a silver platter and parishioners honk and flash their headlights at the pastors to say "Amen." It's quite a scene—and afterward you can go shopping. Dogs are as welcome to attend as anyone. (In fact, you may see Marty the Poodle in one of the cars there. The dapper dog has become a regular since reading about services in this book.) Other animals are also welcome: Peepers the Duck usually makes a weekly appearance as well. (Lucky for Peepers that Marty is a poodle and not a Lab.)

Exit I-80 at Appian Way. The shopping center is just north of the freeway, on the west side of Appian Way, Pinole. For more information, call 510/234-0954.

PLACES TO STAY

Motel 6: Rates are $49 for the first adult and $6 for the second. 1501 Fitzgerald Drive 94564; 510/222-8174.

Martinez

Martinez has a charming historic district right off the entrance to its regional shoreline park, so spend some time walking with your dog around the Amtrak station and antique shops. You'll see plenty of fellow strollers taking a break from the train.

PARKS, BEACHES, AND RECREATION AREAS

4 Hidden Lakes Open Space

🐾🐾🐾🐾🐾 (See Contra Costa County map on page 80)

Although the city park called Hidden Valley Park doesn't allow dogs, the open space to the south of it does. It's crossed by one of the East Bay Regional Parks' trails (the California Riding and Hiking Trail) on its way from the Carquinez Strait Regional Shoreline to where it connects with the Contra Costa Canal Trail. Call 510/635-0135 or see www.ebparks.org for maps of the Contra Costa Regional Trails.

One entrance to Hidden Lakes is off Morello Avenue, where it intersects with Chilpancingo Parkway.

Antioch

Antioch is pretty much a desert for dogs, but south of town are two charming spots of relief.

PARKS, BEACHES, AND RECREATION AREAS

5 Black Diamond Mines Regional Preserve

🐾🐾🐾🐾🐾 (See Contra Costa County map on page 80)

Leash-free dogs, especially leash-free dogs of the male persuasion, think this park is an excellent place to visit. The coal miners who worked and lived here in the 1860s and 1870s planted a variety of drought-tolerant trees not usually found in the East Bay, including something called "trees of heaven." Dogs who sniff these trees seem to know why they're called trees of heaven. Their noses just can't get enough as they press them deep into the bark.

The hills of Black Diamond Mines are jumbled and ragged, looking a lot like the Sierra foothills. From the parking lot, it's a moderate climb to the Rose Hill Cemetery, where Protestant Welsh miners (the tombstones bear the names

Davis, Evans, and Jenkins) buried victims of mine accidents and many of their children, who died of diphtheria, typhoid, and scarlet fever.

Plenty of tunnel openings and piles of tailings have been preserved by the park for walkers to examine. A brochure marks mine sites. You should be alert for rattlers during warm seasons, although any rattler not actually snoozing will probably get out of your way before you even know he's near.

You can walk into this East Bay regional preserve from the Contra Loma Regional Park just below it (see below). But from that direction, the trails are too hot and dry for a dog in summer. Instead, enter from the north by car via Somersville Road and park in the last lot, which has some shady trees.

It's $4 to park here. Dogs are $1 extra. Backpack camping is available for $5. Phone 510/636-1684 for camp info. From Highway 4 at Antioch, exit at Somersville Road and drive south to the park entrance. Keep driving for a bit more than one mile if you want to park in the lot farthest in. You'll pass wonderful old mining-era houses and barns, now used as park headquarters and offices. 510/635-0135 or 925/757-2620.

6 Contra Loma Regional Park

🐾🐾🐾🐾🐕 (See Contra Costa County map on page 80)

This 776-acre park is so well hidden amid the barren hills north of Black Diamond Mines that you might not ever know it was here. A few attractive trails, including a trail leading into Black Diamond Mines Regional Preserve, rise into the surrounding hills for you and your leash-free dog to explore. Dogs can be off leash in the back country. You'll know it when you see it.

Unfortunately, as in all regional parks, your dog may not accompany you in the swimming area. Nor can he take an informal swim himself in the fishing areas, since the park managers want to protect his feet from stray fishhooks. It's probably better not to bring your dog here on a hot day. Instead, save the trip for winter or spring, when the wildflowers burst open.

From Highway 4, take the Lone Tree Way exit. Go south on Lone Tree for a little more than a half mile, then turn right onto Bluerock Drive. Follow Bluerock along the park's east side to the entrance. The fee for parking is $4. The dog fee is $1. 510/635-0135.

Bethel Island

PLACES TO EAT

Rusty Porthole: Picture this: steak, prime rib, chicken, french fries, your dog, you, the California Delta. What more could a dog desire? Dine with your happy pooch at the patio overlooking the water. If you come by boat, the parking's easy, with 200 feet of dock space. 3893 Willow Road; 925/684-3607.

PLACES TO STAY

Sugar Barge RV Park and Marina: Got an RV? Got a dog? Got a boat? Then park them all here in the heart of the Sacramento-San Joaquin River Delta to sample the Delta life with dog. The Sugar Barge has everything from a full-service marina to horseshoe pits. Kids enjoy the swimming pool and playground. Rates are $28–32. 1440 Sugar Barge Road 94511; 800/799-4100; www.sugarbarge.com.

Hercules

PARKS, BEACHES, AND RECREATION AREAS

7 San Pablo Bay Shoreline Park

😺😺😺🐾 (See Contra Costa County map on page 80)

This tiny, undeveloped East Bay Regional Park shoreline is just right if you happen to be in Hercules exploring the old Santa Fe Railroad yard. A paved trail runs about one-eighth of a mile along the tracks. New housing developments and interesting restored Victorian railroad workers' housing surround a small but pretty area of grass, swamp, and eucalyptus trees. Best of all, you and your dog can check it all out without a leash.

If you follow Railroad Avenue to its end, across the line into Pinole, there's a very small and beautifully landscaped city park behind the wastewater treatment plant (which smells fresh as a rose). You must keep your dog on leash here.

From I-80, exit at Pinole Valley Road and travel north. Pinole Valley Road becomes Tennent Avenue, then Railroad Avenue. Park somewhere around the Civic Arts Facility, a cluster of Victorian buildings in a grove of palms and eucalyptus. Call 510/724-9004 or 510/635-0135.

Pleasant Hill

PARKS, BEACHES, AND RECREATION AREAS

8 Paso Nogal Park

😺😺😺😺🐾 (See Contra Costa County map on page 80)

This large open-space park has the best of both worlds: smooth dirt trails along gentle oak-dotted slopes, where leashed dogs can hike to their hearts' content, and a fenced park where they can throw off their leashes and run like the wind. The dog park has benches, tables, water, and good parking. It's grassy and surrounded by trees. The trees within the park are nothing but glorified sticks right now, but they'll grow.

The dog park is open Monday–Saturday and is closed Sunday for maintenance. To help preserve the lush grass, it's also closed when the ground is wet. (This can be weeks at a time during rainy season.) The park is at Morello Avenue and Paso Nogal Road. 925/682-0896.

Concord

PARKS, BEACHES, AND RECREATION AREAS

9 The Paw Patch

🐾🐾🐾🐾🐕 (See Contra Costa County map on page 80)

The grass truly is always greener on the other side of the fence at this wonderful 2.5-acre dog park. It's so green and lush that it has other dog parks green with envy. Dog parks with grass (aka turf) often struggle in vain against a tide of pounding paws. The grass can end up anything but green and rather downtrodden. But not the grass here. The park district folks work hard to maintain it. In fact, they recently won a coveted award for their turf management from the California Parks and Recreation Society.

There's more to this park than grass, though. It's got benches, water, poop bags, a smaller fenced area for small dogs, and lots of toys. The lucky dogs who come here get to sniff through a toy box and pick out a favorite toy to play with here. Or they find them scattered around the grass.

The park is within the lovely 126-acre Newhall Community Park. You can take your dog around the park on a leash. From the top of the hill you're rewarded with great views of everything from Mount Diablo to the Carquinez Straits. (This is where you'll also find a Vietnam War memorial.) The park is at Turtle Creek Road and Ayres Road. 925/671-3444.

10 Lime Ridge Open Space Recreation Area

🐾🐾🐾🐾🐕 (See Contra Costa County map on page 80)

This open space reserve is huge, sprawling across parts of both Walnut Creek and Concord. It's undeveloped and open to lucky leash-free dogs. You can sometimes find a creek, depending on the time of year and status of drought, and that's a real relief during the long, hot summers.

The only entry point from Concord is from the parking lot on Treat Boulevard west of Cowell Road. 925/671-3270.

PLACES TO STAY

Holiday Inn Concord: Rates are $79–133. Dogs require a $100 deposit. 1050 Burnett Avenue 94520; 925/687-5500.

Clayton

PARKS, BEACHES, AND RECREATION AREAS

🔟 Clayton Dog Park

😋😋🐕 (See Contra Costa County map on page 80)

Big oaks are adjacent to this dog park, but there's very little shade within. It has a water meter but no water (yet). A dirt lot has wood chips, but dog people pine for grass. Yet for all its little foibles, this is a perfectly decent place to take a dog for an off-leash romp. It may not be the Ritz, but it's not a dive either. It has picnic table, two benches, and poop bags, and it's along the Creek Trail, which makes for a fine leashed dog walk. The park is on Marsh Creek Road and Regency Drive, across from Clayton Park. 925/673-7300.

🔢 Morgan Territory Regional Preserve

😋😋😋😋🐕 (See Contra Costa County map on page 80)

Morgan Territory, named after a farmer who owned the land long before it became part of the East Bay Regional Parks system, is as far away from the Bay Area as you can get while still being in the Bay Area. From its heights, on a rim above the Central Valley, you see the San Joaquin River, the Delta, the valley, and, on a clear day, the peaks of the Sierra. Eagles and hawks soar above as you and your leash-free pooch explore ancient twisted giant oaks and lichen-covered sandstone outcrops below. Morgan Territory is close to the end of the earth and well worth the journey.

As the crow flies, Morgan Territory is equidistant from Clayton, Danville, San Ramon, Livermore, Byron, and Brentwood. And "distant" is the key word.

This 4,147-acre preserve has miles of hiking and riding trails. If you don't want to climb much but want great views of the Central Valley, try the Blue Oak Trail, which starts at the entrance. You'll even see the "backside" of Mt. Diablo. It's an unusual vantage point for Bay Area folks.

Most of the creeks are dry in the summer, though your dog can splash into cattle ponds, if he's so inclined. Watch for wicked foxtails in these grasses. These are the sticky wickets that help make veterinarians a well-off breed.

The easiest access is from Livermore in Alameda County. From I-580, take the North Livermore Avenue exit and drive north on North Livermore Avenue. Shortly after the road curves left (west), turn right, onto Morgan Territory Road, and follow it 10.7 miles to the entrance. From the Walnut Creek/Concord area, take Clayton Road to Marsh Creek Road, then turn right onto Morgan Territory Road. The entrance is 9.4 miles from Marsh Creek Road. 510/635-0135 or 925/757-2620.

PLACES TO EAT

Skipolini's Pizza: The folks here serve New York–style pizza, as well as salads and sandwiches. They welcome dogs at their outdoor tables. 1033 Diablo Street; 925/672-5555.

Richmond

Point Richmond, the Richmond neighborhood tucked between the Richmond-San Rafael Bridge and Miller-Knox Regional Shoreline, is a cheerful small-town hangout for you and your dog. Consider stopping by for a snack on your way to some of the magical, four-paw shoreline here.

Sit on a bench in the Point Richmond Triangle, the town center. You'll be surrounded by nicely preserved Victorian buildings, the Hotel Mac, and many delis and bakeries, some with outdoor tables. We were asked not to mention one by name because it welcomes cats as well as dogs. Grrrr. The Santa Fe Railroad rattles past periodically, blowing the first two notes of "Here Comes the Bride."

From I-580, on the Richmond end of the Richmond–San Rafael Bridge, exit at Cutting Boulevard and drive west to town. Bear right on Richmond Avenue. The Triangle is at the intersection of Richmond and Washington Avenues and Park Place.

PARKS, BEACHES, AND RECREATION AREAS

13 Point Pinole Regional Shoreline

🐾🐾🐾🐾🐕 (See Contra Costa County map on page 80)

Of all the East Bay Regional Parks' shorelines, this is the farthest from civilization and its discontents, and thus the cleanest and least spoiled. It's also huge and a heavenly walk for dog or owner, with its views of Mt. Tamalpais across San Pablo Bay, and its docks, salt marsh, beaches, eucalyptus groves, and expanses of wild grassland waving in the breeze. Some of the eucalyptus trees are so wind-carved they could be mistaken for cypresses.

The park has fine bike paths, and your dog should be leashed for safety on these, but he's free on the unpaved trails—even on the dirt paths through marshes, such as the Marsh Trail. Just make sure he stays on the trail and doesn't go into the marsh itself. Dogs may not go on the fishing pier or on the shuttle bus to the pier.

From I-80, exit at Hilltop Drive, go west and take a right on San Pablo Avenue, then left on Atlas Road to the park entrance. There's a $4 parking fee and a $1 dog fee. 510/635-0135.

14 Wildcat Canyon Regional Park

🐾🐾🐾🐾🐕 (See Contra Costa County map on page 80)

This is Tilden Regional Park's northern twin. Tilden (see the Berkeley section of the Alameda County chapter) has its attractive spots, but it's designed for people. Wildcat seems made for dogs, because not much goes on here. Dogs really dig this. Who needs all those human feet passing by anyway? (Unless, of course, they're tracking eau du cow patty or some other savory scent.) Best of all, you can leave your dog's leash tucked away in your pocket.

Large coast live oaks, madrones, bay laurels, and all kinds of chaparral thrive on the east side. And since the area was ranchland from the days of Spanish land grants and traces of house foundations remain, it isn't surprising that a lot of exotic plants flourish here alongside the expected ones. You'll find berries, nasturtiums, and cardoon thistle, which looks like an artichoke allowed to grow up. All kinds of grasses and wildflowers cover the western hillsides.

At the entrance parking lot is Wildcat Creek, which gets low but usually not entirely dry in summer. Then you can follow the Wildcat Creek Trail (actually an abandoned paved road); it travels gently uphill and then follows the southern ridge of the park. Or follow any of the nameless side trails, which are wonderfully wild and solitary. You can hear train whistles all the way up from Emeryville and the dull roar of civilization below, but somehow it doesn't bother you up here.

Other trails lead through groves of pines or follow Wildcat Creek. The park is roughly three miles long. If you come to the boundary with Tilden, remember that dogs aren't allowed in the nature area across the line. You can get on the East Bay Skyline National Recreation Trail (Nimitz Way), running along the park's north side. Don't branch off onto the Eagle's Nest Trail, however; it belongs to the East Bay Municipal Utility District, which requires a permit and frowns on dogs. But there's plenty of room here. You and your dog could spend several blissful days in Wildcat.

From I-80, southbound, take the McBryde exit and turn left on McBryde Avenue to the park entrance. If you're northbound, take the Amador/Solano exit. Go three blocks north on Amador Street and turn right (east) on McBryde to the entrance. 510/635-0135 or 510/236-1262.

15 Kennedy Grove Regional Recreation Area
🐾🐾🐾 (See Contra Costa County map on page 80)

This is a large picnic and play area for folks who like softball, volleyball, and horseshoes. Dogs must be leashed. The best part of this park is that you can get to the Bay Area Ridge Trail from here from a gate to the right as you enter the park, or from a trailhead at the Senior Parking Area. You'll cross some East Bay Municipal Utility District land (no permits necessary in this section) and San Pablo Dam Road. The trail ascends and soon becomes the Eagle's Nest Trail. If you're really inspired and your pooch isn't pooped, you can then climb all the way to Inspiration Point in Tilden Regional Park (see the Berkeley section of the Alameda County chapter). Dogs like Joe firmly put their paw down when it comes to such rigorous tasks. Whenever we visited, he would just sit there riveted to the ground like a fire hydrant. You could almost see him shaking his head "no way."

From I-80, take the San Pablo Dam Road exit and go south; the entrance is a quarter mile past the intersection of Castro Ranch Road. The parking fee is $4 and there's a $1 dog fee. 510/635-0135 or 510/223-7840.

16 Miller-Knox Regional Shoreline
🐾🐾🐾🐾🐕 (See Contra Costa County map on page 80)

Hooray! Wooooof! Yap! Although your dog must be leashed in developed areas, she can run free on the hillside trails east of Dornan Drive in this 259-acre park.

West of Dornan is a generous expanse of grass, pine, and eucalyptus trees with picnic tables, a lagoon with egrets (so there's no swimming), and Keller Beach (dogs are prohibited). It's breezy here and prettier than most shoreline parks by virtue of its protecting gentle hills, whose trails offer terrific views of the Richmond-San Rafael Bridge, Mt. Tamalpais, Angel Island, and San Francisco. Ground squirrels stand right by their holes and pipe their alarms. Although you can't bring your dog onto Keller Beach, there's a paved path above it along riprap shoreline, where your dog can reach the water if he's so inclined. In the picnic areas, watch for discarded chicken bones!

You can also tour the Richmond Yacht Harbor by continuing on Dornan

DIVERSION

Foof 'Er Up: Is your pooch starting to smell like a dog? If you go to Point Isabel, you can give your dog both the walk of his life and a bath. **Mudpuppy's Tub and Scrub,** the park's very own dog wash, offers full- or self-service scrubbings in several elevated tubs. The cost is very reasonable, considering it includes shampoo, drying, and someone else to clean the tub afterward. And not only can your dog get unmuddy and downright gorgeous here, he can go home with some pretty doggone nice pooch items, too. Mudpuppy's offers a full line of dog toys, treats, and gifts. Owners Eddie Lundeen and Daniel Bergerac provide a fun, clean atmosphere. Call or stop by before your walk in the park to reserve your tub. (The earlier you do so, the better, especially on weekends.)

And here's some great news for your dog's best friend. (That would be you.) Mudpuppy's now has a café just down the road: It's called Mudpuppy's Sit and Stay Café. It has a walk-up window so you and your dog can go and get some delectable goodies for humans, including espresso, tasty pastries, warming soups (usually featuring one veggie variety and something hearty), great sandwiches, salads, and ice cream. The café makes this area one of the most dog-friendly and dog-person–friendly around. Eat, drink, walk, talk, buy, suds, scrub, enjoy.

Mudpuppy's is in the first parking lot inside the park, off Isabel Road, Richmond. 510/559-8899; www.mudpuppys.com.

Drive south to Brickyard Cove Road, a left turn past the railroad tracks. Or, from Garrard Boulevard, drive south till you see the Brickyard Cove housing development. The paved paths lining the harbor offer views of yachts, San Francisco, Oakland, and the Bay Bridge.

From either I-80 or I-580, exit at Cutting Boulevard and go west to Garrard Boulevard. Go left, pass through a tunnel, and park in one of two lots off Dornan Drive. 510/635-0135.

🔳 Point Isabel Regional Shoreline

😺😺😺😺 🐕 (See Contra Costa County map on page 80)

With so many Bay Area beaches either outright banning dogs or enforcing new leash demands, it not easy being a water dog around here these days. Thank goodness for this 21-acre patch of utter water-dog heaven! Dogs are so happy when they come here that some howl as they arrive in their cars. (Some owners do, too, but they're another story.)

Point Isabel is an exception to the East Bay Regional Parks' rule that dogs must be on leash in "developed" areas. This is a decidedly unwild but terrific shoreline park with plenty of grass and paw-friendly paved paths. It's swarming with dogs. In a recent census by the park district, 558,930 people and 784,370 pooches visited in one year. Fortunately, people here are generally very responsible, and the park looks pretty good, despite being accosted by more than four million feet and paws annually.

The large lawn area is perfect for fetching, Frisbee throwing, and chasing each other around. And the bay and the sand—ahh: These are a water dog's delight. The surf here is usually very tame, making dog paddling a joy.

There are benches, picnic tables, restrooms, a water fountain for people and dogs, and many racks full of bags for scooping. Cinder paths run along the riprap waterfront, where you can watch sailboarders against a backdrop of the Golden Gate and Bay Bridges, San Francisco, the Marin Headlands, and Mt. Tamalpais. On a brisk day, a little surf even splashes against the rocks.

After a wet and wonderful walk, you may want to take your pooch to Mudpuppy's Tub and Scrub, which is right here, for a little cleaning up. And after that, if you've been a very good human, you can treat yourself to a cuppa joe and some café cuisine at the new Mudpuppy's Sit and Stay Café. Talk about a people and pooch paradise. (See the Diversion Foof 'Er Up.)

From I-80 in Richmond, exit at Central Avenue and go west to the park entrance, next to the U.S. Postal Service Bulk Mail Center. For more info on the park or its wonderful doggy user group, PIDO (Point Isabel Dog Owners and Friends—why isn't it called PIDOF?), see www.pido.org. 510/635-0135.

El Cerrito

PARKS, BEACHES, AND RECREATION AREAS

18 Hillside Park

🐾 (See Contra Costa County map on page 80)

This is not the prettiest park around; the southern end is mostly an eroded hillside of scrubby grass with power lines. But off Schmidt Lane is the much more attractive El Cerrito Foundation Memorial Grove. A bumpy dirt path leads up through coyote brush to eucalyptus groves at the hilltop, overlooking El Cerrito, the Golden Gate and Bay Bridges, and Mt. Tamalpais. The trail doesn't go far into the open space.

Enter off Schmidt Lane, which runs north off San Pablo Avenue. 510/215-4300.

Orinda

PARKS, BEACHES, AND RECREATION AREAS

19 San Pablo Dam Reservoir

🐾🐾🐾 (See Contra Costa County map on page 80)

This reservoir is a top fishing spot in the Bay Area. It's stocked with more trout than any lake in California. That's great news for humans, but dogs could not care less. They're not allowed to set paw in this magnificent body of water (and neither are people), so hanging out alongside a human angler is out of the question. You can't even take your pooch out on your own boat.

The paved and dirt trails around the reservoir are lovely and often empty once you and your leashed dog wind into the hills. The dirt trails get rougher as you leave the popular fishing areas. You'll have to ford some creek beds or streams, and there's too much poison oak for comfort if your dog doesn't step daintily right down the middle of the trail. The trails are wild and woodsy, though, and dogs recommend them highly.

The entrance fee is $6.50 for parking and $1 for dogs. You can buy a season ticket for $88 a car or $85 a boat. Fishing is $4, and you'll need your fishing license, of course. The lake itself is open mid-February–mid-November.

From I-80, exit at San Pablo Dam Road and drive east about six miles. From Highway 24, exit at Camino Pablo/San Pablo Dam Road and go north about 5.5 miles. 510/223-1661.

20 Robert Sibley Volcanic Regional Preserve

🐾🐾🐾🐾🐕 (See Contra Costa County map on page 80)

We're not exactly talking Mt. St. Helens here, but this 371-acre park has some pretty interesting volcanic history. Geologically inclined dogs can wander leashless as you explore volcanic dikes, mudflows, lava flows, and other evidence of extinct volcanoes.

The preserve is actually closer to Oakland than Orinda, but it lies in Contra Costa County. From the entrance on Skyline Boulevard, you can get on the East Bay Skyline National Recreation Trail and walk north to Tilden Regional Park (see the Berkeley section of the Alameda County chapter) or south to Redwood Regional Park (see the Oakland section of the Alameda County chapter). Or, for a shorter stroll, take the road to Round Top, the highest peak in the Berkeley Hills, made of volcanic debris left over from a 10-million-year-old volcano.

More attractive and less steep is the road to the quarries. It's partly paved and smooth enough for a wheelchair or stroller, but it becomes smooth dirt about halfway to the quarries. Both trails are labeled for geological features. (Pick up a brochure at the visitor center.) At the quarry pits, there's a good view of Mt. Diablo. This is a dry, scrubby, cattle-grazed area, but in the rainy season your dog may be lucky enough to find swimming in a pit near the quarries. In the spring, look for poppies and lupines.

From Highway 24 east of the Caldecott Tunnel, exit on Fish Ranch Road, drive north to Grizzly Peak Boulevard, and then take a left. Go south on Grizzly Peak to the intersection with Skyline Boulevard. Go left on Skyline. The entrance is just to the east of the intersection. 510/635-0135.

PLACES TO EAT

High Tech Burrito: The burritos and fajitas here are really, really good. The ingredients are fresh and combined in very interesting ways. Try the veggie burrito. It's *muy bueno*. Dogs can dine with you (no spicy scraps, please!) at the many courtyard tables at Theatre Square. 2 Theatre Square; 925/254-8884.

Lafayette

PARKS, BEACHES, AND RECREATION AREAS

🐾 Briones Regional Park

🐾🐾🐾🐾🐕 (See Contra Costa County map on page 80)

From both main entrances to this park, you can walk one-quarter of a mile and be lost in sunny, rolling hills or cool oak woodlands. Unless you stick to the stream areas, it's not a good park for hot summer days. But with a good supply of your own water, you and your dog, who may run blissfully leashless, can walk gentle ups and downs all day on fire roads or foot trails.

The north entrance requires an immediate uphill climb into the hills, but you're rewarded with a quick view of Mt. Diablo and the piping of ground squirrels, all of whom are long gone safely into their burrows by the time your dog realizes they might be fun to chase. If your dog is a self-starter, this end of the park is fine for you. The Alhambra Creek Trail, which follows Alhambra

Creek, does offer water in the rainy season. Stay away from the John Muir Nature Area (shaded on your brochure map), where dogs aren't allowed.

When we're feeling lazy, we prefer the south entrance at Bear Creek, just east of the inaccessible (to dogs) Briones Reservoir. Here you have an immediate choice of open hills or woodsy canyons, and the land is level for a few miles. The Homestead Valley Trail leads gently up and down through cool, sharp-scented bay and oak woodlands.

Watch for deer, horses, and cattle. Some dogs near and dear to me love rolling in fresh cow patties—an additional hazard of the beasts existing in close proximity.

From Highway 24, take the Orinda exit; go north on Camino Pablo, then right on Bear Creek Road to Briones Road, to the park entrance. The parking fee is $4 and the dog fee is $1. 510/635-0135.

Walnut Creek

Walnut Creek's big secret is its beautiful creeks and canals, former irrigation ditches that now adorn golf courses and housing developments. Walnut Creek, San Ramon Creek, the Contra Costa Canal, and the Ygnacio Canal all pass through town. Dogs must be leashed everywhere, except in a new dog park and the undeveloped areas of city-owned open spaces, as we describe below.

PARKS, BEACHES, AND RECREATION AREAS

22 Acalanes Ridge Open Space Recreation Area

🐾🐾🐾🐾🐕 (See Contra Costa County map on page 80)
In 1974, the city of Walnut Creek set aside a few open spaces for a limited-use "land bank." Dogs must be "under voice or sight command" (translation: off leash if obedient). Hoo boy! The trails are open to hikers, dogs, horses, and bicycles, however, so on a fine day, your dog may have some competition.

Acalanes Ridge, close to Briones Regional Park (see the Lafayette section), is crossed by the Briones to Diablo Regional Trail. Like the others, it lacks water.

A good entry point is from Camino Verde Circle, reached by driving south on Camino Verde from the intersection of Pleasant Hill and Geary Roads. For information on any of the open spaces, call 925/943-5899.

23 San Miguel Park

🐾🐾🐾🐾🐕 (See Contra Costa County map on page 80)
Dogs who are early risers love waking up, throwing on their leashes, coming to this park, and then throwing off their leashes. From 6–9 A.M. daily, this grassy four-acre park goes to the dogs. It's positively poochy here during the morning canine commute. It's not a fenced area, and that's fine with dogs. Boy dogs and shade-seekers like the park's trees.

The park is a few minutes northeast of the I-680/Highway 24 interchange. From northbound I-680, take the exit toward Ygnacio Valley Road and turn right in a little over a half mile onto Ygnacio Valley Road. In about two miles, turn right on San Carlos Drive and in .3 mile, go left at San Jose Court. The park is at San Jose Court, off Los Cerros Avenue. 925/943-5855.

24 Shell Ridge Open Space Recreation Area

🐾🐾🐾🐾🐾 (See Contra Costa County map on page 80)

Dogs may run off leash everywhere but in the developed areas (parking lots, picnic grounds), but "must be under positive voice and sight command." The people who write these rules must be retired military document writers or part-time computer-manual writers.

Within the Shell Ridge Open Space is the Old Borges Ranch, a demonstration farm staffed irregularly by rangers. The ranch house is sometimes open noon–4 P.M. on Sunday. Call first to check. For information or to make a reservation to visit, call 925/943-5860.

You can enter by the Sugarloaf-Shell Ridge Trail at the north edge. From I-680, take the Ignacio Valley Road exit, go east on Ignacio Valley Road to Walnut Avenue (not Boulevard), turn right and right again on Castle Rock Road. Go past the high school, turn right, and follow the signs. 925/943-5899.

PLACES TO EAT

Walnut Creek's "downtown," your respite from mallsville, is Main Street. Here, you'll find several welcoming outdoor restaurants, benches for just sitting, and good weather. One of our favorites follows.

Original Hot Dog Place: Every kind of hot dog is served in this tiny shop with a neat hot dog mural on the wall and a wooden Indian outside next to the tables. 1420 Lincoln Avenue at Main Street; 925/256-7302.

PLACES TO STAY

Holiday Inn: A few months before I originally wrote about this, I got a letter from Daniel Fevre, then the general manager of this hotel. "My first question (when I took this job) was—you guessed it—'Do we take pets?' The answer was 'No.' My reply was 'We do now!' To test the program, I stayed with my two dogs (and one cat) for several days until the movers arrived, and the staff was great."

Fevre is no longer with the hotel, but his legacy—the dog-friendly policy—is intact. It has a pool, which humans enjoy, but what's really special about this place is its proximity to a hiking trail. The staff will tell you about it at the front desk. Rates are $79–169. There's a $25 fee for the length of your dog's stay. 2730 North Main Street 94598; 925/932-3332.

Walnut Creek Motor Lodge: Very small dogs only, please (15 pounds or under). Rates are $70–85. 1960 North Main Street 94596; 925/932-2811.

Danville

PARKS, BEACHES, AND RECREATION AREAS

25 Las Trampas Regional Wilderness

🐾🐾🐾🐾🐕 (See Contra Costa County map on page 80)

This regional wilderness is remarkable for its sense of isolation from the rest of the Bay Area. You can experience utter silence at this 3,298-acre park, and the views from the ridge tops are breathtaking.

Rocky Ridge Trail (from the parking lot at the end of Bollinger Canyon Road) takes you and your leash-free pooch on a fairly steep .75-mile ascent to the top of the ridge, where you'll enter the East Bay Municipal Utility District watershed. Since dogs aren't allowed here and permits are required even for humans, it's better to head west on any of several trails climbing the sunny southern flanks of Las Trampas Ridge.

Creeks run low or dry during the summer, so bring plenty of water. Your dog should know how to behave around cattle, deer, and horses.

From I-680 about six miles north of the intersection with I-580, take the Bollinger Canyon Road exit and head north on Bollinger Canyon Road to the entrance. (Go past the entrance to Little Hills Ranch Recreation Area, where dogs aren't allowed.) 510/635-0135 or 925/837-3145.

26 Oak Hill Park

🐾🐾🐾 (See Contra Costa County map on page 80)

Here's a very clean, beautiful park run by the city of Danville. It's about as good as a park designed for people can get, offering picnic tables, a pond with ducks and geese and waterfalls, volleyball and tennis courts, and an unusually attractive children's play area with swings, a slide, and its own waterfall. The rest of the park is natural oak-studded hillside laced by an equestrian/hiking/exercise dirt trail, from which there is a fine view of Mt. Diablo. Dogs will enjoy this path, but they must remain on leash. No wading in the pond, either. The park is at Stone Valley Road and Glenwood Court. 925/314-3400.

27 Hap Magee Ranch Canine Corral

🐾🐾🐾🐕 (See Contra Costa County map on page 80)

In the summer of 2004, this 1.5-acre park had been opened just three weeks when it was hit by a doggy tragedy. A big dog and a Jack Russell terrier blind-sided each other while running around, and the Jack Russell died. The accident immediately resulted in a "time share" arrangement, where big dogs were allowed at odd hours, small dogs at even hours. There are plans for a separate area for smaller dogs to be constructed so that all dogs will be able to use the park at the same time.

The park is a pretty mix of grass and wood chips, with a little shade. From I-680 going north, exit at El Cerro Boulevard and turn right onto El Cerro at the light. At the second light, go right at La Gonda Way. The park is on the left after the stop sign. Park in the paved lot. 925/314-3400.

San Ramon

PARKS, BEACHES, AND RECREATION AREAS

28 Memorial Park Dog Park

🐾🐾🐾🐕 (See Contra Costa County map on page 80)

Once a dog's paws get used to the decomposed granite that's on the surface of this park, this place is a positively peachy for poochies. It's 1.3 acres, with a separate section within for dogs under 20 pounds. (These are the ones Jake would pick up and carry around a park in his mouth ever so gently when we first adopted him at six months.) There will be shade trees here one day, but until the saplings grow, manmade shade structures do the trick. The park has water, poop bags, benches, and picnic tables.

The park is on the northwest side of town. Exit I-680 at Bollinger Canyon Road and drive west less than a quarter mile to San Ramon Valley Boulevard, where you'll find parking straight ahead on the south side of Bollinger. 925/973-3200.

29 Del Mar Dog Park

🐾🐾🐾🐕 (See Contra Costa County map on page 80)

This one-acre fenced park is covered with cedar wood chips. Jake, unfortunately, is content to trot around a little and then settle down to see how many wood chips he can chew to smithereens before I can get him to start acting more like a dog, less like a termite. But normal dogs love gallivanting around here. The park has all the usual amenities, including water, benches, and shade structures (no shade trees yet). The park is on the south side of town, at Del Mar Drive and Pine Valley Road. 925/973-3200.

PLACES TO STAY

San Ramon Marriott at Bishop Ranch: The folks who run this attractive hotel are very friendly to creatures of the doggy persuasion. Rates are $79–199. Dogs pay a $75 fee for the length of their stay. 2600 Bishop Drive 94583; 925/867-9200.

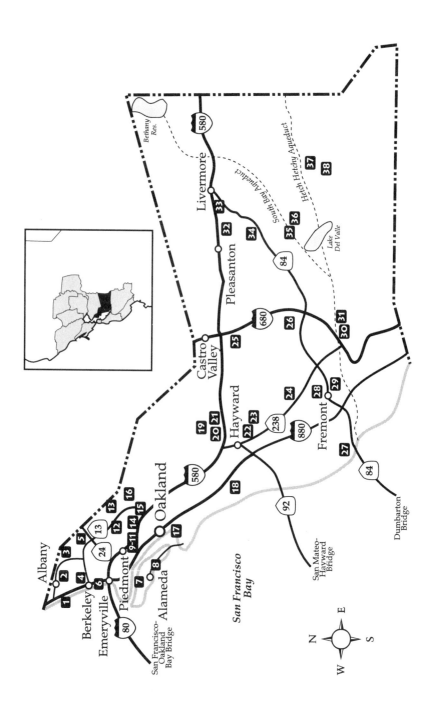

CHAPTER 5

Alameda County

From the hallowed hippie havens of Berkeley's Telegraph Avenue to the pleasing suburban pleasantries of Pleasanton, Alameda County is like California in miniature: It has nearly every level of population density and type, and nearly every temperate natural environment. Somehow, it all works.

Dogs dig it here, whether they're rasta dogs or shaved shih tzus. The county is like the creek it's named after—it's been lined with concrete, filled with trash, and dammed into oblivion, yet it still manages to gush joyfully onward. Some of the wildest country in the Bay Area is in this county, full of hidden gems of nature. So many of these parks are off-leash havens that your dog may think he's dreaming.

The 12-mile Alameda Creek Regional Trail (see Fremont section) is a favorite among dogs. They can run off leash on most of the trail, but where signs say leashes are required, heed the message.

As if all this weren't enough good news, your dog's hair will stand on end when he learns that unless he's a pit bull, he's allowed to run leashless on thousands of acres of parkland within the East Bay Regional Park District. Some 59 parks and recreation areas and 29 regional interpark trails—95,000

PICK OF THE LITTER—ALAMEDA COUNTY

BEST BAYSIDE OFF-LEASH AREA
César Chávez Park, Berkeley (pages 106–107)

BEST LEASH-FREE HIKES
Tilden Regional Park, Berkeley (pages 108–109)
Redwood Regional Park, Oakland (pages 117–118)
Chabot Regional Park, Castro Valley (pages 121–122)
Sunol Regional Wilderness, Fremont (pages 127–128)

COOLEST DOG PARK
Drigon Dog Park, Union City (page 124)

MOST DOG-FRIENDLY PLACES TO EAT
Flippers, Montclair District, Oakland (page 120)
Montclair Malt Shop, Montclair District, Oakland (page 120)
Noah's Bagels, Montclair District, Oakland (page 120)
Café Paradiso, Livermore (page 131)

BEST HIKING BUDDIES
Sierra Club's Canine Hike Unit (page 108)

acres in all—fall under the district's jurisdiction. Poop-bag dispensers are installed at the most heavily used areas, such as Point Isabel Regional Shoreline in Richmond (Contra Costa County).

The only places where dogs must be leashed within the district's parks are in developed areas, parking lots, picnic sites, lawns, and in posted Nature Areas. They aren't permitted on beaches (Point Isabel Regional Shoreline is a major exception), wetlands, marshes, or in the Tilden Nature Area. In addition, the district was deciding whether dogs have to be leashed along Redwood Regional Park's Stream Trail. Call 510/635-0135 for more information on the East Bay Regional Park District. You can also check out more details about the dog rules and hiking tips by going to www.ebparks.org and looking for the "Dogs" section. (Special rules and permits apply to anyone bringing more than three dogs. This was primarily designed for dog walkers, but if you have a gaggle of dogs yourself, you should check out the info on the site.)

All this is great, but Alameda County dogs are waggier than ever these days: They've got a few wonderful new parks that are devoted to their off-leash selves! In fact, the county is home to the very best fenced dog park in the state. It's in Union City and well worth a visit. (See Drigon Dog Park in the Union City section.)

A final note: Berkeley is the home of *The Bark*, the best dog magazine on dog's green earth. It doesn't even seem right to call it a dog magazine. *The Bark* bills itself as "the magazine of the modern dog culture," and "the magazine about life with dogs." It's smart, hip, beautifully designed, and a joy to read. *The Bark* grew out of a regional newsletter, *The Berkeley Bark*, created by Claudia Kawczynska. At the time I called it "the best regional dog newsletter I've ever seen." Its grown-up form is even better. If you appreciate good writing, gorgeous design, and you love dogs, check out *The Bark*'s website: www.thebark.com.

Berkeley

Berkeley, well known for its tolerance of eccentricity, is equally eccentric when it comes to dogs. Like most of Alameda County, it features strict leash laws: You break the law, you pay the price—which can be above $100 for the second offense.

But there is a unique loophole. If your dog is obedience-trained, Berkeley doesn't require him to be leashed. If an animal control officer sees you with your unleashed dog, you'll be asked to demonstrate that your dog is under

DIVERSION

Sniff Out a Good Book: Just try leaving your dog tied up outside when you visit either of the two **Cody's bookstores** in Berkeley. As soon as you're immersed in a dog-eared volume, you will be jolted back to reality by an announcement: "Will the guardian of the small yellow dog who is tied up outside please go get him and bring him in the store? Dogs are welcome in Cody's." Indeed they are. In fact, on some weekends the number of dogs here equals the number of humans at other bookstores. And the workers here can't remember the last time a dog gave a book a one-leg salute. Good work, dogs.

Cody's bookstores are known for having the best selection of books in the Bay Area. You can get almost anything you want here. And if you and your dog can't sniff out a title you're seeking, the staff here will be happy to help you track it down. The two store locations and phone numbers: 2454 Telegraph Avenue, Berkeley, 510/845-7852; 1730 4th Street, Berkeley, 510/559-9500.

absolute voice control. If the officer is not persuaded, you'll be cited and asked to appear in court with your dog, where you'll have another chance to prove it. (I can just picture Jake sitting, lying down, and rolling over in court. Well, maybe if a treat were involved. Nahhh.)

Whether they're all under absolute voice control or not, you'll see a lot more unleashed dogs in Berkeley than in any other Bay Area city. The University of California at Berkeley also has a leash law, but the campus is swarming with loose dogs, too.

Berkeley created the country's first official dog park, Ohlone Dog Park. Still, it was a big battle recently when it came to opening a 17-acre chunk of dog heaven at César Chávez Park at the Berkeley Marina. Foes included the Sierra Club and a blind woman. (Fortunately, the Girl Scouts and the pope stayed out of the melee.) The dogs triumphed, and the park just keeps getting better.

PARKS, BEACHES, AND RECREATION AREAS

1 César Chávez Park

🐾🐾🐾🐾 ✖ (See Alameda County map on page 102)

Urban pooch paradise doesn't get much better than this. Dogs who come here get to feel the bay breeze blowing through their fur as they frolic with their friends on 17 acres of prime land on the San Francisco Bay. Trails meander up and down the rolling hills and wind through a couple of quiet meadows. There's grass, grass everywhere.

The views of San Francisco, the Golden Gate Bridge, and the Bay Bridge are some of the best around. The park is equipped with plenty of poop-bag stations crammed to the gills. Use them. In fact, while you're at it, pick up an "orphan" poop if you see one lying around. Many people worked very hard for a very long time to get this park established, and the goal is to keep it beautiful and dog-friendly.

This is also a great place to fly a kite, and there are plenty of instructions posted on how to do it safely around here.

Take University Avenue west past the I-80 interchange and follow the signs to the Berkeley Marina and César Chávez Park. 510/981-5150.

② Ohlone Dog Park

🐾🐾🐕 (See Alameda County map on page 102)

For years after it opened as the first leash-free dog park in America in 1979, Ohlone provided a model for other cities considering opening a dog park. But sadly, the park is often in pretty bad shape these days, with mud happening before rainy season and in winter overtaking everything, including the mulch and woodchips used for covering the mud.

Still, it's a decent place for an off-leash romp in a safely fenced area. You'll find a water faucet, complete with a dog bowl set in concrete, and two picnic tables for owners who want to relax while their dogs socialize. The grass isn't always green here, but it's definitely better than what's on the other side of the fence. (Speaking of which, some of the park's neighbors have been making moves to limit hours or even to move the park out of the neighborhood. We'll update you about this sad situation in the next edition. This should not be happening to the nation's first dog park.)

The park is at Martin Luther King Jr. Way and Hearst Street. 510/981-5150.

DIVERSION

Take a Hike!: East Bay dogs who enjoy the great outdoors are very lucky indeed. Berkeley is the home base for the San Francisco Bay chapter of the **Sierra Club.** The club holds dozens of fun hikes for dogs each year, via its Canine Hike unit, and most of the hikes are in the East Bay. Dogs get to hike and play off leash, as long as they're well behaved and under voice control. Hikes are of varying difficulties and lengths. Some involve easy swimming (Jake is drooling), some involve camping, some even involve meeting the love of your life (when Sierra Singles and their dogs come out to play). The folks who participate in the canine hikes are almost as friendly and fun-loving as their dogs. Phone 510/848-0800 for info on the dog hikes, or to find out how to join the Sierra Club. You don't have to be a member to do the hikes, but one of the benefits of membership is that you'll receive a schedule of all Sierra Club events—including doggy hikes—every two months.

🐾 Tilden Regional Park

🐾🐾🐾🐾 🐕 (See Alameda County map on page 102)

Humans and dogs alike give Tilden a big thumbs-up (dewclaws-up). Leash-free dogs find the scents from its western ridge delectable and humans find the ridge's breathtaking views of the entire San Francisco Bay equally enticing.

Escapes from civilization are everywhere in this 2,078-acre park. Try the trails leading east from South Park Drive. They connect with the East Bay Skyline National Recreation Trail.

You can pick up the Arroyo Trail at the Big Springs sign and take it all the way to the ridge top. There's a great stream at the trailhead that you can follow through laurel, pine, toyon, and scrub on your low-grade ascent. Your dog may want to take a dip in the stream for refreshment.

After the trail veers from the stream, it steepens and leads into cypress-studded meadows and eucalyptus groves. Eventually it feeds into the Skyline National Recreation Trail, also known as the Sea View Trail, offering vistas over the bay along the way.

Dogs aren't allowed in the large nature area at the northern end or in the Lake Anza swimming area. Leashes are required in all the developed areas, including picnic grounds and ball fields. Remember to watch your step in the areas frequented by dogs, as some owners neglect to clean up after their furry friends. There's nothing like stepping in a steaming pile of dog dung to put a damper on a day of exploring nature.

DIVERSION

Ride a Dog-Sized Train: If your dog's not an escape artist or the nervous type, he's welcome to ride with you on **Tilden Regional Park's miniature train.** The open-car train takes you for a 12-minute ride through woods and past stunning views of the surrounding area. Adventurous dogs like it when the train toots its whistle as it rumbles past a miniature water tower, a car barn, and other such train accessories. When Joe Dog appeared on KRON-TV's *Bay Area Backroads* riding the train, he was fine until we hit the little tunnel—then he decided he wanted to go home. He was relieved that part ended up on the cutting-room floor.

The Redwood Valley Railway Company runs trains between 11 A.M. and 6 P.M. weekends and holidays (not Thanksgiving or Christmas) only, except during spring and summer school vacations, when it also runs weekdays, noon–5 P.M. and weekends until 6 P.M. Tickets are $1.75; kids under two and dogs ride free. You must keep the dog on a tight leash and make sure he doesn't jump out. It's in the southeast corner of Tilden Regional Park in Berkeley. From the intersection of Grizzly Peak Boulevard and Lomas Cantadas, follow the signs. 510/548-6100.

Speaking of steaming, be sure to check out Tilden's miniature steam train for a riveting good time.

From Highway 24, take the Fish Ranch Road exit north (at the eastern end of the Caldecott Tunnel). At the intersection of Fish Ranch, Grizzly Peak Boulevard, and Claremont Avenue, take a right on Grizzly Peak and continue north to South Park Drive. One more mile north brings you to Big Springs Trail. During peak season, continue on Grizzly Peak to the Shasta Gate. 510/635-0135.

4 Aquatic Park

 (See Alameda County map on page 102)

Take advantage of this city park for a quick stroll by the water. Conveniently situated off I-80, it's fairly tranquil, even with the lagoon's powerboats and water-skiers whizzing by. The lagoon's banks are planted with a mixture of grass, willows, cypress, and eucalyptus. Boy dogs have lifted many a leg in homage here.

Thanks to its greenery, birds are plentiful. Dogs like to bird-watch from the paved paths and the parcourse fitness trail. The pooch paddle is banned, and wading dogs are frowned upon, too.

Should you choose to walk to greener pastures, there's now a grand pedestrian crossing that takes you and your pooch over the freeway and lets you

DIVERSION

Go Shopping in 1969: You and your dog can shop in the autumn of love when you stroll through the sidewalks of **Telegraph Avenue** near the UC Berkeley campus. Street vendors sell tie-dyed clothes, crystals, pottery, and T-shirts airbrushed with clouds. Street performers sing, juggle, beg for money, or do whatever else comes naturally. Incense and other herbaceous odors waft through the air, but dogs prefer the scents of all the nondeodorized humans.

Dogs who reminisce about the 1960s really dig it here. They're perceived as totally cool dudes and given major amounts of love from people who like to hug dogs hard. When we last visited, Jake was wearing his favorite psychedelic bandana, and he received a few "duuuudes" per block.

Some dogs—and humans—may find the weekend crowds a sensory overload. If your schedule allows, try a cool afternoon. From I-80, take the Ashby exit, go about two miles east to Telegraph, and turn left (north). The street-merchant part begins around the intersection of Dwight Way.

---

off within walking distance of César Chávez Park. (It's at least a half-hour walk to get to Chávez from here via the walkway, but it's a beautiful walk.) You can't miss it.

From I-80, take the Ashby exit and turn north on Bay Street. There's a small parking lot. If you come from the north side of the park, you can park at a couple of areas on Bolivar Drive, along the park's east side. 510/981-5150.

5 Claremont Canyon Regional Preserve

🐾🐾🐾🐾🦮 (See Alameda County map on page 102)

This large park is full of steep hillside trails that lead to crests with stunning views of the university and the surrounding hills and valleys. If your dog likes eucalyptus trees and doesn't like leashes, take him here. It's one of those tree-filled, leashes-optional parks.

From Highway 13 (Ashby Avenue), drive north on College Avenue. Turn right on Derby Street, past the Clark Kerr Campus of UC Berkeley. The trailhead is at the southeast corner of the school grounds, near the beginning of Stonewall Road. 510/635-0135.

PLACES TO EAT

So many restaurants here have outdoor tables where dogs are welcome. Because of space, we list just a handful.

Bel Forno: Dine with your doggy under a shade-giving awning and next to a couple of trees. The turkey pesto sandwiches are tasty. Thirsty dogs get water. 1400 Shattuck Avenue; 510/644-1601.

Fontina Caffe Italiana: Dogs like dining with their people at the five umbrella-topped tables here. The food is snout-licking good. But what they like even better is that Fontina is right next door to the Shattuck Cat Clinic. Poor Joe Dog never knew the pleasures of Fontina, because he knew too well the pleasures of cats. 1730 Shattuck Avenue; 510/649-8090.

La Méditerranée: This delicious and inexpensive Middle Eastern restaurant has built up quite a following; there's usually a line on weekends when Cal is midsemester. The folks here will let your dog sit quietly at your feet at the outdoor tables, which have the added benefit of an outdoor heater on cool nights. You might want to tie your dog up on the sidewalk outside the fence separating the tables if it's especially crowded. 2936 College Avenue; 510/540-7773.

NeFeli: The light Greek cuisine at NeFeli really hits the spot. Try the Athenian panini if you like your Greek sans meat. It's a real treat. Dogs get to join you at tables under the awning in front. 1854 Euclid Avenue; 510/841-6374.

Peet's Coffee: Not only Peet's but various other cafés and shops encircle a sunny patio with benches. Nearly every morning, crowds of hungry bicyclists and amblers congregate to sit in the sun, argue (this is Berkeley), eat pastries, and sip Peet's coffee, which many call the best in the Bay Area. Dogs' noses don't stop quivering, and they can often meet other frustrated dogs. 2916 Domingo Avenue off Ashby. 510/843-1434.

Rick and Ann's Restaurant: Dogs feel really at home here, because Rick and Ann and their staff love dogs. There's always a bowl of water for your thirsty pooch. This is also a popular place among people. The food is delicious and all-American. Joe's favorites were meatloaf and creamy macaroni and cheese. It may take you a while to choose something from the imaginative menu, but just about anything you select will be great. The restaurant is next to Peet's, at 2922 Domingo Avenue; 510/649-8538.

Sea Breeze Market and Deli: Smack in the middle of the I-80 interchange, you won't even notice the traffic as you and your dog bask at sunny picnic tables, where crab claws crunch underfoot and begging is outstanding. Dogs are perfectly welcome so long as they don't wander into the store itself. You can buy groceries, beer, wine, classy ice cream, or a meal from the deli: fresh fish-and-chips, calamari, prawns, scallops, chicken, and quiche. The deli serves croissants and coffee early; if you live in the East Bay, you can zip in for a quick croissant and a dog walk at César Chávez Park before work. It's at the foot of University Avenue, past the I-80 entrance. 598 University Avenue; 510/486-0802.

DIVERSION

Flea to the Market: If your dog has the itch to shop, and promises not to do leg lifts on furniture even when it's outdoors and looking an awful lot like the tree it came from, you can have a relaxed time at the **Ashby Flea Market.** Good dogs love the easy camaraderie they'll find here. Crowds will be tolerant, but keep him on a short leash and watch out for chicken bones and abandoned cotton candy. (Jake Dog always does!)

This market is held every Saturday and Sunday at the Ashby BART station parking lot in Berkeley. From I-80, take the Ashby exit and drive about 1.5 miles east to the intersection of Adeline Street.

PLACES TO STAY

Golden Bear Inn: Rates are $89–99. Dogs pay a $15 fee for the length of their stay. 1620 San Pablo Avenue, 94702; 510/525-6770; www.goldenbearinn.com.

Emeryville

PARKS, BEACHES, AND RECREATION AREAS

🐾 Emeryville Marina Park

🐾🐾 (See Alameda County map on page 102)

If you're a human, this is a fine park. If you're a leashed dog, it's just so-so. A concrete path follows the riprap shoreline past cypress trees and through manicured grass. A quick and scenic stroll down the north side will give you a fine view of the marina and a miniature bird refuge where egrets, sandpipers, blackbirds, and doves inhabit a tiny marsh. Dogs who like to bird-watch think it's cool here.

Dogs who like to fish don't have it so easy. Pooches aren't allowed on the fishing pier. But if you console them with an offer to picnic at tables with grand views of the Bay Bridge, they usually snap out of their funk.

From I-80, take the Powell Street exit at Emeryville and go west on Powell to the end of the marina. It has lots of free parking. 510/577-6080.

PLACES TO STAY

Woodfin Suite Hotel: This is a big, friendly hotel for people, who get a full hot and cold breakfast buffet in the morning, and drinks and hors d'oeuvres in the evening, plus a pool, spa, and fitness center. Dogs just get to stay in an all-suites hotel, and only if they're not too big. "About 50 to 60 pounds" is the limit, says a front-desk clerk. Rates are $145. Dogs are $5 extra and require a $150 deposit. 5800 Shellmound 94608; 510/601-5880 or 888/433-9042.

Alameda

PARKS, BEACHES, AND RECREATION AREAS

7 Alameda Point Dog Run

😺 🐕 (See Alameda County map on page 102)

While this fenced park encompasses two acres along the Oakland Estuary, it's not much to look at—or to be in, for that matter. There are no trees. The ground is pretty much rock-hard, having baked in the sun and weathered through the years. Being just 100 feet back from this part of the estuary does provide a breeze, but the super-nice park supervisor, Fred, says the breeze tends to be a bit strong here. Your dog's ears may flap in the breeze, but more likely they'll just stream straight back. There's no water, either. It's a good place to take a dog if you're near the ferry terminal, because it's on Main Street, adjacent to the terminal. It's better than nothing. 510/748-4568.

8 Alameda Dog Exercise Area

😺😺😺😺🐕 (See Alameda County map on page 102)

Wahoo! This is one of the bigger fenced-in dog parks we've encountered. It's nearly six acres, shaded here and there by some wonderful big cypress and pine trees. The ground wants to be grass, but it's pretty much packed dirt at this point. Dogs have a howling good time chasing each other around big brush patches here and there. Among the amenities: benches, a separate section for small dogs, water, and poop bags. But the best amenity here is a natural one: a fresh bay breeze. The park is right off the bay. You can see the masts of the boats in the harbor from the dog park.

The park is set beside Crown Memorial Beach, which bans dogs. The dog park is actually part of Alameda's largest park, Washington Park. That park has lots of great amenities for people, including wonderful playgrounds and ball fields. Leashed dogs enjoy the wide green expanses, the bike path, and the edge of the marsh here. Unfortunately for hungry dogs, pooches aren't permitted at the picnic areas. Your best bet is to stick to the dog exercise area. They're more than welcome at the picnic tables there. The dog park is at 8th Street and Central Avenue. It's to the left of Washington Park's tennis courts. 510/748-4568.

PLACES TO EAT

Aroma Restaurant: Any restaurant that has something about smell in its name is a sure-fire winner in a dog's book. And this places smells mahhhvelous! It looks pretty terrific, too. It's right on a narrow bit of the Oakland Estuary, just a bone's throw from the Park Street Bridge. The outdoor dining area (where dogs can join their humans) looks like something you'd see in a wedding banquet, with lots of tables under white awnings. The food? A wonderful cuisine defies

DIVERSION

Seize the Bay from Oakland and Alameda: Water-loving dogs just about swoon when they learn they're allowed on the **Blue and Gold Fleet's ferries** that run between Oakland/Alameda and San Francisco. Fares are $5.25 one-way for adults. The Oakland ferry terminal is at the foot of Clay Street in Jack London Square. The Alameda dock is at the Gateway Center, 2991 Main Street. Phone 415/705-8200 for schedules and more information, or 415/705-5555 for tickets; www.blueandgoldfleet.com.

a succinct description. There's a little of everything—Italian, French, Asian-Pacific—and it all has a California twist. The seafood is fresh, and the weekend brunches are eggy and tasty. 2237 Blanding Avenue; 510/337-0333.

Good and Plenty Cafe de Ballena: This wonderful café is a veritable Noah's Ark. Animals of all kinds come to the outdoor tables here with their people. It's not uncommon to see cats on laps and birds on shoulders. But dogs are by far the best—er, most common—critters who visit while their people dine on delicious deli food. Kira, a 100-pound malamute who moved here from Arizona to live on a boat, convinced her "dad" to write and tell us that the food servers "welcome pets with open arms and have been known to get suckered out of a snack or two by the appropriate big, brown-eyed doggy look…. Kira gives this place a four-paw rating with no hesitation." The café is near the Ballena Isle Marina at 1132 Ballena Boulevard; 510/769-2132.

Piedmont

Piedmont is almost entirely residential, and very proper and clean. This means you won't be able to find a stray scrap of paper to scoop with, so be prepared. Its quiet streets are delightful for walking, offering views from the hills.

The parks below allow dogs off leash—but only if they have a permit from the city's police department. Licensed dogs from any city can get one, but it'll cost you more if you don't live in Piedmont, and more still if your dog is not spayed or neutered. The police department's animal services division issues these permits during limited hours on Thursdays only. Phone 510/420-3000 for details.

PARKS, BEACHES, AND RECREATION AREAS

🅖 Linda Off-Leash Area

😺 🐕 (See Alameda County map on page 102)

This is just a strip of pavement running down a dirt area (formerly grass) about the length of one city block. There's some shade. The "park" is set along a hill, but it's too close to a couple of roads for true off-leash comfort as far as my dogs are concerned. For some reason it gets tremendous use.

Beach Park is across from Beach School, at Linda and Lake Avenues. You'll see the little doggy signs. A permit is required for your off-leash use. Please see above for more information. 510/420-3050.

10 Dracena Park

🐾🐾🐾🐾 🐕 (See Alameda County map on page 102)

Parts of this park are grassy, with tall shade trees here and there. But the part dogs long for is the off-leash section. It's a lovely area, with a paved path up and down a wooded, secluded hill. Tall firs and eucalyptus provide plenty of shade, and sometimes it's so quiet here you can hear several kinds of birds. The area isn't fenced, and at the top and bottom there's potential for escape artists to run into the road, so be careful and leash up at these points if you have any doggy doubts.

Poop bags are provided. The trail takes about 15 minutes round-trip, if you assume a very leisurely pace. We like to enter on Artuna Avenue at Ricardo Avenue, because it's safest from traffic and parking's plentiful on the park side of the street. But lots of folks enter at Blair and Dracena Avenues. A permit is required for off-leash use. Please see above for more information. 510/420-3050.

11 Piedmont Park

🐾🐾🐾🐾 🐕 (See Alameda County map on page 102)

The huge off-leash section (by permit only; see above) of this beautiful park is one of the best examples of a leash-free dog area in the state. A few salmon-pink concrete pathways lead you and your happy dog alongside a gurgling stream and up and down the hills around the stream. It's absolutely gorgeous and serene back here. (On our last visit, a hummingbird greeted us at the entrance and was back again when we left.) The park smells like heaven, with eucalyptus, redwood, acacia, pine, and deep, earthy scents wafting around everywhere. It reminds me of a serene Japanese garden, minus the Japanese plants.

The stream is fed year-round by a spring higher in the hills. This is pure bliss for dogs during the summer. The trails for dogs and their people run on the cooler side anyway, with all the tall trees. Almost the entire leash-free section is set in a deep canyon, so it's very safe from traffic. A leisurely round-trip stroll will take you about an hour, if you want it to. Poop bags are supplied at a few strategically located stations along the paths. Use them.

A hint if you want your walk to be as peaceful as possible: Don't come here during the school year around lunchtime or quittin' time for school. The high school at the top of a hill on the other side of the stream can spew some very loud students at those times. On one ill-timed visit, a couple of them were throwing glass bottles into the stream. Joe Dog almost got thwacked right in the ol' kisser.

To get to the leash-free section of this elegant park, come in through the main entrance at Highland and Magnolia Avenues. You'll see a willow tree just as you enter. Continue on the path past the willow tree and follow it down to the left side of the stream. You'll see signs for the dog area. Be sure to leash up in other parts of the park, should you explore beyond the stream area. 510/420-3050.

Oakland

Oakland, the most urban city in the East Bay, is also blessed with a collection of generous and tolerant city parks. Unfortunately, what we call the "white gloves" part of Oakland—the parklands ringing Lake Merritt and the Oakland Museum—is off-limits to dogs. But read on. Pooches who enjoy the bay are thrilled to learn that they're allowed on the Blue and Gold Fleet's ferries that run between Oakland and San Francisco. Fares are $5.25 one-way for adults. The ferry terminal is at the foot of Clay Street at Jack London Square. Phone 415/773-1188 for schedules and more information; www.blueandgold-fleet.com. The city now even has a leash-free dog park, and a few more were in the early planning stages.

If you're looking for a super dog-friendly neighborhood, look no further than Montclair. The bookstore, the florist, the pet store, and the hardware store have all been very kind to four-legged friends, including an anonymous doggy tipster who emailed me about this dog-loving community. In addition, the three dog-friendly Montclair eateries listed below really go all out for dogs.

PARKS, BEACHES, AND RECREATION AREAS

🐾 Joaquin Miller Park

🐾🐾🐾 (See Alameda County map on page 102)

This large, beautiful city park is nestled at the western edge of the huge Redwood Regional Park. If it weren't for the Oakland city parks' rule that dogs must always be leashed, Joaquin Miller would be dog heaven.

Dogs can't enter some of the landscaped areas, such as around Woodminster Amphitheater. On the deliciously cool and damp creek trails below, however, you and your dog will feel as if you own the place.

The West Ridge Trail, reachable from Skyline Boulevard, is popular with mountain bikers. It's waterless, but it's still a good run. The best trails can be entered from the ranger station off Joaquin Miller Road. The Sunset Trail descends about one-eighth of a mile to a cool, ferny stream winding through second- and third-growth redwoods, pines, oak, and laurel. It then ascends to a ridge overlooking cities and the bay. In spring, the ridge is peppered with wildflowers. Plenty of picnic tables and water fountains are scattered throughout the park.

From Highway 13 in Oakland, take the Joaquin Miller Road exit and go one-half mile east to the ranger station. 510/238-7275.

🔟🔟 Redwood Regional Park

🐾🐾🐾🐾🐕 (See Alameda County map on page 102)

Although it's just a few miles over the ridge from downtown Oakland, Redwood Regional Park is about as far as you can get from urbanity while still within the scope of the Bay Area. Dogs who love nature at its best, and love it even more off leash, adore the 1,836-acre park. People who need to get far from the madding crowd also go gaga over the place.

The park is delectable year-round, but it's a particularly wonderful spot to visit when you need to cool off from hot summer weather. Much of the park is a majestic forest of 150-foot coast redwoods (known to those with scientific tongues as *Sequoia sempervirens*). The redwoods provide drippy cool shade most of the time, which is a real boon for dogs with hefty coats. Back in the mid-1800s, this area was heavily logged for building supplies for San Francisco, and it wasn't a pretty sight. But fortunately, sometimes progress progresses backward, and the fallen trees have some splendid replacements.

There's something for every dog's tastes here. In addition to the redwoods, the park is also home to pine, eucalyptus, madrone, flowering fruit trees, chaparral, and grasslands. Wild critters like the park, too, so leash up immediately if there's any hint of a deer, rabbit, or other woodland creatures around. Many dogs, even "good" dogs, aren't able to withstand the temptation to chase.

Dogs have to leash up along the beautiful Stream Trail, which runs along the environmentally sensitive stream. You'll see the leash signage if this "trial" is still going on during your visit. On or off leash, mud is inevitable if you follow the Stream Trail, so be sure to keep a towel in the car. Water dogs may try to dip their paws in Redwood Creek, which runs through the park. But please don't let them. This is a very sensitive area. Rainbow trout spawn here after migrating from a reservoir downstream, and it's not an easy trip for them. If you and your dog need to splash around somewhere, try the ocean, the bay, or your bathtub.

No parking fee is charged at Skyline Gate at the north end (in Contra Costa County—the park straddles Contra Costa and Alameda Counties). Entering here also lets you avoid the tempting smells of picnic tables at the south end. The Stream Trail leads steadily downhill, and then takes a steep plunge to the canyon bottom. It's uphill all the way back, but it's worth it. From Highway 13, exit at Joaquin Miller Road and head east to Skyline Boulevard. Turn left on Skyline and go four miles to the Skyline Gate.

If you prefer to go to the main entrance on Redwood Road, exit Highway 13 at Carson/Redwood Road and drive east on Redwood Road. Once you pass Skyline Boulevard, continue two miles on Redwood. The park and parking will be on your left. The Redwood Road entrance charges a $4 parking fee and a $1 dog fee. 510/635-0135.

14 Dimond Park

 (See Alameda County map on page 102)

Dimond Park is a small jewel of a canyon, dense and wild in the midst of the city. Your leashed dog's eyes will sparkle when she sees this lush place. The Dimond Canyon Hiking Trail begins to the east of El Centro Avenue. There's a small parking lot at El Centro where it bisects the park. A short foot trail goes off west of El Centro, ending quickly at the Dimond Recreation Center and an attractive jungle gym for children.

The main trail is wide and of smooth dirt. It starts on the east side and follows Sausal Creek about a quarter of a mile up the canyon. At that point, the trail becomes the creek bed, so you can continue only in dry season. But what a quarter mile! The deciduous tangle of trees and ivy makes the canyon into a hushed, cool bower, and the creek is wide and accessible to dogs longing for a splash. When the water level is high enough, there are falls and, except in the driest months, there's enough for a dog pool or two. After the trail goes into the creek bed, the going is a little rougher, but you can follow it all the way to the ridge at the eastern end.

From I-580, take the Fruitvale Avenue exit north to the corner of Fruitvale and Lyman Road, the eastern entrance. Or, to park at the trailhead, take the Park Boulevard exit from Highway 13 and turn left (south) on El Centro Avenue. 510/482-7831.

15 Hardy Dog Park

(See Alameda County map on page 102)

This two-acre park in the Rockridge district has easy freeway access and plenty of shade. That's because it's under the freeway. But that's OK. It's a huge improvement from its previous incarnation as a fenced quarter-acre patch of dirt. Now it's big and grassy, with benches, water, and poop bags.

To get to the park from Highway 24, take the Claremont exit and follow Claremont Avenue back under the freeway. The park is under the freeway, at Claremont and Hudson Street. 510/238-3791.

16 Leona Heights Regional Open Space

(See Alameda County map on page 102)

Unmarked on most maps, and devoid of most amenities (water and restrooms, for instance) this 271-acre open space is good for dogs who like to get away from the crowd. You won't find many bikes or horses here. Since it's part of the East Bay Regional Park District, your dog need not be on leash.

The open space stretches from Merritt College south to Oak Knoll, and from I-580 east to Chabot Regional Park. A bumpy fire trail goes from Merritt

College downhill to the southern entrance, just north of Oak Knoll. The best way to enter is to park at a lot off Canyon Oaks Drive, next to a condominium parking lot. Right at this entrance is a pond, but you won't see any more water as you ascend. It's a dry hike in warm weather.

The 2.7-mile fire trail leads gently uphill all the way to Merritt, through coyote brush and oak woodland. In spring, it's full of wildflowers and abuzz with the loud hum of bees. Watch out for poison oak.

From I-580, exit at Keller Avenue and drive east to Campus Drive. Take a left (north), then a left on Canyon Oaks Drive. 510/635-0135.

🐾 Martin Luther King Jr. Regional Shoreline

🐾🐾 (See Alameda County map on page 102)

The Oakland shoreline doesn't have much to offer a dog besides this park (formerly known as the San Leandro Bay Regional Shoreline), which is well maintained by the East Bay Regional Park District. And it has a major flaw: The district classifies the whole thing as a developed area, so you must leash. The kind of fun a dog most wants—running full-out across grass or swimming in the bay—is illegal.

But you can have a genteel good time on a sunny day that's not too windy, ambling together along the extensive paved bayside trails. Amenities for people are plentiful: picnic tables, a few trees, fountains, a parcourse fitness trail, a tiny beach, and a huge playing field.

A wooden walkway crosses over some mudflats for watching shorebirds and terns fishing. For bird-watching, go at low tide. Keep your dog firmly leashed and held close to you and hike along the San Leandro Creek Channel to Arrowhead Marsh. If you enter from Doolittle Drive, walk along the Doolittle Trail. There's a small sandy beach here, but dogs aren't allowed to swim. (The usual East Bay Regional Park rules apply: No dogs allowed on beaches.)

From I-880, exit at Hegenberger Road in Oakland. Go west on Hegenberger and turn on Edgewater Drive, Pardee Drive, or Doolittle Drive. Parking is free at each of these entry points. 510/635-0135.

PLACES TO EAT

Oakland's College Avenue, in the Rockridge district, has a tolerant family atmosphere. Lawyers with briefcases buy flowers on the way home from the BART station, and students flirt over ice cream. I've never seen anyone in this neighborhood who didn't love dogs.

The avenue is known to be a food lover's paradise, and among the attractions are a string of restaurants with outdoor tables, several of which follow. The Montclair district also has a couple of hits with the dog crowd.

Cafe Rustica: The pizza here is elegant. Eat it at the outdoor tables with your drooling dog. 5422 College Avenue; 510/654-1601.

Crepevine: This popular café serves yummy sweet and savory crepes, pastas, salads, and all-day breakfast. The patio and street tables are available year-round and sometimes the overhead heaters will warm you and your pooch as you enjoy the exotic crepe concoctions. 5600 College Avenue, two blocks from Rockville BART; 510/658-2026.

Flippers: The servers at this Montclair-district eatery are very dog-friendly. They'll bring your dog water, and when possible, they manage to find a meaty treat to "sneak" to your pet (with your permission, of course). Flippers serves breakfast all day here, but it's really known for its burgers. 2080 Mountain Boulevard; 510/339-2082.

Montclair Malt Shop: Don'tcha just hate it when you go to an ice cream parlor and your dog's eyes almost tear up with the anticipation of a single drop of yummy cold cream falling from your cone to the ground so he can lap it off the sidewalk? You won't have to deal with those pleading eyes if you visit this delightful ice creamery: Dogs can order their very own special brew of pooch-friendly ice cream, known as Frosty Paws. Then you can dine together at the bench outside, or just stand around and talk with other dog people while your dog inhales his frozen treat. The place is known for its dog business; on a recent hot summer afternoon, 17 dogs were outside, downing their ice creams with delight. "We love dogs here," says super-friendly Diane, who makes the best malt this side of the bay. (She will be the first to tell you this, and she speaks the truth.) 2066 Mountain Boulevard; 510/339-1886.

Noah's Bagels: We initially learned about this dog-friendly Montclair-district bagelry from a letter to the editor in the *San Francisco Chronicle*. The author of the letter wrote that she finds dogs in public offensive, which is why it gives such pleasure to offer her "tip." In her own words, "If you're not a dog lover, don't go to Noah's Bagels in Montclair on any weekend morning. I've even seen dog dishes outside the store. I avoid this area altogether now...." Sounds like our kind of place. Not only do dogs get water in doggy bowls, but they also get "floor bagels" when available. These are bagels that have been dropped on the floor, either by customers or employees. Do dogs care that their bagel has taken a little roll on terra firma? No! They're still snout-licking good anyway. Dine with your dog at several outdoor tables here. 2060 Mountain Boulevard; 510/339-6663.

Oliveto Cafe: This café and Peaberry's, next door, share a building with the Market Hall, God's own food emporium. The food's the best, but for a dog, the atmosphere is congested. It's not for nervous dogs. Oliveto serves very classy pizza, tapas, bar food, desserts, coffees, and drinks, but alcohol is not allowed at the sidewalk tables. 5655 College Avenue, just south of Rockridge BART; 510/547-5356. •

Peaberry's: Enjoy coffees, pastries, and desserts at the outdoor tables here. This is a favorite with BART commuters. 5655 College Avenue; 510/653-0450.

Royal Coffee: This is a cheery and popular place with very good coffee (in the bean or in the cup), tea, and supplies. On weekend mornings, it's dog central. 307 63rd Street at College Avenue; 510/653-5458.

PLACES TO STAY

Oakland Airport Hilton: Dogs have to be under 30 pounds to stay here. Rates are $169–189. Dogs require a $300 deposit. 1 Hegenberger Road 94614; 510/635-5000; www.hilton.com.

San Lorenzo

PARKS, BEACHES, AND RECREATION AREAS

🔟🖐 San Lorenzo Dog Park

🐾🐾🐾🐕 (See Alameda County map on page 102)

It's just ducky with your dog if you want to take him to this pretty dog park: Part of it curves around a duck pond. The quackers sometimes waddle right by, somehow knowing that their canine friends can't get to them through the fence. It's almost like a cartoon at times, with a duck strutting his stuff while a dog looks on with almost embarrassed disbelief that there's no way on dog's green earth that he'll be having duck for dinner that night.

The dog park is only about two-thirds of an acre, but it has all the good pooch-park amenities, including water, benches, and poop bags. It's grassy with some decomposed granite. There's not much shade, although the back end has some big trees on the outside perimeter, and they can provide shade at times.

The dog park is toward the back of San Lorenzo Community Park, at the very west end of Via Buena Vista. The address is 1970 Via Buena Vista. 510/881-6700.

Castro Valley

PARKS, BEACHES, AND RECREATION AREAS

🔟🟡 Chabot Regional Park

🐾🐾🐾🐾🐕 (See Alameda County map on page 102)

You and your leash-free dog can throw your urban cares to the wind when you visit this 4,972-acre park filled with magnificent trails and enchanting woodlands. Except for the occasional sounds of gunfire, you'll scarcely believe you're in the hills east of metropolitan Oakland. But fear not—the guns you'll hear are merely being used for target practice at the park's marksmanship range.

The trails at Chabot (sha-BO) are so secluded that if no one is firing a gun, the only sounds you may hear are those of your panting dog and the singing birds. Adventure-loving dogs like to take the Goldenrod Trail, starting at the southern terminus of Skyline Boulevard and Grass Valley Road. It connects with the East Bay Skyline National Recreation Trail, which winds through

Grass Valley and climbs through eucalyptus forests. Lucky dogs can be off leash everywhere but in developed areas.

Campsites are $16–20. Dogs are $1 extra. Reserve by phoning 925/373-0144. No reservations are taken October 1–March 31, when the 23 sites are first-come, first-served.

From the intersection of Redwood Road and Castro Valley Boulevard in Castro Valley, go north on Redwood about 4.5 miles to Marciel Gate. (The campground is about two miles inside the gate.) From Oakland at the intersection of Redwood Road and Skyline Boulevard, go about 6.5 miles east on Redwood to Marciel Gate. For general park info, call 510/635-0135.

20 Castro Valley Dog Park

🐾🐾🐾🐾 (See Alameda County map on page 102)

This is a fun place to take a dog for some leash-free exercise. It's about two-thirds of an acre and has water, poop bags, and benches. It's set within the beautiful Earl Warren Park, whose walking path is worth sniffing out despite the on-leash requirement. The park is at 4660 Crow Canyon Road. Exit I-580 at Crow Canyon Road and head north several blocks. 510/881-6700.

21 Cull Canyon Regional Recreation Area

🐾🐾🐾🐾 (See Alameda County map on page 102)

Dogs may be off leash up on the grassy slopes laced with eucalyptus stands, but they have to wear their leashes in the areas designed for human fun. It's not such a bad fate, considering that there are plenty of grassy slopes away from developed areas.

In summer, fishing and swimming are popular here. But pooches may not go near the swimming complex, which includes an attractive pavilion and sandy beach. Leashed dogs may visit picnic areas, the Cull Creek area, and the willow-lined reservoir that sports a wooden bridge and a handful of ducks and coots.

From I-580, take the Center Street/Crow Canyon Road exit. Go left on Center Street and take a right on Castro Valley Boulevard. Follow it to Crow Canyon Road and take a left. Take another left on Cull Canyon Road. It's a half mile to the park entrance. 510/635-0135.

PLACES TO STAY

Chabot Regional Park: See Chabot Regional Park, above, for camping information.

Hayward

PARKS, BEACHES, AND RECREATION AREAS

22 Hayward Memorial Park Hiking and Riding Trails

🐾🐾🐾 (See Alameda County map on page 102)

For humans, Memorial Park offers all kinds of amenities, including an indoor pool, tennis courts, kids' swings and slides, picnic tables, a band shell, and even a slightly funky cage full of doves. But really, if you're a dog, the big question is, "Who cares?"

The fun for dogs begins when you get on the Wally Wickander (poor guy) Memorial Trail and enter the greenbelt part of the park, laced with dirt fire trails designed for hikers and horses. Dogs must remain leashed, but the trail is so beautiful that it doesn't seem to matter. It follows a steep-sided creek lined with a thick tangle of oak, laurel, maple, and lots of noisy birds. The trash pickup is a little lax, but if you're looking for solitude in a city park, you'll find it here.

You can enter through Hayward Memorial Park, at Mission Boulevard (Highway 238) just south of the intersection of Highway 92. You can also enter at the parking lots on East Avenue through East Avenue Park on the north end, or on Highland Boulevard through Old Highland Park on the south end. 510/881-6715.

23 Garin Regional Park and Dry Creek Regional Park

🐾🐾🐾🐾 🐕 (See Alameda County map on page 102)

Garin Regional Park is about one mile and one century away from one of the busiest streets in Hayward. It's a fascinating place for you and your dog to learn about Alameda County farming and ranching. The parking lot next to Garin Barn—an actual barn, blacksmith's shop, and tool shed that is also Garin's visitor center—is strewn with antique farm machinery.

A total of 20 miles of trails, looping among the sweeps of grassy hills, beckon you and your dog. Off-leash dogs are fine on the trails once you've left the visitor center. Dogs seem to like to think they're on their own farm here, looking for all the world as if they're strutting down their very own property and watching out for evil feline intruders.

Dry Creek, which runs near the visitor center, was a delightful small torrent one day when we were there after a March storm. There isn't much shade on hot days, though. That's when you might want to try cooling your paws at tiny Jordan Pond. It's stocked with catfish, should your dog care to join you on his kind of fishing excursion.

From Highway 238 (Mission Boulevard), Tamarack Drive takes you quickly up the hill to Dry Creek Regional Park. Garin Avenue takes you to Garin, or you can enter Garin from the California State University, Hayward campus. The parking fee is $4. Dogs are $1 extra. 510/635-0135.

PLACES TO STAY

Motel 6: Rates are $46–62 for the first adult, $6 for the second. 30155 Industrial Parkway Southwest 94544; 510/489-8333.

   Vagabond Inn: Rates are $80–100. Dogs are $10 extra. 20455 Hesperian Boulevard 94541; 510/785-5480.

Union City

PARKS, BEACHES, AND RECREATION AREAS

24 Drigon Dog Park

🐾🐾🐾🐾🐕 (See Alameda County map on page 102)

A dogbone-shaped walkway dotted with pawprints? Doggy tunnels, hoops, jumps, and other fun agility toys? Fire hydrants galore? A gated entrance featuring a giant dog bone and big concrete pillars with huge paw prints? What is this—dog heaven or something?

   Yes! Drigon (DRY-ghin) Dog Park is pooch paradise that happens to be firmly planted on grassy terra firma. It is paws down the most well designed of California's fenced dog parks. The design is the brainchild of two dog-loving park district planners—a $300,000 shining gem that's utterly to drool for. You drive by, you see it, you can't help but smile, even if you don't have a dog. It's like real-world-meets-cartoon-fantasy—something you could find around the corner if you lived in Toontown.

   The park is 1.5 acres, with a small section for wee dogs. It has water, poop bags, nicely designed benches, and shade in the form of a permanent awning. Everything here is doggy: The concrete around the newly planted trees has embedded paw prints. The hydrants are concrete (they can't rust or corrode from boy dog bladder activities) and have drainage. This helps keep the grassy area pretty green.

   The park, named for a heroic police dog who is in a more ethereal dog heaven now, is closed Mondays for maintenance. It's in the middle of a residential suburban neighborhood, at 7th Street and Mission Boulevard. 510/471-3232.

Pleasanton

PARKS, BEACHES, AND RECREATION AREAS

🐾 Muirwood Park Dog Exercise Area

🐾🐾🐾🐾 (See Alameda County map on page 102)

Dogs enjoy galloping around this very long, narrow park in part because it's so easy on their paws. The ground cover is affectionately known as "forest floor material," which is basically degraded wood chips mixed with leaf and branch litter. Much as you'd find in the real Muir Woods in Marin, the stuff makes for cushy walks and runs—it's great for the joints of older dogs.

If your dog likes chasing far-flung balls, this is a perfect place for it. The park is about 300 feet long by 40 feet wide, which means there's plenty of room to use your tennis ball launcher to its full capacity. The park has all the usual dog-park amenities, including benches, water, and poop bag dispensers. There's ample shade from evergreen acacias—a popular food with giraffes. (You won't likely see any giraffes wandering through the dog park, but park workers have been known to collect leaves and branches for the giraffes at the Oakland Zoo.)

The park is at 4701 Muirwood Drive. The cross street is Las Positas Boulevard. 925/931-5340.

🐾 Pleasanton Ridge Regional Park

🐾🐾🐾🐾 (See Alameda County map on page 102)

This fairly recent and beautiful addition to the East Bay Regional Parks system is an isolated treat. Dogs may run off leash on all the secluded trails here as soon as you leave the staging area.

You can reach Pleasanton Ridge from either Foothill or Golden Eagle Roads. At the Foothill Staging Area, there are fine picnic sites at the trailhead. Climb up on the Oak Tree fire trail to the ridgeline, where a looping set of trails goes off to the right. The incline is gentle, through pasture (you share this park with cattle) dotted with oak and—careful—poison oak. Wildflowers riot in spring. It's a hot place in summer. At the bottom of the park, however, is a beautiful streamside stretch along Arroyo de la Laguna. There's no water above the entrance, so be sure to carry plenty.

From I-680, take the Castlewood Drive exit and go left (west) on Foothill Road to the staging area. 510/635-0135.

PLACES TO STAY

Crown Plaza: Rates are $69–179. Dogs pay a $50 fee for length of their stay, and may stay only in ground-floor rooms, which are also smoking rooms. 11950 Dublin Canyon Road 94588; 925/847-6000.

Fremont

PARKS, BEACHES, AND RECREATION AREAS

🐾 Coyote Hills Regional Park

😺😺😺 (See Alameda County map on page 102)

This park is a paradox. It's a working research project on Ohlone Indian history, a teeming wildlife sanctuary, and a family picnic and bicycling mecca—all rolled into 966 acres.

Dogs used to be able to run leashless in the small hills that give the park its name, but leashes are now the law. We understand. (Waaah.) Wildlife is abundant here. You'll see red-tailed hawks, vultures, and white-tailed kites that swoop down on unsuspecting squirrels.

The beautiful Bayview Trail climbs quickly behind the visitor center. From the crest of Red Hill—green even in the dry season because its ground cover is drought-tolerant—you look down on varied colors of marsh grasses, waterfowl, and wading birds, and the shallow salt ponds in the bay. Most of the park is a fragile sanctuary, and dogs must stay on the little hills or at the picnic area by the visitor center.

From I-880, take the Decoto Road/Highway 84 exit in Fremont. Go west on Highway 84 to the Thornton Avenue/Paseo Padre Parkway exit. Go north on Paseo Padre about one mile to Patterson Ranch Road/Commerce. A left on Patterson Ranch Road brings you to the entrance. When the kiosk is staffed, the parking fee is $4. The dog fee is $1. For information on tours and activities, call 510/795-9385. For general information, call 510/635-0135.

🐾 Alameda Creek Regional Trail

😺😺😺🐕 (See Alameda County map on page 102)

This 12.4-mile trail runs from the bayshore to the East Bay hills, and dogs can actually be off leash in many sections. But they may be disappointed when they discover that it's not as pristine a trail as the name might imply. First of all, the trail is paved. Second of all, the creek is paved. (You'll see what I mean.) But more important, the trail doesn't just pass through farmland and greenbelt areas. It also runs alongside railyards, industrial lots, and quarries. Junkyard dogs like it. Wilderness dogs just shrug their hairy shoulders. A scenic stretch of this paved trail is at the Niles Canyon end. Dogs find it especially interesting in winter after a storm, when there's actually water in the concrete-lined creek and ducks and coots splash around.

Although the East Bay Regional Park District's usual liberal leash rules apply here, it has posted a good many areas with "leash up" symbols. If you see one, do so. On this trail, as on any you share with other hikers, horses, and bicycles, just use common sense.

You may enter this trail at many points near the creek's mouth—in the salt flats of the bay by Coyote Hills Regional Park. The trail officially begins in Fremont's Niles district, at the intersection of Mission Boulevard (Highway 238) and Niles Canyon Road (Highway 84). 510/635-0135.

29 Fremont Dog Park

🐾🐾🐕 (See Alameda County map on page 102)

A park with male-pattern baldness? That's what you get when you visit this fenced one-acre park. The surface is grass, but in the middle, there's a big bald patch. But dogs don't care about the aesthetics. They're just happy to be able to cruise around off leash. The park has benches, poop bags, and water. There's no shade, so it can get toasty at times.

The park is within the beautiful, 450-acre Central Park, which leashed dogs are welcome to explore. The dog section is on Stevenson Boulevard, just west of Gallaudet Drive, near the softball fields. 510/790-5541.

30 Mission Peak Regional Preserve

🐾🐾🐾🐾🐕 (See Alameda County map on page 102)

Smart Fremont dwellers take their dogs to this 2,596-acre park. It's a huge expanse of grass, dotted with occasional oak groves and scrub. Unfortunately for humans who get short of breath, the foot trails head straight up. Trails to the top rise 2,500 feet in three miles. (Pant, pant.)

Leash-free dogs love this place. The entrance at Stanford Avenue offers a gentler climb than the entrance from the Ohlone College campus. You'll pass Caliente Creek if you take the Peak Meadow Trail, but in hot weather, there won't be much relief from the sun. Be sure to carry water for yourself and your dog. The main point of puffing up Mission Peak is the renowned view stretching from Mt. Tamalpais to Mt. Hamilton. (On very clear days, you can see to the Sierra's snowy crest.) Your dog may not care much for the scenery, but she'll probably appreciate the complete freedom of the expanse of pasture here.

From I-680, take the southern Mission Boulevard exit in Fremont (there are two exits; the one you want is in the Warm Springs district). Go east on Mission to Stanford Avenue, turn right (east), and in less than a mile, you'll be at the entrance. 510/635-0135.

31 Sunol Regional Wilderness

🐾🐾🐾🐾🐕 (See Alameda County map on page 102)

You and your leash-free dog will howl for joy when you visit this large and deserted wilderness treasure. It's like going to a national park without having to leave your poor pooch behind.

One of the best treats for canines and their companions is a hike along the Camp Ohlone Trail, which you reach via the main park entrance, on Geary

Road. The trail takes you to an area called Little Yosemite. Like its name-sake, Little Yosemite is magnificent. It's a steep-sided gorge with a creek at the bottom, lofty crags, and outcrops of greenstone and basalt that reveal a turbulent geological history. Its huge boulders throw Alameda Creek into gurgling eddies and falls. There's no swimming allowed here, much to Jake's dismay.

You can return via the higher Canyon View Trail or head for several other destinations: wooded canyons, grassy slopes, peaks with peeks of Calaveras Reservoir or Mt. Diablo. The park brochure offers useful descriptions of each trail. Dogs may run leashless on trails except for on the Backpack Loop.

Dogs are allowed only at the Family Campground site at headquarters and not at the backpacking campsites farther in. Sites are $12. The dog fee is $1. Dogs must be leashed in the campground or confined to your tent. (Anyone whose dog has ever chased off after a wild boar in the middle of the night understands the reason for this rule, and this park has plenty of boars.) Call 510/636-1684 to reserve. Reserved sites are held until 5 P.M. The day-use parking fee is $4, plus $1 extra for your dog.

From I-680, take the Calaveras Road exit, then go left (east) on Geary Road to the park entrance. The park may be closed or restricted during fire season, June–October. 925/862-2244.

PLACES TO STAY

Best Western Garden Court: Rates are $59–99. Dogs are $10 extra. 5400 Mowry Avenue 94538; 510/792-4300.

Sunol Regional Wilderness: See the Sunol Regional Wilderness, above, for camping information.

Livermore

PARKS, BEACHES, AND RECREATION AREAS

Livermore is barking up the right tree: Plans are in the works for two more dog parks. Meanwhile, dogs are greatly enjoying the current three.

32 May Nissen Dog Park

🐾🐾🦴 (See Alameda County map on page 102)

At one-third of an acre, this is the smallest of Livermore's dog parks. But there's still enough room for dogs to have a decent time. There's water, some grass, and shade-providing trees. A double-gated entry helps prevent escape artist pooches from bolting when someone leaves or enters the park.

The dog park is set within May Nissen Park. It's on Rincon Avenue, just south of Pine Street. 925/373-5700.

33 Vista Meadows Park

🐾🐾🐾 🐕 (See Alameda County map on page 102)

Your dog can't quite live out a favorite nursery rhyme and go 'round the mulberry bush here, but he can go under a mulberry tree (or do a leg lift on it, which is a popular pastime with some dogs here). This .75-acre fenced park has some mulberry trees on its back end. There's even a bench under them, should you feel like relaxing in their shade. The grass here is pretty worn down, but it can come back again with the help of the wonderful parks department. Amenities include water, poop bags, and a double-gated entry. The park is at Westminster and Lambeth Road. 925/373-5700.

34 Max Baer Dog Park

🐾🐾🐾 🐕 (See Alameda County map on page 102)

This .6-acre, fenced-in dog park is level and grassy, with lots of shady trees. It's double-gated, for your dog's safety. Inside the park are poop bags, a water fountain and bowls, and chairs where people can hang out while their dogs romp. On summer evenings, as many as 25–30 dogs enjoy the park. "Everybody loves it," says veterinarian Martin Plone, who was behind the park's birth in 1993. "It's become a meeting place for people. While their dogs are playing, people form friendships."

The dog park is part of the popular Max Baer Park. It's at Murdell Lane and Stanley Boulevard. 925/373-5700.

35 Sycamore Grove Park

🐾🐾🐾 (See Alameda County map on page 102)

Sycamore Grove is an unusual and attractive streamside park. In rainy times, it can look semiswampy, as most of the Central Valley used to look. In fact, it is Lake Del Valle's floodplain, and federal flood controllers occasionally send runoff into this park's stream, Arroyo Del Valle, when Lake Del Valle rises too high.

With its low hills, tall grass, and loud sounds of birds and squirrels, it's almost an African savanna. Blackbirds and swallows swoop over the stream and marshy spots, grabbing insects. Poppies are plentiful in spring. Kids, dogs, miniature horses, potbellied pigs, and llamas live in harmony here, mostly because everyone obeys the leash law. Water dogs and their kin love wading in the stream pools near the picnic tables. Follow the paths far enough and the place becomes satisfyingly wild.

The park is quite flat, perfect for dogs who don't do well in low gear. Take I-580 to Livermore; exit to Portola Avenue. Go east to North Livermore Avenue and turn right. After 2.5 miles, North Livermore turns into Arroyo Road. Turn right on Wetmore Road. There's a $2 fee. 925/373-5700.

36 Del Valle Regional Park

🐾🐾🐾🐾🐕 (See Alameda County map on page 102)

This popular reservoir is best known for swimming, boating, fishing, and camping. Like Chabot Regional Park (see the Castro Valley section), it's primarily a manicured and popular human recreation area, with neat lawns and picnic tables (where dogs must be leashed).

But, glory be to dog, the park sports several unspoiled trails for leash-free hiking in the surrounding hills. And, unlike at Lake Chabot, here you're permitted to take a dog on a rented boat. Every dog can have his day here.

From this recreation area, you can enter the Ohlone Wilderness Trail—29 miles of gorgeous trail through four regional parks. (See Ohlone Regional Wilderness, below.)

The 150 sites at Family Camp allow dogs, but only on leash or confined to your tent. Sites are $15–20. Reserve by calling 510/636-1684.

From I-580, take North Livermore Avenue from downtown Livermore. It will become South Livermore Avenue, then Tesla Road. Take a right (south) on Mines Road, and then turn right on Del Valle Road. The parking fee is $6. The dog fee is $1. 510/635-0135.

37 Ohlone Wilderness Trail

🐾🐾🐾🐾🐕 (See Alameda County map on page 102)

Some of the area's most remote and peaceful wilderness areas are accessible only by way of this 29-mile trail. The trail stretches from Mission Peak, east of Fremont, through Sunol Regional Wilderness and Ohlone Regional Wilderness to Del Valle Regional Park, south of Livermore. You and your occasionally leash-free dog (signs tell you when it's allowed) will hike through oak and bay woods and grassy uplands that are carpeted with wildflowers in spring.

You'll also see abundant wildlife—if you're quiet and lucky, you might even see an endangered bald eagle. If your dog can't take the pressure of merely watching as tule elk and deer pass by, you should keep him leashed.

A permit is required. (See Ohlone Regional Wilderness, below, for permit details.) Because of some restrictions, you won't be able to do all 29 miles at once with your dog. That's OK. In fact, that's probably just fine with your dog. 510/635-0135.

38 Ohlone Regional Wilderness

🐾🐾🐾🐾🐕 (See Alameda County map on page 102)

The centerpiece of this magnificent parkland is the 3,817-foot Rose Peak—only 32 feet lower than Mt. Diablo. Leash-free dogs are in heaven on earth as they explore the surrounding 6,758 acres of grassy ridges. Wildlife is abundant, so if your dog isn't obedient, it's best to keep her leashed. The tule elk appreciate it, and your dog will appreciate it, too, should you run into a mountain lion.

The regional parks system shares the wilderness with the San Francisco

Water District, which wants to limit the human presence here. Dogs may not stay overnight in the campgrounds.

To enter this wild and breathtaking area east of Sunol Regional Wilderness, you must pick up a permit (which includes a detailed trail map and camping information) for $2 at the East Bay Regional Park District headquarters or at the Del Valle and Sunol kiosks, and at the Coyote Hills Visitors Center (Fremont). 510/635-0135.

PLACES TO EAT

Café Paradiso: "Start your day in paradise," says a manager here. And the food here is heavenly. Try the Bird of Paradise sandwich for a real taste treat. The lucky dogs who dine at the umbrella-topped outdoor tables get not only water, but treats! 53 Wright Brothers Avenue; 925/371-2233.

PLACES TO STAY

Del Valle Regional Park: See Del Valle Regional Park, above, for camping information.

Residence Inn Livermore: These are convenient little apartments/suites if you need more than just a room. Rates are $169–224, and there's a $75 fee per doggy visit, so you might want to stay a while. 1000 Airway Boulevard 94550; 925/373-1800.

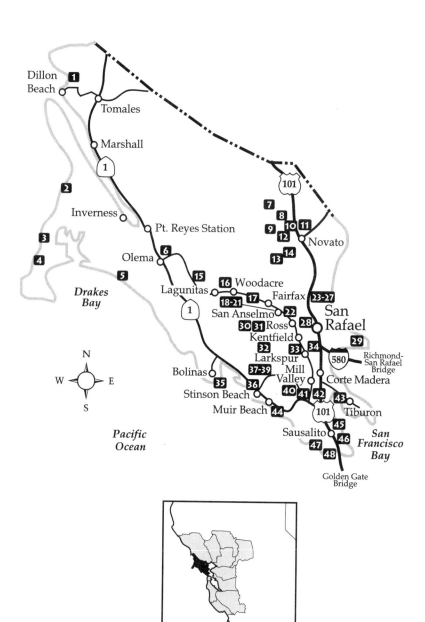

Dillon
Beach **1**

Tomales

Marshall

1

2

Inverness

Pt. Reyes Station

3

4

Olema **6**

5

*Drakes
Bay*

15

Lagunitas

1

16 Woodacre

17 Fairfax

18-21

San Anselmo **22**

30 31 Ross

Kentfield

32

33

Larkspur

37-39

Bolinas

35

36

Stinson Beach

Muir Beach

44

7

101

8

9 **10** **11**

12

13 **14**

Novato

23-27

28

**San
Rafael**

29

34

580

Richmond-
San Rafael
Bridge

Mill
Valley

Corte Madera

40 **41** **42** **43**

101 Tiburon

45

Sausalito **46**

*San
Francisco
Bay*

47

48

Golden Gate
Bridge

N

W — E

S

*Pacific
Ocean*

CHAPTER 6
Marin County

This is a good place to be a dog or a well-heeled human. For four-legged friends, it's got it all, from the bay to the ocean to the redwoods and hilly parklands in between. Throw in some dog-friendly restaurants, inns, and cottages, and you've got the makings of a pooch paradise.

Unfortunately, the once-leash-free Golden Gate National Recreation Area lands require leashes these days. It's a huge loss to dogs, who could once gallavant buck-naked on dozens of trails and a couple of beaches. It's enough to make a dog want to take off his bandanna and cry into it. (Try not to let him blow his nose into it, though. That's always a bit of a mess.) This rule is being evaluated, and we hope that by the next edition of this book we'll have good news.

One large park entity still allows dogs off leash, but this may not be forever, either. Marin County operates 33 Open Space District lands. The landscapes include grassy expanses, wooded trails, redwood groves, marshes, and steep mountainsides. The idea is to set aside bits of land so that Marin never ends up looking like Santa Clara Valley. The Open Space parks are free and completely undeveloped. Until fairly recently, dogs were permitted off leash just about

PICK OF THE LITTER—MARIN COUNTY

BEST OFF-LEASH BEACH
Dillon Beach Resort, Dillon Beach (page 135)

BEST REMOTE BEACH
Kehoe Beach, Inverness (page 136)

PLACE TO HIKE OFF LEASH IN THE HEAT
Indian Tree Open Space Preserve, Novato (page 144)

BEST BREAD
Bovine Bakery, Point Reyes Station (page 139)

MOST DOG-FRIENDLY PLACE TO EAT
Fish, Sausalito (page 168)

MOST MAGICAL LODGINGS
The Ark, Inverness (pages 137–138)
Manka's Inverness Lodge, Inverness (pages 138–139)
Rosemary Cottages, Inverness (page 139)
The Old Point Reyes Schoolhouse Compound, Point Reyes Station (pages 140–141)
The Olema Inn, Olema (pages 142–143)

everywhere on these lands. But now they can run leashless only on designated fire roads. They must be leashed on trails. It's still a pretty good deal, since most dogs don't mind the wide berth. Speaking of wide berth, you're not allowed to bring more than three dogs at a time to open space lands. This rule keeps commercial dog walking at bay. See www.marinopenspace.org for more park info, or phone 415/499-6387.

Life on a leash isn't the same as the untethered life. But it's not always a drag. Marin offers some real gems to leashed pooches. Most dogs are surprised to discover that if they wear a leash, they're permitted to explore a bit of beautiful Mt. Tamalpais (see Mount Tamalpais State Park and Mount Tamalpais–Marin Municipal Water District Land in the Mill Valley section).

Dogs' mouths also tend to drop open when you mention they can visit parts of the 65,000-acre Point Reyes National Seashore. Because it's a delicate ecosystem and a national treasure, dogs are banned from campgrounds, most trails, and several beaches. Point Reyes National Seashore is home to 350 species of birds and 72 species of mammals (not including dogs). Where dogs are permitted, they must be on leash. It's a small price to pay to be able to peruse the place with the pooch at all. Kehoe Beach, Point Reyes Beach South, and Point Reyes Beach North are the seashore's most dog-friendly areas.

I don't normally mention doggy day-care facilities (after all, the book is about places you can go with your dog), but Camp K-9 of Marin is worthy of a little rule-breaking. It offers training, day care, and overnight boarding, but it also has a do-it-yourself dog wash and even a "campground rental," which is a large, enclosed outdoor area with everything you'll need for a private dog park for that special event, or simply to work on training. If you do nothing else, check out Camp K-9's fun, hip, very retro website, www.campk-9ofmarin .com. (It makes me want to sip a neat cocktail while wearing a little apron and listening to 1960s smooth lounge music.) Phone 415/924-CAMP (415/924-2267) for more info.

Dillon Beach

PARKS, BEACHES, AND RECREATION AREAS

1 Dillon Beach Resort

🐾🐾🐾🐾🐾 (See Marin County map on page 132)

Don't let the name fool you: This is a beach, not a high-end hotel with dozens of spa treatments. What really gets dogs excited is that not only are they allowed on the beach, but at a certain point that seems to confuse everyone we've spoken with there, they can throw their leashes to the wind. The rule says something to the effect that from the parking lot to the high tide line, dogs must be leashed, and from the tide line and into the water, dogs can be leash free. Check with the person at the kiosk when you drive in. Please make super-sure your dog is truly under voice control before letting her go, because this a rare privilege these days. (The next leash-free beach to the north is in Humboldt County; to the south it's in Pacifica.)

The beach is privately run and very well maintained. If you notice broken glass or anything that's not in keeping with a clean, safe beach, the staff asks you to report it.

There's a $5 fee per vehicle. It's worth the price. The beach is the northernmost beach in Marin County. So far north, in fact, that it has the Sonoma County area code. The address is One Beach Avenue; 707/878-2696.

PLACES TO STAY

Lawson's Landing and Resort: When you camp here, you camp in a grassy meadow along the sand dunes. There are no set campsites, just the open meadow. That's great, because sometimes you can have the whole place to yourself. Other times you have to share the meadow with lots of other outdoorsy sorts of folks. Camping is $17. Weekly rates are available. Lawson's Landing is easy to find once you're in Dillon Beach. The address is 137 Marine View Drive, P.O. Box 67, Dillon Beach, CA 94929; 707/878-2443; www.lawsonslanding.com.

Inverness

This sweet, quiet village on Tomales Bay is one of the most attractive in Marin. The dog-friendly beaches, cafés, and lodgings are to drool for. What's not to love about this place?

PARKS, BEACHES, AND RECREATION AREAS

2 Kehoe Beach

🐾🐾🐾🐾 (See Marin County map on page 132)

This is our favorite of the Point Reyes National Seashore beaches that allow dogs, since it's both the most beautiful and the least accessible. The only parking is at roadside. You take a half-mile cinder path through wildflowers and thistles, with marsh on one side and hill on the other. In the morning, you may see some mule deer. Then, you come out on medium-brown sand that stretches forever. Since the water is shallow, the surf repeats its crests in multiple white rows, as in Hawai'i. Behind you are limestone cliffs. Scattered rocks offer tidepools filled with mussels, crabs, anemones, barnacles, snails, and sea flora.

In such a paradise of shore life, the leash rule makes sense. The chief reasons for leashing dogs (or banning them altogether) at the Point Reyes National Seashore beaches are the harbor seals that haul out onto the beaches. They're in no position to get away fast from a charging dog. The snowy plover, a threatened shorebird that nests on the ground, also appreciates your dog obeying the leash law. In fact, sections of this beach and the other Point Reyes beaches may become closed long-term because of these birds. Restricted areas will be posted so tell your dog to keep her eyes peeled.

From Inverness, follow Sir Francis Drake Boulevard to the fork. Bear right on Pierce Point Road and go about four miles; park beside the road where you see the sign and walk about a half mile to the beach. 415/464-5100.

3 Point Reyes Beach North

🐾🐾🐾🐾 (See Marin County map on page 132)

Point Reyes Beach North is a generous, functional beach. There's no long trail from the parking lot, no special tidepools or rocks, just a long, clean, beautiful running beach for the two of you. Officially, however, dogs must be leashed.

From Inverness, take Sir Francis Drake Boulevard. Follow signs for the lighthouse. Go about 10 miles. The turnoff for the beach is well marked. 415/464-5100.

🐾 Point Reyes Beach South

🐾🐾🐾 (See Marin County map on page 132)

Point Reyes Beach South is a little narrower and steeper than Point Reyes Beach North, and it has a few interesting sandstone outcrops with wind-carved holes. It has a bit less of that wide-open feeling. Leash the dog.

Follow the directions for Point Reyes Beach North; it's the next beach southward. 415/464-5100.

PLACES TO EAT

Inverness Store: Lots of dogs visit this little grocery store, which has been around for more than 80 years. The folks here are kind to doggies and welcome them to munch a lunch at the picnic table at the dike here. They even invite dogs and their people to bring a blanket and make it a real picnic. (No ants, though.) 12784 Sir Francis Drake Boulevard; 415/669-1041.

Manka's Inverness Lodge: This magnificent lodge is home to a mouth-watering restaurant, if wild game is the type of dish that makes your mouth water. (See Places to Stay for more information.)

Priscilla's Pizza and Cafe: The salads, pizzas, pastas, and sandwiches here are a delight. Dine with doggy at the large side patio. 12781 Sir Francis Drake Boulevard; 415/669-1244.

PLACES TO STAY

The Ark: Don't expect 40 days and 40 nights of rain during your stay at The Ark. But be assured that even if it's raining cats and dogs, you'll still have a wonderful time here. That's because this two-room cottage is cozy and charming, with vast skylights, a soaring ceiling, a nifty loft, and the down-home comfort of a woodstove. It's furnished with lovely wood pieces and locally handcrafted items. The Ark is far removed from the hustle and bustle of downtown Inverness, and it is adjacent to a wildlife preserve, replete with trees. If you enjoy singing birds, open a window and let the songs stream in. Or walk outside to the beautiful, private area surrounding the cottage.

The Ark was built in 1971 by a class of UC Berkeley architecture students under the guidance of maverick architect Sim Van der Ryn. The class was called "Making a Place in the Country." If you took a class in the result of this project, it would probably be called "Making a Place in Your Heart." Your dog won't soon forget a vacation here, and neither will you. As long as your dog doesn't take a stab at the subjects of "Making a Hole in the Yard" or "Making Pee-Pee on the Floor," he'll be as welcome here as the humans in his party.

The Ark sleeps up to six people. Rates are $215 for two people, $25 per additional person. Dogs pay a flat fee for their visit: $25 for one dog, $35 for two dogs. Healthful, delicious, organic breakfast fixings (described below in mouthwatering detail in the listing for the Ark's sister property, Rosemary

Cottages) are $20 extra. You'll get the address when you make your reservation; 415/663-9338 or 800/808-9338; www.rosemarybb.com (click on The Ark).

Manka's Inverness Lodge: Often, humans and their dogs spend the night here, eat breakfast, and decide never to return home. It's an old hunting lodge, surrounded by woods and the beaches and mudflats of Tomales Bay—and the owners love dogs.

The lodgings are super-cozy, fun, and funky. Features vary from one to the other, and include fireplaces, huge tubs, antiques, and a variety of surprising decorative touches. Views are either of Tomales Bay or the surrounding woods.

Dogs can stay in the cabins or one suite. Rates for dog-friendly accommodations are $265–385. Dogs are $50 extra for the length of their stay.

The food here is exceptional. The lodge's restaurant has received many an award. The vegetarian and fish dishes are exotic and mouthwatering. But it's all the wild game dishes that make dogs vote it a four-paw restaurant. If dogs accompany you for a meal at the outdoor tables here, they'll drool over every mouthful you eat.

Look for the uphill turn off Sir Francis Drake Boulevard and take Argyle Way about 400 yards to the lodge. P.O. Box 1110, Inverness, CA 94937; 415/669-1034 or 800/58-LODGE (800/585-6343); www.mankas.com.

Rosemary Cottages: The two gorgeous cottages that share this spacious, wooded property are the kind of places you and your dog will not leave easily. The Fir Tree Inn and The Rosemary Cottage are set in a secluded spot, each with a wall of windows looking out at the stunning forest scenery of the Point Reyes National Seashore. A deck overlooks a sweet-smelling herb garden. The inside of the cottages are cozy and beautifully crafted, with a full kitchen and many homey details. Snuggle up near the wood-burning stove on chilly evenings after a day of whale-watching and dog-walking at nearby beaches. Hearth-type dogs love it here.

There's plenty of privacy: Although the cottages share the garden and hot tub (which uses chemicals other than chlorine and its harsh brethren), many guests spend their vacation here and never even know just where the other cottage is.

Owner Suzanne Storch wants your stay to be as restful and healthful as possible, and she provides a "green" environment (only more-natural cleansers are used) and the most delectable organic breakfast fixings, including a basket of oranges and other fruit, granola, yogurt, pancake mix, maple syrup, homemade jam (made by Suzanne), and eggs from her chickens. You don't have to have these amazing organic foods, and it'll be $20 less if you don't, but where else can you find a deal like this for such a sumptuous feast?

The Rosemary Cottage is $245 for up to two people, and The Fir Tree is $265. If you want the breakfast fixings at either cottage, add $20. If you have one dog, you'll pay a $25 flat fee. For two dogs you'll pay a $35 flat fee. You'll get the address when you make your reservation. 415/663-9338 or 800/808-9338; www.rosemarybb.com.

Point Reyes Station

This community is the commercial hub of West Marin. But that's not saying much, because it's not exactly Development Central out here. In fact, there are probably more cows than people. You'll find some terrific places to eat and to spend the night with your dog. We list some below, but a great resource for information on the entire West Marin area, and additional places to stay with a dog, is Bobbi, who runs the West Marin Network, a lodging service. Give her a jingle at 415/663-9543.

PLACES TO EAT

Bovine Bakery: The bread here will make you drool, which will make your dog embarrassed. Dine on bread or pizza or "killer monster cookies" at the bench in front. 11315 Highway 1; 415/663-9420.

DIVERSION

If Only Dogs Could Read: Point Reyes Books once sent me a letter that ended like this: "We welcome genteel canines, whether a reading rover or a browsing bowser—or just a patiently waiting companion. *Se habla* milkbone." So of course, next time we found ourselves pawing around for a good book, Joe hounded me to drive with him to this wonderful little bookstore. He immediately fell in love with the place. Dogs get lots of loving and a crunchy biscuit. After a recent visit, his protégé, Jake, decided that instead of chewing books, he'd simply make dog-eared pages. Anything to go back.

This store really is a treat—for dogs and humans. It has a big selection of new and used books, with a strong outdoor book section. Combine a visit here with a hike and a lunch, and you've got yourselves a doggone great day. 11315 Highway 1, Point Reyes Station; 415/663-1542; www.ptreyesbooks.com.

Cafe Reyes: The patio on the café's side is big and very attractive, with excellent views of local scenery. Even dogs seem to enjoy its ambience. The food is great, too. Bring it to the 15 umbrella-topped tables and wolf it down with your pooch at your side. The cuisine is best described as Tex-Mex with a California leaning. Try one of the Thai burritos for a true international experience. You can also get baked goodies and strong coffee, for those lazy, foggy days here. There's not really a street address. It's on Highway 1 and is big and wooden. You can't miss it. 415/663-9493.

PLACES TO STAY

The Berry Patch Cottage: This delightful garden cottage is surrounded by trees and has a private yard with plenty of berries (thus the name), fruit trees, and nut trees. The cottage owners live next door, and they invite guests to share their vegetable garden. Some times of the year, it's pretty much food city here. It's a terrific getaway from the urban lifestyle. The cottage is a charmer, with a full kitchen that opens to a redwood deck, a living room with a wonderful little reading nook (and books to read in that nook), and a bedroom that's warmed by an old Sears & Roebuck potbelly stove. Rates are $100 to $150. Dogs are $5 extra. The mailing address is P.O. Box 712 94956. You'll get the physical address when you make a reservation. 415/663-1942 or 888/663-1942; www.berrypatchcottage.com.

The Old Point Reyes Schoolhouse Compound: The three glorious getaway cottages that make up the old schoolhouse area are the cat's meow for dogs and their people. On a serene stretch of rolling pastureland in Point

Reyes Station, the cottages have a sweet country theme and seem perfectly at home in their surroundings. Dogs love it here, because each cottage is adorned with its own private enclosed patio and garden. They're wonderful places to relax outside with your pooch.

The cottages also have fully equipped kitchens that come with a real bonus: a lovely picnic basket and all the gear that goes with it (excluding the food). Now there's no excuse for not taking your pooch on a picnic. In addition, each cottage has access to a wonderful organic garden and a secluded garden hot tub. The larger two have fireplaces and full kitchens.

Jasmine Cottage is the smaller of the two romantic hideaways. It's sequestered in a country garden at the top of a hill and has small flower gardens, vegetable gardens, and even a flock of chickens, who provide guests with their morning eggs. A full, simple breakfast is included in your stay at this cottage. The chickens are in a protected area, but if your dog has a hankering for KFC, best keep her away. When we visited, Joe Dog went cuckoo over the cock-a-doodle-doos. We had to drag him kicking and screaming back inside the cottage for fear he would give a hen a heart attack.

Gray's Retreat is just as enchanting, but chicken-free and bigger. It's more geared toward families, since it sleeps up to six and comes with a high chair and a portable crib. Breakfast is not provided, but the kitchen is stocked with enough basic dry goods (including organic breakfast goodies) that with a few groceries, you can have yourself a feast. The newest addition, the Barn Loft, is the smallest, but it offers the best views and the best price. (No breakfast here, either.)

Rates for the cottages: Jasmine, $220; Gray's, $245; Barn Loft, $185. Stay seven days, and get the seventh night free. Dogs are $50 extra for the length of their stay. The cottages are on the historic Old Point Reyes Schoolhouse Compound. The mailing address is P.O. Box 56, Point Reyes Station, CA 94956; 415/663-1166; www.oldpointreyesschoolhouse.com.

Point Reyes Station Inn: Dogs are welcome to stay in one room at this recently built inn. It's a first-floor room with a private entrance, its own patio, a fireplace, and a whirlpool tub for two (that would be two humans, lest your water dog gets any ideas). Rates are $135–165. 11591 Highway 1 94956; www .pointreyesstationinn.com.

Seven Grey Foxes Bed and Bath: These two sweet apartments are tucked away on a quiet country road in a cozy neighborhood just outside the village. It's very peaceful here. The two-room apartment (aka the cottage) is very attractive, with huge windows overlooking beautiful gardens, and a Franklin fireplace. The one-room apartment is just a smaller version of the other, and it doesn't have the wall of windows. Rates are $95 for the smaller, $150 for the larger. You'll get the address when you make your reservation. 415/663-9543; www.sevengreyfoxes.com.

Olema

PARKS, BEACHES, AND RECREATION AREAS

5 Limantour Beach

😺😺😺😺 (See Marin County map on page 132)

This bountiful beach at Point Reyes National Seashore is most people's favorite, so it's often crowded. From the main parking lot, walk a quarter of a mile through tule marsh, grasses and brush, and scattered pines, past Limantour Estero. Dogs are prohibited on the side trails south of the parking lot.

Rules for leashed dogs are clearly marked—a refreshing exception to the obscure and contradictory rules in so many parks. For example, approaching Limantour Beach on the path, you'll see a sign that says dogs are prohibited to your right, allowed to your left. This beach is plenty big, so it's an excellent arrangement that keeps dog owners and dog avoiders equally happy. You may walk with your dog to Santa Maria Beach.

From Highway 1, look for the turnoff to Bear Valley Road, which runs between Olema and Inverness Park. Take Bear Valley from either direction to Limantour Road; turn south on Limantour all the way to the beach. 415/464-5100.

6 Bolinas Ridge Trail

😺😺😺😺 (See Marin County map on page 132)

This Golden Gate National Recreation Area trail, part of the Bay Area Ridge Trail, is not for sissies—canine or human. It climbs steadily for 11 miles from the Olema end, giving you gorgeous views of Tomales Bay, Bolinas, and the ocean, and ends up at the Bolinas-Fairfax Road below Alpine Lake.

You must keep your dog leashed. One good reason for this is that there are cattle roaming unfenced along the trail. And the trail is very popular with nonsissy mountain bikers. (The trail is wide, but made of dirt and rock.) From the western end, you'll walk through rolling grassland with cypress clumps. Rock outcrops sport crowns of poison oak, so watch it.

You may be able to cope with 11 miles of this, but remember your dog's bare pads and don't overdo it. Also, it isn't much fun for man or beast to walk 11 miles attached by a leash.

Unfortunately, only the Bolinas Ridge Trail is open to dogs; you can't take any of the spur trails going south.

The western end begins about one mile north of Olema on Sir Francis Drake Boulevard. There's roadside parking only. 415/556-0560 or 415/663-1092.

PLACES TO STAY

The Olema Inn: This absolutely enchanting inn is exactly 100 years younger than our nation. It opened on July 4, 1876. That's a long, long time ago by

California standards. The inn has obviously been revamped a bit since then, but it still retains the elegant charm of the era. The six beautiful rooms feature antique furniture mingling with up-to-date luxuries such as super-comfortable European Sleepworks mattresses topped with down comforters. (No dogs on the bedding, please.) A fresh breakfast of croissants, local artisan cheeses, fruit, and beverages comes with your stay. Eat it in the dining room or enjoy it in the pretty garden, the lush green grounds, or the big porch out front. Rates are $145–185. 10,000 Sir Francis Drake Boulevard 94950; 415/663-9559; www.theolemainn.com.

Olema Ranch Campground: It's hard to find a campground that's decent for both RVs and tent campers, so we were mighty pleased to find Olema Ranch. RV folks get all the hookups they need, and tenters get a choice of scenic meadow or forest campsites. Many sites come with water. The campground features amenities such as a kitchen, laundry facilities, and a supply store, so we're not exactly talking the big wilderness adventure here. But still, it's a terrific spot to set up a tent with a dog who doesn't mind a little civilized camping. Rates are $23–35. Dogs are $1 extra. 10155 Highway 1, P.O. Box 175, Olema, CA 94950; 415/663-8001 or 800/655-CAMP (800/655-2267); www.olemaranch.com.

Novato

PARKS, BEACHES, AND RECREATION AREAS

7 Mount Burdell Open Space Preserve

🐾🐾🐾🐾🐕 (See Marin County map on page 132)

Mount Burdell is the largest of Marin's open space preserves. You'll share it with cattle, but there's plenty of room. There are several miles of trails, including part of the Bay Area Ridge Trail, that wind through its oak-dotted grasslands. (Dogs have to be leashed on trails, but are permitted to run leash-less on fire roads here.)

A creek is about one-eighth of a mile up the trail starting at San Andreas Drive, but it's dry in summer. In winter, you might find the preserve's Hidden Lake. In summer, there are lots of foxtails and fire danger is high. No fires are ever allowed. Camping is allowed by permit, but there are no facilities.

From San Marin Drive, turn north on San Andreas Drive. Park on the street. 415/499-6387.

8 Miwuk Park

🐾🐾🐾 (See Marin County map on page 132)

This is one of the best city parks we've visited. Dogs must be on leash, but it offers a great combination of dog pleasures and human amenities. Paved paths, good for strollers, wind through pine trees. You will find boccie ball courts, horseshoes, a kids' gym, and a lovely shaded picnic area with grills.

Outside the Museum of the American Indian in this park is an intriguing display of California native plants that the coastal Miwuk used for food, clothing, and shelter.

Best of all for canines, Novato Creek flows deep and 30–40 feet wide (even in summer). A woman we encountered with a golden retriever told us that the muddy bottom can sometimes be soft and treacherous, so keep a close eye on your dog if he goes swimming. The park is at Novato Boulevard and San Miguel Drive. 415/897-4323.

9 Indian Tree Open Space Preserve

🐾🐾🐾🐾 🐕 (See Marin County map on page 132)

This is a great choice for a hike if the weather is hot: Your ascent to the top (and to terrific views) takes you through cool, shaded woodlands of oak, madrone, and bay. You'll also encounter redwoods and ferns along the way. At the top, the open area isn't parched and sun-baked like so many areas around here in summer: It's often cool and drippy with fog. Jake the dog, who lives in a foggy area of the city and can't take the heat, is very happy here. You needn't leash on fire roads here, but watch out for horses. Leashes are the law on the preserve's trails.

From U.S. 101, exit at San Marin Drive/Atherton Avenue; drive west on San Marin. After San Marin turns into Sutro Avenue, take a right onto Vineyard Road. Park along the dirt county road that begins at the trailhead. 415/499-6387.

10 Dogbone Meadow Dog Park

🐾🐾🐾🐾 🐕 (See Marin County map on page 132)

Lucky dogs who visit here have two fenced acres of off-leash running room and all the "playground equipment" they could want. The park sports tunnels, ramps, jumps, hanging tires, and other fun agility equipment. Big dogs have big toys, and little dogs have littler toys. Everyone's happy here.

The park is a pretty combination of grass and landscaping bark, with the rolling hills of O'Hair Park in the background. (You can walk your dog on leash in this 100-acre city park.) The volunteers who worked so hard to make this park a reality have planted 35 trees, but it will take many years before they're shade-giving. Until then, people gather under shade structures on hot, sunny days. If your dog is dirty from all the romping around, you can use the dog-wash station near the entrance/exit. The park is at San Marin Drive and Novato Boulevard, on the left as you're heading west. 415/897-4323.

11 Deer Island Open Space Preserve

🐾🐾🐾🐾 🐕 (See Marin County map on page 132)

This preserve is called an island because it's a high point in the floodplain of the Petaluma River, an oak-crowned hill surrounded by miles of dock and tules. You can easily imagine it surrounded by shallow-water Miwuk canoes slipping through rafts of ducks. The trail is a 1.8-mile loop of gentle ups and downs above ponds and marshy fields. There are some sturdy old oaks among the mixed deciduous groves, and lots of laurels. The trail is partly shaded and bans bikes. Dogs have to be leashed on the trails but are permitted off leash on fire roads here.

From U.S. 101, exit at San Marin Drive/Atherton Avenue; drive east about 1.5 miles and take a right on Olive Avenue, then a left on Deer Island Lane. Park in a small lot at the trailhead, by a small engineering company building. 415/499-6387.

12 Indian Valley Open Space Preserve

🐾🐾🐾🐾🐕 (See Marin County map on page 132)

Lots of dogs come here to trot around in leashless ecstasy on the fire road. On hiking trails, they have to trot around in leashed ecstasy. The hiking trails and fire roads are partly sunny, partly shaded by laurels, and much-revered by canines. Take the Waterfall Trail if you love waterfalls and don't mind leashes. You'll be rewarded at the end, unless of course it's dry season.

From U.S. 101, exit at DeLong Avenue and go west on DeLong, which becomes Diablo Avenue. Take a left on Hill Road and a right on Indian Valley Road. Drive all the way to the end; park on this road before you walk left at the spur road marked "Not a Through Street," just south of Old Ranch Road. Cross Arroyo Avichi Creek right at the entrance (dry in summer). 415/499-6387.

13 Lucas Valley Open Space Preserve

🐾🐾🐾🐾🐕 (See Marin County map on page 132)

This space of rolling, oak-dotted hills affords great views of Novato and Lucas Valley developments. The summit here is 1,825 feet—the second-highest in Marin. We like to take the scenic Big Rock Trail up to the Big Rock Fire Road. It's a gentle grade for beasts and their people.

The preserve has a dozen access points, most from Lucas Valley and Marin-wood. One access point is reached by turning left (north) off Lucas Valley Road on Mount Shasta Drive, followed by a brief right turn on Vogelsang Drive. Park near this dead end and walk in. Keep in mind that all Marin Open Space Preserves require pooches to be on leash except on fire roads. 415/499-6387.

14 Loma Verde Open Space Preserve

🐾🐾🐾🐕 (See Marin County map on page 132)

This rugged open space connects to a couple of others, which makes for a vigorous hike if you and your dog aren't fair of paw. There are two access points to this open space, where dogs are allowed off leash on fire roads. One, south of the Marin Country Club, is a waterless, tree-covered hillside with a fire road. Bikes are allowed, so be sure to keep your leash-free dog under voice control. It's a good road if you like easily reachable high spots; there are fine views of San Pablo Bay. Exit U.S. 101 at Ignacio Boulevard. Go west to Fairway Drive and turn left (south), then left on Alameda de la Loma, then right on Pebble Beach Drive. Access is at the end of Pebble Beach.

The second access point is through the Posada West housing development. From Alameda del Prado, turn south on Posada del Sol. The trail opening is at the end of this street. 415/499-6387.

PLACES TO STAY

Inn Marin: Any lodging that boasts three "dog pot stations" on the property has got to be doggone dog-friendly (and doggone clean, too). These stations are actually just waste cans coupled with plastic bag dispensers, but we appreciate the inn's discreet name for them. The 70-room inn is stylish, clean, and convenient to U.S. 101. It features excellent amenities for people traveling on business (data ports, two-line speaker phones, large desks) and people with disabilities (seven rooms have special features for wheelchairs, and for sight- or hearing-impaired guests). Rates are $99–169. Dogs are $20 total for the first six days, and then $40 per week after. (And get this: "You can have up to four per room!") 250 Entrada Drive, Novato, CA 94949; 415/883-5952 or 800/652-6565; www.innmarin.com.

TraveLodge: Rates are $59–99. Dogs are $10 extra. 7600 Redwood Boulevard 94945; 415/892-7500.

Lagunitas

PARKS, BEACHES, AND RECREATION AREAS

15 Samuel P. Taylor State Park

 (See Marin County map on page 132)

An exception among the state parks: Dog access is generous. You can take a dog into the picnic areas, and that's worth doing here. The main picnic area right off Sir Francis Drake Boulevard is cool and often lively with the grinding call of jays. It's an easy place to bring out-of-state visitors who may just want to eat a sandwich, hug a redwood, and go home. The park has hollow trees stretching 20 feet across that you can actually stand inside.

But best of all, you and your dog may spend a whole day on the wide fire trails—roughly 10 miles of them—clearly differentiated on the map you get at the entrance. Dogs may not go on the foot trails, but the fire trails are delightful enough. You can take the bicycle/horse trail from near the entrance along Papermill Creek, rising for four miles to Barnabe Peak, at 1,466 feet. Unfortunately, your dog must stay leashed, but you may actually appreciate that when you see the excellent artist's drawing of a poison oak cluster on the park's map—it's everywhere.

The park has 60 campsites. Sites are $18–20. From April through October, call for reservations: 800/444-7275. The park's day-use fee is $6. The entrance is on Sir Francis Drake Boulevard about two miles west of Lagunitas. 415/488-9897.

PLACES TO EAT

Lagunitas Grocery: Grab a sandwich at the deli inside and feast on it at the outdoor tables with your dog. Thirsty dogs can ask for a bowl of water. 7890 Sir Francis Drake Boulevard; 415/488-4844.

PLACES TO STAY

Samuel P. Taylor State Park: See Samuel P. Taylor State Park, above, for camping information.

Woodacre

PARKS, BEACHES, AND RECREATION AREAS

16 Gary Giacomini Open Space Preserve

😊😊😊😊 🐾 (See Marin County map on page 132)

The most recent addition to Marin's open-space lands is this 1,600-acre gem. The preserve stretches for seven miles along the southern edge of the San Geronimo Valley. Stands of old-growth redwoods shade the ferny lower regions of the park. The higher you go, the more grassy it gets. Dogs such as Jake (i.e., male) prefer the trees, but they can get the best of both worlds by following one of the wide fire trails and sniffing out various areas along the way.

Pooches may go leashless on the fire roads but not on the more narrow hiking trails. Come visit before the rest of the doggone world finds out about this hidden treasure.

From U.S. 101, take Sir Francis Drake Boulevard west to San Geronimo Valley Drive and turn left. You can park at the intersection of Redwood Canyon Drive, just west of Woodacre, and begin your hike at the nearby trailhead. This is a fun route to take with your dog, since it brings you from thick forest to the top of the ridge. 415/499-6387.

Fairfax

This small, friendly, progressive town is known as the birthplace of the mountain bike. That's not news that will put a wag in your dog's tail, but this will: Secret Agent Dog, a pooch with impeccable taste, had his person write to tell me that "Fairfax is…one of the most dog-friendly places we've ever lived." Mutt Mitt dispensers are placed strategically through town, and there are two drinking fountains (one by the baseball field, one by town hall) for both humans and dogs. People here love to see dogs with their people; some stores will welcome your dog if it's not busy, but we'll leave that on a case-by-case basis.

PARKS, BEACHES, AND RECREATION AREAS

17 Cascade Canyon Open Space Preserve

🐾🐾🐾🐾 🐕 (See Marin County map on page 132)

As on all of Marin's open space lands, dogs can cavort about off leash on the fire roads. The fire road here is vehicle-free except for rangers. It's a pleasant walk that leads all the way into the Marin Municipal Water District lands of Mt. Tamalpais. (Once you enter these, you must leash.)

These days, dogs must be leashed on all open-space hiking trails. But the trails are so enticing that they're actually worth trying despite the new leash law. The main trail sticks close to San Anselmo Creek, which is reduced to a dry creek bed in summer. A no-bicycles trail branches off to the right and disappears into the creek; the left branch fords the creek. When the water's high, you may be stopped right here. But in summer, you can walk a long way. Side trails lead you into shady glens of laurel and other deciduous trees, but there's lots of poison oak, too.

The park is at the end of Cascade Drive. There's a Town of Fairfax sign saying "Elliott Nature Preserve," but it's official open space. Please don't park at the end of Cascade. Spread out so the folks who live at the end of Cascade don't get so inundated with dogs. Pooches have been a problem for some residents, whose beautiful flowers and lawns have succumbed to dog feet and pooch poop. Be courteous, and think how you'd feel if the shoe were on the other paw. 415/499-6387.

San Anselmo

San Anselmo Avenue provides you and your mellow pooch a laid-back stroll, and you can both cool your paws in San Anselmo Creek, which runs through town. Your well-behaved pooch can even be off leash, provided she's under voice control. A group has been trying for years to get a dog park at Red Hill Park, behind the Red Hill Shopping Center at the end of Shaw Drive. For more information on this noble effort, call 415/258-4645.

PARKS, BEACHES, AND RECREATION AREAS

18 Creek Park

🐾🐾🐾 (See Marin County map on page 132)

San Anselmo Creek runs between Sir Francis Drake Boulevard—which has a wide variety of antique shops—and San Anselmo Avenue, the main shopping street. A bridge connects the two streets.

Creek Park is small, but handy and clean. It's next to a free public lot with some shady spaces. Along the creek banks on the Sir Francis Drake side are picnic tables on a lawn with beautiful willows and maples. Lots of people lounge on the grass. Wooden steps lead down to the water. You'll find plenty of shade in which to picnic or lie on the grass while resting between shopping binges for antiques.

Turn into the parking lot from Sir Francis Drake Boulevard, near "The Hub" (intersection of Sir Francis Drake and Red Hill Avenue). 415/258-4645.

19 Loma Alta Open Space Preserve

🐾🐾🐾🐾 🐕 (See Marin County map on page 132)

A little canyon amid bare hills, lined with oaks, bay laurel, and buckeye, this is an exceptional open-space preserve. Shade is plentiful. The trail follows White Hill Creek, which is dry in the summer. Leashes are required on the trails, but obedient dogs can throw their leashes to the wind on the fire road.

You can park at the trailhead at the end of Glen Avenue, a turn north off Sir Francis Drake Boulevard. 415/499-6387.

20 Memorial Park

🐾🐾🐾 🐕 (See Marin County map on page 132)

This pleasant and popular city park has tennis courts, three baseball diamonds, and a children's play area. Next to the diamonds is a dog-exercise area, where leash-free dogs romp joyfully, fetching, chasing Frisbees, or socializing. Even a creek runs nearby. There's a hitch—dogs can be off leash only before 8 A.M. and from one hour before sunset to, well, sunset. The park is at Veterans Place, a quick jog east from San Francisco Boulevard. 415/258-4645.

21 Sorich Ranch Park

🐾 🐾 🐾 🐾 🐕 (See Marin County map on page 132)

The biggest and by far the wildest city park in San Anselmo is Sorich Ranch Park, an undeveloped open space soaring to a ridge top from which you can see a distant make-believe San Francisco skyline across the bay. From the very top of the ridge, you also can see Mt. Tamalpais and most of San Rafael, including the one-of-a-kind turquoise and salmon Marin County Civic Center, designed by Frank Lloyd Wright. (Some Marinites are glad there's only one.)

The entrance from the San Anselmo side is at the end of San Francisco Boulevard, and the path is pretty much straight up. But if you aren't up to a 10-minute puffing ascent, you can just stroll in the meadows at the bottom. No leash is required, and the park is uncrowded and often pleasantly breezy. No water is available, and it can be scorching in summer. 415/258-4645.

PLACES TO EAT

Bubba's Diner: If you found an eatery by this name in many other towns, you might be inclined to stride by with nary a glance, lest you absorb grease and saturated fat just by looking at it. But being that this Bubba's Diner is in San Anselmo, grease is not the main ingredient of most dishes, and the saturated fat is at least upscale saturated fat.

Bubba's is a really fun, unpretentious place to bring a dog for some extra-tasty American-style eats. The cheery owner, Beth, likes to see well-behaved dogs dining at the two awning-shaded tables and benches in front of the restaurant. But she warns people not to tie dogs to the benches, lest the dog drag away the bench. (One small pooch actually went exploring the neighborhood, pulling the hefty pine bench behind him!) Take Beth's advice and hook your dog to the pay phone if you're dining alone and need to run in to place your order.

Choose from dozens of yummy dishes here. The food varies from healthful and delicious (oyster salad, grilled salmon with asparagus and sautéed spinach) to decadent and delicious (pot roast, fried chicken, burgers, mashed potato pancakes). If you're pining for some fried green tomatoes, look no further. Bubba's is famous for them. Thirsty doggies can get water here. 566 San Anselmo Avenue; 415/459-6862.

San Rafael

PARKS, BEACHES, AND RECREATION AREAS

We can't officially recommend Red Hill Park, behind the Red Hill Shopping center, because it's still not a real dog park. One of these days…. Meanwhile, there are plenty of other places for pooch paws to be happy.

22 Terra Linda–Sleepy Hollow Divide Open Space Preserve

🐾🐾🐾🐾🦮 (See Marin County map on page 132)

This ridgeline preserve has many entrances, but generally the best are the highest on the ridge. We'll describe the one that starts you at a good high point, so that you don't have to climb. From the entrance at the end of Ridgewood Drive, you can walk into Sorich Ranch Park (see the San Anselmo section).

From this ridge, you can see the city of San Rafael, U.S. 101, the wonderful turquoise-roofed Marin County Civic Center, the bay, and the hills of Solano County. No leash is necessary on fire roads, unless you're worried about your dog's tangling with deer. But pooches must be leashed on trails.

Park near the very end of Ridgewood Drive. The entrance is unmarked, and you have to step over a low locked gate. 415/499-6387.

23 Field of Dogs

🐾🐾🐾🐾🦮 (See Marin County map on page 132)

We love the name, love the park. The people behind Field of Dogs worked really hard to make the park a reality. It took about six years. It's not only real now, but it's a great place to take a dog for off-leash exercise.

The one-acre park has little trees, big trees, a double-gated entry, benches, picnic tables, poop bags, and very nice park-goers—of both the pooch and people variety. Some trees are in the middle of the park, and we've heard about more than one head-on canine collision with a tree during chase games. After the swirling stars and tweeting birds wear off, the dogs are just fine.

The park is behind the civic center, at 3540 Civic Center Drive. It's an easy jaunt from U.S. 101. Exit U.S. 101 and continue east to Civic Center Drive, which is the first light.Turn left and the park will be on your right just past the post office and firehouse. 415/485-3333.

24 John F. McInnis County Park

🐾🐾🐾🦮 (See Marin County map on page 132)

This is an all-around, got-everything park for people. Among its riches are two softball fields, two soccer fields, tennis courts, a picnic area, a scale-model car track, a nine-hole golf course, miniature golf, batting cages, and a dirt creekside nature trail.

Best of all for trustworthy dogs, they can be off leash, so long as they're under verbal command and out of the golf course. This park isn't particularly pretty, but it's very utilitarian. From U.S. 101, exit at Smith Ranch Road. 415/499-6387.

25 San Pedro Mountain Open Space Preserve

🐾🐾🐾🐾 ✖ (See Marin County map on page 132)

A narrow footpath rises moderately but inexorably upward through a madrone forest. But if you make it up far enough, you'll be rewarded with terrific views of the bay and Marin's peaks. Deer are plentiful, so it's kind to leash your dog if you don't trust him completely to stay by your side.

Park at the entrance at the end of Woodoaks Drive, a short street off North Point San Pedro Road just north of the Jewish Community Center of Marin. 415/499-6387.

26 Santa Margarita Island Open Space Preserve

🐾🐾🐾 (See Marin County map on page 132)

What a wonderful, secret place this is. Gallinas Creek, fortified by levees, is lined with rickety piers and small boats, like a bit of the Delta. You can cross to a tiny island via a footbridge and climb the hill you'll find here, covered with oaks and boulders, or walk around the edge on a dirt path. Watch for poison oak on the hill. Though of course it isn't true, you can feel as if no one has been here before you except Coast Miwuks. Dogs are supposed to be leashed at this open space.

From North Point San Pedro Road, turn west on Meadow Drive. Where it ends, at the western end of Vendola Drive, is the footbridge. You can park on the street. Carry water if you plan to stay long. 415/499-6387.

27 Santa Venetia Marsh Open Space Preserve

🐾🐾🐾🐾 (See Marin County map on page 132)

Dogs are very lucky to be able to visit this saltwater marsh. Only leashed pooches on their best behavior should come here, because the preserve is home to an endangered bird, the California clapper rail. Keep your eyes peeled: It looks like a chicken (and apparently tastes something like one, too—it was heavily hunted during the Gold Rush, when its meat was considered a delightful delicacy), but it has a long beak.

Mmm, doggy, the scents can be mighty strong here sometimes. They're so doggone nose-flaring good your dog may not even notice he's wearing a leash. You may not feel the same about the odor, but hey, just keep saying to yourself "it's a natural smell."

It's cool and breezy here, but gentler than any San Francisco Bay shore park. The grasses and pickleweed make a pretty mixture of colors, and swallows dart above the ground hunting insects.

Vendola Drive has two distinct parts, and you can get to the marsh from the end of either. At the western end of the creekside segment of Vendola, at the corner of Meadow Drive, is a footbridge leading to Santa Margarita Island (see above). 415/499-6387.

2·8 Boyd Park

🐾🐾 (See Marin County map on page 132)

This is not a very doggy park, until you drive past the Dollar mansion (now the Falkirk Community Cultural Center) into the hills on Robert Dollar Scenic Drive to the undeveloped section. The only parking is at a turnout off the drive, but at that spot, the drive becomes a dirt fire trail, closed to autos, that mounts the ridgecrest in a steady uphill climb through brush, oak, and madrone.

Leash your pup and start walking. You'll get a breathtaking view of the Richmond–San Rafael Bridge, the Bay Bridge, the Oakland skyline, and Mt. Tam. Robert Dollar Scenic Drive begins at the end of Laurel Place. 415/485-3333.

2·9 China Camp State Park

🐾🐾🐾 (See Marin County map on page 132)

You shouldn't miss a drive through this lovely park, although it's not terribly hospitable to dogs except at Village Beach, the site of the 1890s Chinese fishing village for which the park is named. As you drive in, you'll see a rare piece of bay, marsh, and oak-covered hills as the Miwuks saw it. The hills, like islands, rise from salt-marsh seas of pickleweed and cordgrass. You'll see the "No Dogs" symbol at every trailhead, in case you're tempted. However, with your dog you may visit any of three picnic grounds on the way, via North Point San Pedro Road. Buckeye Point and Weber Point both have tables in shade or sun overlooking San Pablo Bay, mudflats at low tide, and the hills beyond the bay. Bullhead Flat lets you get right next to the water, but there's no shade at the tables.

Watch for the sign to China Camp Village, a left turn into a lot, where there's some shade. You'll see the rickety old pier and the wood-and-tin village. Park, leash your dog, and walk down to the village and the beach. On weekdays, this park is much less crowded. There are more picnic tables overlooking the water by the parking lot, an interpretive exhibit and, on weekends, a refreshment stand serving shrimp, crab, and beer. You can eat at picnic tables right on the beach—small, but pleasantly sheltered by hillsides, with gentle surf.

Swimming is encouraged here, and it's often warm enough. Derelict fishing boats and shacks are preserved on the beach. You can walk all the way to a rocky point at the south end, but watch out for the luxuriant poison oak in the brush along the beach. You may occasionally find broken glass.

There are 31 primitive walk-in campsites here. As in all state parks, dogs must always be leashed or confined to your tent. Sites are $15–20. To reserve (recommended April–October), call 800/444-7275. From U.S. 101, take the North Point San Pedro Road exit and follow it all the way into the park. (Don't go near McNears Beach County Park just south of China Camp. Dogs are strictly forbidden.) 415/456-0766.

PLACES TO EAT

Cento Stelle: We really enjoy eating at Cento Stelle, which in Italian means 100 stars. Besides being in love with the name, we're also in love with the very good Italian food. Dine with dog at the four sidewalk tables. 901 Lincoln Avenue; 415/485-4422.

Phyllis' Giant Burgers: Dogs dig this drive-in burger joint. Order your meat-eater one of the giant burgers. Or if your pooch is in a no-beef mode, try a veggie burger. 2202 4th Street; 415/456-0866.

Shaky Grounds: The shaky grounds here refer to coffee, not earthquakes (we think). If coffee isn't your cup of tea, you can order pastries, smoothies, soups, salads, and sandwiches. 1800 4th Street; 415/256-2420.

PLACES TO STAY

China Camp State Park: See China Camp State Park, above, for camping information.

Villa Inn: This place recently got much more dog-friendly: There are no more dog fees, and dogs don't have to be shrimps to stay here; any size dog is welcome. Rates are $69–125. 1600 Lincoln Avenue 94901; 415/456-4975 or 888/845-5246.

Ross

PARKS, BEACHES, AND RECREATION AREAS

30 Natalie Coffin Greene Park

🐾🐾🐾 (See Marin County map on page 132)

Leashed dogs are welcome at this enchanted mixed forest of redwood and deciduous trees. The picnic area has an old-fashioned shelter built of logs and stone.

The park borders generic Marin Municipal Water District land, and from the park, you can pick up the wide cinder fire road leading to Phoenix Lake, a five-minute walk. Bikers, hikers, and leashed dogs are all welcome on this road, but the lake is a reservoir, so no body contact is allowed—for man or beast.

The road continues, depending how far you want to walk, to Lagunitas Lake, Bon Tempe Lake, Alpine Lake, and Kent Lake. (No swimming in any of them; sorry, dogs.) Combined, the water district offers 94 miles of road and 44 miles of trail in this area, meandering through hillsides, densely forested with pine, oak, madrone, and a variety of other trees. For a trail map, send a self-addressed, stamped envelope to Sky Oaks Ranger Station, P.O. Box 865, Fairfax, CA 94978, Attention: Trail Map.

At the corner of Sir Francis Drake Boulevard and Lagunitas Road, go west on Lagunitas all the way to the end, past the country club. You'll find a parking lot and some portable toilets. 415/453-1453.

Kentfield

PARKS, BEACHES, AND RECREATION AREAS

🐾 Baltimore Canyon Open Space Preserve

🐾🐾🐾🐾🐕 (See Marin County map on page 132)

If you don't like heat, this 175-acre open space is a fine place to come for a summer stroll. You have less chance of getting roasty-toasty here than at many other nearby parks: The big oaks, madrones, bays, firs, and even redwoods tend to keep things cool in the canyon. It even has a year-round creek and a seasonal 30-foot waterfall. It's worth the hike to the end of the canyon to see this cascade.

From this open space you have good access to a lot of fire roads through the ridges connecting with Mt. Tamalpais and water-district lands. Leashes aren't required on the fire roads, but bikes are also allowed on these trails, so be careful. Dogs must be leashed on regular hiking trails.

Two access points are at the ends of Crown Road and Evergreen Drive. 415/499-6387.

Larkspur

PARKS, BEACHES, AND RECREATION AREAS

🐾 Blithedale Summit Open Space Preserve

🐾🐾🐾🐾🐕 (See Marin County map on page 132)

The access point at the end of Madrone Avenue—the north end of this open space—is a delightful walk in hot weather, through cool redwoods that let some light filter through. This isn't one of those really dark, drippy canyons; you're at a medium-high altitude on the slopes of Mt. Tamalpais. The trail follows Larkspur Creek, which retains some pools in summer. Cross the footbridge and follow the slightly rough foot trail. Unfortunately, leashes are now the law on these trails. But you can let your dog off his leash once you hit the fire road.

The drive up narrow Madrone Avenue is an adventure in itself; redwoods grow right in the street. According to a sign at the entrance, the part of this space belonging to the city of Larkspur requires dogs to be leashed. 415/499-6387.

🐾 Creekside Park

🐾🐾🐾 (See Marin County map on page 132)

This is the small, attractive park where the multipurpose Bon Air Path starts. The 1.8-mile paved trail goes from Bon Air Road, following Corte Madera Creek, westward to the town of Ross and eastward to the Larkspur Landing shopping

center, near the ferry terminal. There are lots of paths by Corte Madera Creek, and a kids' gym. You must leash your dog and be sure to keep him out of marshy areas. A bulletin board displays excellent bike-trail maps and descriptions of local flora and fauna.

From Sir Francis Drake Boulevard, turn south on Bon Air Road; from Magnolia Drive, turn north. The park entrance is across from Marin General Hospital. You can get more information on the county's bike trails from the Bicycle Trails Council of Marin at 415/456-7512. For more park information, call 415/499-6387.

34 Canine Commons

🐾🐾🐾🐕 (See Marin County map on page 132)

Canine Commons is popular with common canines. It isn't a very big dog park, but it was the first in Marin, opening its doggy gates in 1989. That's ancient history in the annals of dog parkdom. It's a basic dog park, with water, poop bags, and tennis balls.

Canine Commons is set within Piper Park, where you can play or watch softball, volleyball, tennis, and even cricket. Outside Canine Commons, dogs must be leashed. The park is between Doherty Drive and Corte Madera Creek. Canine Commons is at the west end of the park. Note: At press time, the dog park was closed while some work was being done there. There's a chance it may end up being moved to a new location. (Jake Dog says he hopes not many dogs are in it on moving day. That could get pretty interesting for the movers.) 415/927-5110.

PLACES TO EAT

The Left Bank: Your dog doesn't have to be a poodle to enjoy dining at this terrific French restaurant. Because it's a French place, management knows that dogs and restaurants really do mix. But because they're in America, they have to abide by local health regulations and keep doggies from dining inside. That's OK, though, because there are plenty of outside tables. When it's crowded, managers ask that you tie your dog to the railing that surrounds the outdoor area. You can still dine right beside your pooch. Thirsty pooches can get a bowl of water. 507 Magnolia Avenue; 415/927-3331.

Marin Brewing Company: The brewery makes its own beer here, and it's really good. Swig some with your dog and your sandwich at the nine outdoor tables. 1809 Larkspur Circle; 415/461-4677.

Bolinas

Bolinas is famous for trying to hide from curious visitors—thereby drawing hordes of them. They keep coming, even though town citizens regularly take down the turnoff sign on Highway 1. So if you're coming from the east (San Francisco area), turn left at the unmarked road where Bolinas Lagoon ends. If you're coming from the west, turn right where the lagoon begins.

Sometimes it seems as if half the inhabitants of Bolinas are dogs, most of them black. They stand guard outside bars, curl at shop owners' feet, snooze in the middle of the road. You'll find no city hall in Bolinas, an unincorporated area, and no chamber of commerce. Dogs are always welcome here, but cars, horses, bicycles, and too many unleashed dogs compete for space. Be thoughtful and keep your pooch leashed in town.

PARKS, BEACHES, AND RECREATION AREAS

Alas, dogs are no longer officially allowed on beautiful Agate Beach.

35 Bolinas Beach

🐾🐾🐾🐕 (See Marin County map on page 132)
At the end of the main street, Wharf Road, is a sand-and-pebble beach at the foot of a bluff. Dogs are free to run off leash. But watch for horses—with riders and without—thundering past without warning. It's animal anarchy here, and it's not the cleanest beach in Marin. We give it points for fun, though. 415/499-6387.

PLACES TO EAT

Coast Cafe: This is a very dog-friendly spot for breakfast, lunch, and dinner, beer, wine, and ice cream. "Dogs are great!" has been the mantra of more than one waiter we've met here through the years. Dogs can dine with you at the street tables and sometimes the patio tables (ask first). A bowl of water is available on request, and in the morning, a coffee kiosk sells dog biscuits. Yum! 46 Wharf Road; 415/868-2298.

Stinson Beach

It's fun to poke around Stinson, which is swarming with surfers and tourists on beautiful days. You'll find a relaxed attitude toward dogs at the outdoor snack-shop tables. Bolinas Lagoon, stretching along Highway 1 between Stinson Beach and Bolinas, is tempting but environmentally fragile, so you should picnic along the water only if your dog is controllable. You'll also be taking a chance with muddy paws in your car. Don't go near Audubon Canyon Ranch, where herons and egrets nest.

PARKS, BEACHES, AND RECREATION AREAS

36 Stinson Beach ("Dog Beach")

🐾 🐾 🐾 🐾 (See Marin County map on page 132)

Highway 1 to Stinson and Bolinas is worth the curves you'll negotiate. Don't be in a hurry. On sunny weekends, traffic will be heavy. Try it on a foggy day—it's otherworldly. Anyway, dogs often don't care whether or not the sun is shining.

Before setting out, we asked around. "Go to Stinson," said a friend. "There are dogs everywhere." "Dogs aren't allowed on Stinson Beach," said a Golden Gate National Recreation Area ranger. "Stinson is swarming with dogs," said another friend.

A kind woman in the Muir Woods bookstore solved the mystery. "No dogs on Stinson," she said sternly, "but there's this little part at the north end that isn't Stinson. We call it 'Dog Beach.'"

Indeed, the county-managed stretch where private houses are built at the north end does allow dogs on leash. This is itself a bit of a contradiction, because as you walk along with your obediently leashed dog, dogs who live in the houses lining the county stretch, and who don't have to wear leashes, come prancing out like the local law enforcement to check out the new kid. Leashed and leashless, dogs are indeed everywhere at Stinson. It's merry and there's plenty of room for them.

You and your dog will be equally happy on Stinson Beach, with its backdrop of low hills and lining of dunes. Keep the dog off the dunes where they're roped off, being "repaired" by the forces of nature. Dogs are allowed in Stinson Beach's picnic area by Eskoot Creek, a pretty setting redolent with tantalizing smells.

Take the beach turnoff from Highway 1. Turn right at the parking lot and park at the far north end. Walk right by the sign that says, "No Pets on Beach"—you can't avoid it—and turn right. Where the houses start is the county beach. You'll see a sign dividing the two jurisdictions saying, "End of Guarded Beach." 415/868-0942.

PLACES TO STAY

Beachtime Beach House: This wonderful three-bedroom vacation rental puts the "Oh!!!" in ocean views. It's right on the dog-friendly beach, with sand truly just in front of the house. (The owners try to keep it there, and not inside, which is why they have an outdoor shower and hose, plus slate tile floors and hardwood floors—no carpeting.) It's an airy, attractive house, with three decks, a hot tub on the back deck, a great fireplace stove in the living room, and windows with views that are beyond droolworthy. Rates are $280 per night, and $1,860–2,260 weekly. There's a $60 cleaning fee for the length of your stay. During winter you can rent the house on a monthly basis for a greatly reduced price. You'll get the address when you book the house. 415/383-7870; www.beachtime.org.

Redwoods Haus Bed and Breakfast: It's hard to categorize this place. It's funky, it's a little odd, it's clean, it's super-friendly, it's comfy, and it's cheap compared to most other West Marin lodgings. A very masculine boxer friend of Jake (a boxer dog, not the Muhammad Ali variety) stayed in what's called The Pink Room. With its pink bedspread, pink floral curtains, pink lamp, and other pink decorative touches and white girly furniture, it looks rather doll-housey. He didn't mind a bit, mostly because his people promised not to let anyone know that he stayed there. "Fergus would be so embarrassed," says Denise, his person. (Oops…Sorry, Fergus.)

Jake's favorite of the four guestrooms is The Crows Nest, which has soft but more masculine hues than The Pink Room, and sports excellent ocean views. It's the biggest room, too, with a queen bed, a day bed, and a queen futon.

Here's an example of the funky nature of the Redwoods Haus: "All rooms come with…access to our piano, acoustic guitars, video library, charcoal barbecue, biergarten, and buffet area," its literature announces. That's quite a combination of amenities. It continues, "Cats are OK—purrr. Dogs are OK—wooof."

Rooms come with breakfast. It's not gourmet, but with eggs, ham, cereal, fruit, bread, and beverages, it hits the spot. Rates are $55–165. The Redwood Haus is at 1 Belvedere Street (at Highway 1) 94970; 415/868-9828; www.stinson-beach.com.

Mill Valley

PARKS, BEACHES, AND RECREATION AREAS

37 Mount Tamalpais State Park

😽 😽 😽 (See Marin County map on page 132)

Generally, dogs are restricted to paved roads here. But dogs may stay in one of the campgrounds, and there are also a few spots near the summit where you can take your dog. The views from here are something you'll certainly appreciate on a clear day.

Stop for lunch at the Bootjack Picnic Area, west of the Mountain Home Inn on Panoramic Highway and about a quarter mile east of the turnoff to the summit, Pantoll Road. The tables are attractively sited on the hillside under oak trees. This picnic ground is an access point for the Bootjack Trail and Matt Davis Trail. The Matt Davis Trail is off-limits, but you and your dog may—howl-elujah!—use the 100 feet of Bootjack Trail that leads you into Marin Municipal Water District land, where leashed dogs are allowed. (You must travel north on the Bootjack Trail, though, not south; it's all state park in that direction.)

Heading northward, you can hook up with the Old Stage Fire Road and the Old Railroad Grade Fire Road, which are water district roads going almost the whole distance to the summit. You can also enter the Old Stage Fire Road right across from the Pantoll Ranger Station, at the intersection of Panoramic Highway and Pantoll Road. Pooches have special permission to cross the 100 feet or so of state park trail approaching water district trail.

The Bootjack Picnic Area parking lot charges $6 to park. (Once you pay in any state park lot, your receipt is good for any other spot that you hit that day.) The park has 16 developed walk-in campsites that allow dogs. They're at the Pantoll Station Campground. Sites are $15. All sites are first-come, first-served. 415/388-2070.

38 Mount Tamalpais Summit

😽 😽 😽 (See Marin County map on page 132)

The summit of Mt. Tam is worth the $6 fee that you're charged merely to drive here. But in addition to appreciating the magnificent views, you may also take your dog on one trail up here.

You'll find a small refreshment stand, restrooms, a visitor center, and viewing platforms. On clear days, you can see nine counties, whether you want to or not. In summer, white fingers of fog obscure a good part of your view as they creep between the "knuckles" of Marin's ridges.

It's too bad if your leashed dog doesn't care about views. But he will take eagerly to the smoothly paved Verna Dunshee Trail, about one mile long, running almost level around the summit. About three-quarters of this trail is also wheelchair-accessible.

From U.S. 101, take the Stinson Beach/Highway 1 exit. Follow Highway 1 to Panoramic Highway, which will be a right turn. Continue on Panoramic to the right turnoff to Pantoll Road; Pantoll soon becomes East Ridgecrest Road and goes to the summit, and then loops back for your trip down. 415/945-1455.

39 Mount Tamalpais–Marin Municipal Water District Land

🐾🐾🐾 (See Marin County map on page 132)

Your very best bet for a dog walk high on the mountain is to find one of the water district fire roads near the summit. Your dog must be leashed, but at least she can go on the trails with you, and you both can experience the greenness of this wonderful mountain. At this elevation, the green comes from chaparral, pine, and madrone.

Just below the summit on East Ridgecrest Boulevard, watch for the water district's gate and sign. This is the Old Railroad Grade Fire Road, which descends 1,785 feet from the entry point just west of the summit. On the way it intersects Old Stage Fire Road, then emerges at the Bootjack Picnic Area. En route, you'll cross three creeks. For obvious reasons, you'll be happier in warm weather taking this road down, not up; get someone to meet you in a car at the Bootjack Picnic Area.

Another spot to pick up a water district trail is off Panoramic Highway just west of the Mountain Home Inn. Look for the Marin Municipal Water District sign by the fire station. Park at the state park parking lot west of Mountain Home Inn and walk east along this fire road, called Gravity Car Road (though it's unmarked), through mixed pines, redwoods, fir, madrone, and scrub. Keep your eyes open for fast-moving mountain bikes. 415/945-1400.

40 Old Mill Park

🐾🐾🐾 (See Marin County map on page 132)

Refresh your dog under cool redwoods right in the town of Mill Valley. The old mill, built in 1834, was recently restored. A wooden bridge over Old Mill Creek leads to well-maintained paths that run along the creek. The creek is dog-accessible, though pooches are supposed to be leashed.

One picnic table here sits within the hugest "fairy ring" we've ever seen— 40 feet across. Boy dogs like to imagine the size of the mother tree whose stump engendered this ring of saplings. The park is on Throckmorton Avenue at Olive Street, near the public library. 415/383-1370.

41 Camino Alto Open Space Preserve

🐾🐾🐾🐕 (See Marin County map on page 132)

In this accessible open space, your dog may run free on a wide fire trail along a ridge connecting with Mt. Tamalpais. You'll walk through bay laurels, madrones, and chaparral, looking down on soaring vultures and the bay, Highway 1, the hills, and the headlands. A small imperfection is that you can hear the whoosh of traffic. Just pretend it's the wind. Dogs must be leashed on the regular hiking trails here. Park at the end of Escalon Drive, just west of Camino Alto. 415/499-6387.

42 Bayfront Park

🐾🐾🐾🐾 🐕 (See Marin County map on page 132)

This good-looking park is well designed for every kind of family activity and for dogs. It has an exercise course, lawns are green and silky, and picnic areas are clean and attractive. The multiuse trails for bicycles, strollers, and what-not may be used only by leashed dogs (there are bikes galore). But here's the canine payoff: It has a special dog run next to an estuary, where dogs are free to dip their paws.

The dog-use area starts where you see the signs and all the other dogs. Beware, owners of escape artists: The area is a big three acres, but it's not fenced. No scoops or water are furnished, but the Richardson Bay Estuary is right there to jump into.

At the end of the run there's even a marsh that dogs can explore, if you're willing to put a very mucky friend back into the car with you. Luckily, this marsh is all organic muck, free from the dangerous trash that fills many unprotected bay marshes.

For a dog park, this one offers an unparalleled view of Mt. Tam. Horses and bikes pass by harmlessly on their own separate trail in the foreground, and mockingbirds sing in the bushes.

There had been a heap o' controversy over whether this should continue to be a dog-run area. Some people thought soccer players of the young human persuasion should have the area, and that dogs should have to be leashed. But hooray, the dogs won! The city council approved a permanent dog run here. That's thanks to the work of a magnificent, high-energy group called Park People and Dogs. If you want to find out how you can help Park People and Dogs in its continuing efforts to make this park dog heaven, call Barbara Berlenbach at 415/388-0071. Unfortunately, Barbara tells us that there's been more friction between dog people and nondog people of late. She implores dog-park users to keep dogs on leash until they get to the off-leash area, and to be certain to scoop the poop.

The parking lot is on Sycamore Avenue, just after you cross Camino Alto, next to the wastewater treatment plant. Keep your dog leashed near the steep-sided sewage ponds; dogs have drowned in them. Also, be sure to keep your dog leashed until you've reached the grassy dog-run area; there's a $50 ticket if you're caught unleashed. 415/383-1370.

PLACES TO STAY

Mount Tamalpais State Park: See Mount Tamalpais State Park, above, for camping information.

Corte Madera

Dogs are banned from all parks here. But mope not, pooches, because at least you get to munch on café cuisine.

PLACES TO EAT

Book Passage Cafe: Whether your dog is illiterate or erudite, he's welcome to join you at the many shaded tables outside this bookstore/café. You can dine on sandwiches, muffins, and a few assorted hot entrées, as well as tasty coffees and healthful smoothies. Dogs aren't allowed inside the bookstore, so if you want to peruse (and who wouldn't—the bookstore is one of the best we've seen), bring a friend and take turns dog-sitting. 51 Tamal Vista Boulevard; 415/927-1503.

Twin Cities Market: Pick up a fresh deli sandwich (with your dog's favorite cold cuts, of course) and eat it with your pooch at the three tables outside. It's casual, but that's how most dogs like it. 118 Corte Madera Avenue; 415/924-7372.

PLACES TO STAY

Marin Suites Hotel: The guest accommodations here are mostly of the spacious suite variety, which works out great when traveling with a dog. (Too bad your dog has to be small to stay here. The rule is 20 pounds or less. Spacious suites call for spacious dogs, in my opinion.) You'll get a fully equipped kitchen and separate living room and bedroom. Traditional hotel rooms, with kitchenettes, are also available. Rates are $154–204. Dogs are $10 extra. 45 Tamal Vista Boulevard, Corte Madera, CA 94925; 415/924-3608 or 800/362-3372; www.marinsuites.com.

Tiburon

The town of Tiburon is almost too Disneyland-perfect, with its green lawns and fountains, brick sidewalks, and lack of smells. On a sunny day you can't beat the clean, safe street atmosphere for eating and strolling. Dogs, of course, must be as polite and well behaved as their owners. Tiburon did a good job of planning for parking: There's almost none except for one large lot with reasonable prices, which means that cars aren't driving around searching for a spot. Just give up and park there.

PARKS, BEACHES, AND RECREATION AREAS

43 Richardson Bay Park

🐾🐾🐾 (See Marin County map on page 132)

Generally known as the Tiburon Bike Path, this is a terrific multiuse park, unusual because it can be safely enjoyed by both bicyclists and dogs. It stretches two-thirds the length of Tiburon's peninsula and has parking at both ends. The larger lot is at the northern end. A dirt road, Brunini Way (no vehicles), leads into the park at the north end. You'll find a quiet, natural bay shoreline with a bit of marsh. There's some flotsam and jetsam, but only the highest quality, of course.

Keep walking and you'll enter McKegney Green, the wide bike path that runs for two miles along Tiburon Boulevard toward downtown. (It doesn't go all the way, though.) Your dog must be leashed. The path, marked for running trainers, swings past benches overlooking the bay and a kids' jungle gym.

Soon the path splits and goes past both sides of a stretch of soccer fields, fenced wildlife ponds (no dogs), and a parcourse fitness trail. You can take your dog on either side, but be aware that bicyclists use both. You'll also share this path, on a fair weekend day, with roller skaters and parents pushing strollers. On the green are sunbathers and kite fliers.

The view: Mt. Tamalpais and Belvedere, with the Bay Bridge, San Francisco, and the Golden Gate Bridge peeking out from behind. Bring a jacket—it can be breezy here—and carry water for your dog if you're walking far. The only fountains are for people. Going toward town on Tiburon Boulevard, turn right at the sign that says Blackie's Pasture Road. It leads to the parking lot. 415/435-7373.

PLACES TO EAT

Boudins Bakery: Dine on delectable baked goods and café food at the four outdoor tables here. Dogs get water. 221 Main Street; 415/913-1849.

Paradise Hamburgers and Ice Cream: This place furnishes bike racks and lots of outdoor tables. There's always a Fido bowl of water outside the door. The owners adore dogs and occasionally give a pooch a special treat. 1694 Tiburon Boulevard; 415/435-8823.

Muir Beach

PARKS, BEACHES, AND RECREATION AREAS

44 Muir Beach

🐾🐾🐾🐾 (See Marin County map on page 132)

This beach is small, but a real gem, with rugged sand dunes spotted with plants, a parking lot and large picnic area, a small lagoon with tules, and its share of wind. Redwood Creek empties into the ocean here.

You can reach Muir Beach the long way, hiking about five miles from the Marin Headlands Visitors Center (see Rodeo Beach and Lagoon in the Sausalito section), or the easy way, via Highway 1. From Highway 1, watch for the turnoff for the beach. 415/388-2596.

Sausalito

Even if you live here, you should play tourist and stroll around Sausalito's harbor in the brilliant sea light (or luminous sea fog). On weekends, it's especially pleasant early in the day, before the ferries disgorge their passengers. The city's attitude toward dogs is relaxed. It's the perfect place to stop and sniff around for awhile. If you have your sea legs, board the Blue and Gold Fleet's ferry. You and your dog can go from Sausalito to San Francisco for a mere $7.25. That's cheaper than admission to a bad movie, and there are no commercials.

PARKS, BEACHES, AND RECREATION AREAS

45 Dunphy Park

🐾🐾🐾 (See Marin County map on page 132)

This is a small but accessible park by the bay, and it comes complete with grass, willows, picnic tables, and a volleyball court. Best of all, there's a small beach, and canine swimming is fine. You can watch sailing and sailboarding from here, too. Dogs officially must be on leash. The parking lot is at Bridgeway and Bee Streets. 415/289-4100.

46 Remington Dog Park

🐾🐾🐾🐾🐾 (See Marin County map on page 132)

Your leash-free dog can exercise his paws while you both exercise your social skills at this delightful park. Remington Park is named after the dog whose owner, Dianne Chute, helped raise the money to put the park together a few years back. It's more than an acre, all fenced, on a grassy slope with trees. Dogs have the time of their lives tearing around chasing each other, and

DIVERSION

Seize the Bay from Sausalito: Ahoy, dogs, if you love the Bay, then *carpe diem* and take a ride on a **Blue and Gold Fleet** ferry. Lucky dogs get to sail from Sausalito to San Francisco and Tiburon. The one-way fare from Sausalito to San Francisco is $7.25. Dogs pay nothing. The Sausalito ferry dock is at the foot of El Portal, east of Bridgeway. Phone 415/705-8200 for schedules and more information, or 415/705-5555 for tickets; www.blueandgoldfleet.com.

humans have a great time chatting. The park comes complete with an informative bulletin board, a leash rack, benches, poop bags, and water. It even has a tent you can hide under in foul weather! Everything is cozy here.

Best of all, on Friday evening, about 100 human patrons and their dogs gather for cocktail hour, with wine, cheese, bread, and of course, doggy treats. It sounds very Marin, but it's really just very civilized. On a recent summer evening, the park was host to a Mexican happy hour. Margaritas, chips, and salsa made the atmosphere even more festive than the usual Friday night gathering.

From the day it was finished, Remington and his dog friends have made terrific use of this place. "It's the social hub of Sausalito," says cartoonist Phil Frank, "where the elite with four feet meet." What a boon to freedom-loving Sausalito dogs, who otherwise must be leashed everywhere in town.

From U.S. 101, take the Sausalito/Marin City exit, driving west to Bridgeway. Turn right on Bridgeway and drive south the equivalent of a long city block. Turn right at Ebbtide Avenue and park in the large lot at the end of Ebbtide.

47 Rodeo Beach and Lagoon

🐾🐾🐾🐾 (See Marin County map on page 132)

Rodeo Beach is small but majestic, made of the dark sand common in Marin. Large rocks on shore are covered with "whitewash," birders' polite name for guano. Voice-controlled dogs used to be able to go off leash here, but no more. Leashes are now mandatory. Water dogs enjoy this beach, but letting your dog swim in Marin County surf is always risky—currents are strong, and trying to rescue a dog who is being swept away is to risk your own life. With that mandatory leash, he probably won't be doing the pooch paddle anyway. Don't turn your back on the surf here. Especially in winter, a "sneaker" wave can sweep you and your dog away.

If your dog promises not to bark and disturb wildlife, he can join you on an interesting walk around Rodeo Lagoon. The lagoon is lined with tules and pickleweed. Ocean water splashes into the lagoon in winter and rainfall swells it until it overflows, continually mixing salt and fresh water. Birds love this fecund lagoon. It can be almost too much for a bird dog to take. An attractive wooden walkway leads across the lagoon to the beach.

From the Marin Headlands Visitors Center, follow the signs west. 415/331-1540.

48 Marin Headlands Trails

🐾🐾🐾🐾 (See Marin County map on page 132)

From Rodeo Beach (above), you can circle the lagoon or head up into the hills, as long as your pooch is leashed. You're in for a gorgeous walk—or a gorgeous and challenging walk, depending on the weather. Look at a map of the Bay Area, and it will be obvious why the headlands' trees all grow at an eastward slant. In summer especially, cold ocean air funnels through the Golden Gate, sucked in by the Central Valley's heat—chilling the headlands and the inhabitants of western San Francisco with fog and wind. The Bay Area may be "air-conditioned by God," but the headlands sit right at the air inflow, and it's set on "high." Never come here without at least one jacket.

Your dog will love the wind. The combination of fishy breeze and aromatic brush from the hillsides sends many into olfactory ecstasy. What looks from a distance like green fuzz on these headlands is a profusion of wildflowers and low brush. Indian paintbrush, hemlock, sticky monkeyflower, ferns, dock,

morning glory, blackberry, sage, and thousands more species grow here—even some stunted but effective poison oak on the windward sides. (On the lee of the hills, it's not stunted.) Groves of eucalyptus grow on the crests. You hear a lovely low rustle and roar of wind, surf, birds, and insects—and the squeak and groan of eucalyptuses rubbing against each other. Pinch some sage between your fingers and sniff; if you can ever leave California again after that, you're a strong person.

From the beach and lagoon, you can hike the circle formed by the Miwuk Trail starting at the eastern end of the lagoon, meeting the Wolf Ridge Trail, then meeting the Coastal Trail (à la the Pacific Coast Trail), back to where you started. Or you can pick up the Coastal Trail off Bunker Road near Rodeo Beach. Look for the trailhead signs.

Sights along these trails include World War II gun emplacements, the Golden Gate Bridge, and San Francisco. As the trail rises and falls, you will discover a blessing: You'll be intermittently sheltered from the wind, and in these pockets, if the sun warms your back, you'll think you've died and gone to heaven.

Dogs used to be able to legally run off leash on most of these trails, but no longer. The Golden Gate National Recreation Area (GGNRA), which oversees this 12,000-acre chunk of heaven, has become much stricter of late. The "company" line now is that all dogs must be leashed on all Marin GGNRA lands. It's a howling shame.

If you want to hike from Rodeo Beach to Muir Beach (see the Muir Beach section), remember that dogs have to be leashed the entire way now. And sadly, once you get there, leashes are also now the law. This is tick country, so search carefully when you get home. 415/331-1540.

PLACES TO EAT

Just a few of Sausalito's pooch-friendly restaurants:

Fish: This new eatery on the Sausalito waterfront is one of the most fun restaurants around. The fish is fresh, the harborside tables are to drool for, and the servers love dogs. Dogs get big bowls of water and samples of dog treats made with salmon! If your dog likes the treats (and she will), you can buy them here. The website is worth checking out: It's www.331fish.com. You can get the latest fish news and local bay and ocean-related activity schedules there, too. You can even click on the "fish.cam" to see what's happening at the restaurant at any given minute. What we especially love about the restaurant's location is that it's next to a dog-friendly point of land at Clipper Yacht Harbor. You'll see the Mutt Mitt dispenser. Dogs enjoy the bay views and the scents and sounds of the nearby harbor seals. The restaurant is at 350 Harbor Drive; 415/331-FISH (415/331-3474).

Scoma's: Want fresh salmon and a magnificent view of the bay? Come to this waterfront eatery and dine with your dog on the deck. 588 Bridgeway; 415/332-9551.

Tommy's Wok: This fun Chinese restaurant is just a bone's throw from Remington Park, so it's a great place to dine after your dog burns up all his energy. The food is delicious, leaning more toward Szechuan dishes, but accommodating Cantonese-loving palates as well. Dine with your good doggy at the four outdoor tables. 3001 Bridgeway; 415/332-5818.

Treviso Restaurant: Dogs can join you at the four sidewalk tables at this lovely restaurant that serves delectable Mediterranean cuisine. 39 Caledonia Street; 415/332-4500.

Winship's Restaurant: Dogs like coming to the two outdoor tables here for a big breakfast, but the fare later in the day is good, too. It's the usual tasty soup, salad, sandwich, pasta menu, but this stuff always tastes even better with your dog at your side. 670 Bridgeway; 415/332-1454.

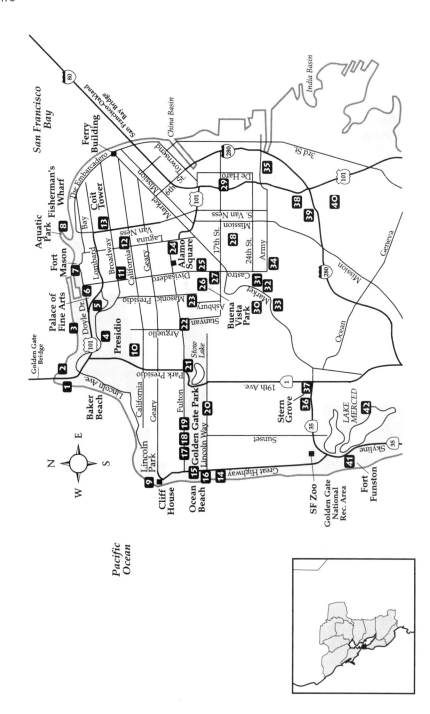

DING! DING!

CHAPTER 7

San Francisco County

For the first three editions of this book, I described San Francisco as being "possibly the most dog-friendly large city on earth." Then the last edition saw Joe Dog weeping into his kibble because of the threats to the oodles of leash-free parks here. But with the fifth edition, life is looking brighter for San Francisco dogs. All of the threatened leash-free areas managed by the city are up and running again, and the city has more leash-free areas than ever. (Dear old Joe went to Dog Heaven—where the cats are slow and all parks are leash-free—before this good news. But he still managed to have one doggone great off-leash life on earth.)

The situation with the formerly off-leash Golden Gate National Recreation Area parklands isn't quite so rosy, but there is some hope. (See the introduction to the Parks, Beaches, and Recreation Areas section for more details on these developments.)

Even with all the roller-coaster events surrounding leash-free areas here, other city attractions have always made dogs feel at home. (Look at Jake Dog. He feels so at home here. Oh, that's right. San Francisco is his home.)

PICK OF THE LITTER—SAN FRANCISCO COUNTY

OFF-LEASH PARK WITH BEST VIEWS
Buena Vista Park (page 187)

PARKS POOCHES ARE PRAYING FOR
Crissy Field (page 175)
Fort Funston (pages 194–195)

CREAMIEST CANINE CANNOLI
Bella and Daisy's (page 196)

MOST DOG-FRIENDLY PLACE TO EAT
Cool Beans (page 197)

MOST DOG-FRIENDLY PLACES TO STAY
Hotel Cosmo (page 204)
Hotel Monaco (pages 204–205)
Hotel Palomar (page 206)
Westin St. Francis (page 209)

BEST WALK WITH/AS A TOURIST
Golden Gate Bridge walk (page 174)

BEST RIDES
Blue and Gold Fleet ferries (page 179)
San Francisco cable cars (page 198)

BEST DAYS TO HAVE A BALL
San Francisco Giants' Dog Days of Summer (page 189)
Bark and Whine Ball (page 197)

No public transportation anywhere compares with San Francisco's, where canines can ride cable cars, streetcars, ferries, and buses. And the finest hotels here permit dogs, as do some of the most popular tourist spots, including Fisherman's Wharf and the Golden Gate Bridge.

Now if we can just get the GGNRA lands to be legally leash-free again, San Francisco will once more be an unparalleled urban paradise for pooches and their people. It would make Joe proud.

San Francisco

San Francisco is the only city in San Francisco County. When you have a city like this, who could ask for anything more?

PARKS, BEACHES, AND RECREATION AREAS

As I mentioned in the beginning of the chapter, the situation with city parks is back on track. This is excellent news for dogs who live here, and for tourist dogs, too. Some dog people would like to see even broader access to city parks. If you would too, contact SFDOG (San Francisco Dog Owner's Group; www.sfdog.org), whose support, in part, is to thank for keeping access to city parks.

The wonderful GGNRA beaches and parks, which had been off-leash heaven on earth until a few years ago, are still sporting signs that say, "Pets on Leash" with a symbol of such underneath (the latter is obviously for dogs who can't read). This is a huge blow to any dog who has ever had the pleasure of running around some of the nation's finest leash-free lands. This sweeping ban on leashless recreation includes the magnificent Fort Funston, Crissy Field, Land's End, Ocean Beach, the Presidio, and Baker Beach. I won't spend time on the reasons in this edition. Suffice it to say that the GGNRA is part of the National Park Service, which maintains a not-so-dog-friendly policy, and that the leash-free lifestyle of GGNRA lands came to the attention of the NPS.

At press time, the GGNRA had received the OK from a federal panel to enter an assessment phase to help determine the leash-free future of its lands. The GGNRA has handed over control of the process to an environmental conflict-resolution organization. User groups from all walks of life—dog people, bikers, equestrians, parents, and environmentalists—will be interviewed during an evaluation phase called negotiated rule-making. It's the beginning of a long and complex process. It could take years before the fate of dogs on GGNRA parklands is determined.

Meanwhile, if you visit GGNRA parks, you may still see other dogs running sans leash. But their people are playing ranger roulette. Citations are inevitable in the areas that had been popular off-leash spots. Legally, dogs are to be leashed until a ruling changes things. Citations start at $50 per pooch. We know a few pups whose people had received tickets at Fort Funston and Ocean Beach. My dog scouts tell me that Crissy Field is the area that's been hardest hit with tickets.

For updates or to find out what you can do to help win back the leash-free lifestyle, go to the SFDOG website, www.sfdog.org. For official updates, check out the GGNRA's website at www.nps.gov/goga. The main page will provide a link to the dog issues pages. You can also phone the GGNRA dog-policy liaisons at 415/561-4732.

DIVERSION

Saunter Across the Golden Gate: Like their people, dogs are thrilled to walk San Francisco's most famous landmark, spanning 1.9 miles from the city to Marin County. It's open 5 A.M.–9 P.M. daily to human and canine pedestrians, no fee.

The **Golden Gate Bridge** folks ask only that 1) if your dog can't contain his excitement over the views, you *please* pick up his poop. (Even if he's not so keen on the scenery and does his number, you'll need to scoop); and 2) your dog wear a leash. You both probably will want to wear sweaters, too—it can be a little nippy when making your way across.

You'll find vista points with parking lots on the northeast (Marin County) and southeast (San Francisco) sides of the bridge. These are the best embarkation points for your walk. The San Francisco side has meters that charge $.25 for 15 minutes. On the Marin side you can park for free for up to four hours. (Ah, but they get you with the $5 bridge toll when you come back to the city.) For more info, call 415/921-5858.

1 Baker Beach

🐾🐾🐾🐾 (See San Francisco County map on page 170)

This beach brings your dog almost within a bone's throw of the Golden Gate Bridge. And what a sight it is. Though in summer you shouldn't hold out much hope for a sunny day here, this sandy shoreline is ideal for a romp in the misty air. And dogs really appreciate Baker Beach in the summer. It's almost always cool and breezy.

If you like to sunbathe without a bathing suit and want to take your dog along, the very north end of the beach (closest to the bridge) is perfect. It's the only official nude beach in Northern California where dogs are welcome. But just make sure he doesn't get too up close and personal with your exposed cobathers.

The south end is also intriguing, with trails meandering through wooded areas and lots of picnic tables for leisurely lunches. Battery Chamberlain, with its 95,000-pound cannon aimed toward the sea, looms nearby.

Leashes have become the law here, but we're hopeful this could change. From either direction, take Lincoln Boulevard to Bowley Street, and then make the first turn into the two parking lots. 415/556-8371.

🐾 Fort Point National Historical Site

🐾🐾 (See San Francisco County map on page 170)

Beneath the Golden Gate Bridge, this mid–19th-century brick fortification stands as a reminder of the strategic military significance San Francisco once had. Now it serves as a tourist attraction and one of the best places to view the skyline, Alcatraz, and the bridge. It's also a magnificent spot for your dog to stand mesmerized by the crashing surf.

By itself, Fort Point doesn't offer much for dogs. They must be leashed and there's only a small patch of grass. We recommend Fort Point as the goal of a long hike that starts at Crissy Field. On this jaunt, you'll come to an old pier. There are actually two piers, but the one you're allowed on is closer to the bridge. Stroll to the end for a close-up view of sailboats being tossed about on the bay. When you finally reach Fort Point, it's a tradition among dog people to continue to the westernmost point and touch the fence. There's no telling why, but you may as well try it.

To get to Fort Point without a long hike, follow the signs from Lincoln Avenue as you approach the Golden Gate Bridge. 415/556-8371.

🐾 Crissy Field

🐾🐾🐾🐾 (See San Francisco County map on page 170)

There's nothing quite like Crissy Field at sunset. As the orange sun disappears behind the Golden Gate Bridge, you'll be viewing one of the most stunning blends of natural and man-made wonders in the world.

Crissy Field, part of the Golden Gate National Recreation Area, is a jewel of a park any time of day. In the past, and perhaps one day again, obedient, leash-free dogs could chase and cavort up and down the beach and jump into the bay whenever they feel like it. But as with other GGNRA lands, leashes are now the law here. (Please see the intro to the Parks, Beaches, and Recreation Areas section for more on this situation.) Rangers do routinely patrol the area and aren't shy about issuing citations.

Leashed or not, your dog will find the views here are to drool for. As you walk westward, you'll see the Golden Gate Bridge before you, Alcatraz and bits of the city skyline behind you. Sailboats sometimes glide so close you can hear the sails flapping in the wind. A newly restored 20-acre marsh lends a satisfying air of swampiness. (For more than $25 million, it should lend something.)

Enter on Mason Street in the Marina district and drive past the warehouses. Go right on Mitchell Street and through the parking lot. If you go too far to the east, you'll run into a sea of sailboarders, so try starting your walk close to the western edge of the parking lot. The beach is bordered by delicate dunes that are undergoing restoration in many places, including the entrance, so keep canines off. 415/556-8371.

DIVERSION

Take Me out to the Ballgame: Can't make it to the San Francisco Giants' Dog Days of Summer? Try a stroll around the outside of SBC Park. A wide promenade flanks right field along **McCovey Cove.** At game time, you and the pooch can get a dog's-eye view of the game alongside other nonticketed folks.

Or make a day of it and walk the entire waterfront of San Francisco with your dog from here. Head west along the promenade, which turns into a sidewalk. You'll come to a grassy marina, complete with a poop-bag station. Continuing west, you'll pass the Embarcadero, Fisherman's Wharf, the Marina District, and, finally, beautiful Crissy Field. Keep walking west and you'll be under the Golden Gate Bridge. SBC Park is at 24 Willie Mays Plaza. Call 415/972-2000 or visit the SF Giants' website: www.sfgiants.com.

🐾 Presidio National Park

🐾🐾🐾🐾 (See San Francisco County map on page 170)

Dogs and their people like to pretend that the Presidio is their very own country estate, complete with acre after rolling acre (1,480 in all!) of secret pathways, open meadows, and dense groves of eucalyptus and pine. It's truly a magnificent spread.

Now that the Presidio is a park, and not a military base, it's expected to draw more visitors than either Yosemite or Yellowstone National Parks. But there are still some out-of-the-way areas that even the most adventurous tourists will have a difficult time finding. A fun tour starts when you park at the golf course parking lot just inside the Arguello Boulevard gate. Cross the street (carefully—it can get busy on this road), and follow the path down the hill. It will quickly widen and loop past wildflowers and seasonal sweet peas. Bear left at the first major fork and hike through a thick forest area, then bear right when that path gives you a choice. You'll hike up and down a gentle sequence of hills. Pull over and enjoy the larger hills to the west. Dogs thrill at dragging their people up and down them for no apparent reason. You'll run into a few more side trails along the way.

A more tame walk starts to the west of the playground on West Pacific Avenue. Again enter on Arguello, but immediately bear right. Parking will be on your right on the bottom of the hill. Cross the street and you'll see a plastic-bag dispenser for scooping the poop. That's where you want to start.

Leashes are now the law throughout the Presidio, but at some point, this could change so that at least some of segments are once again their good old leash-free selves. (Please see the intro the Parks, Beaches, and Recreation Areas section for more on this situation.) 415/556-8371.

5 Palace of Fine Arts

🐾🐾🐾 (See San Francisco County map on page 170)

The glory of ancient Rome embraces you even as you approach this relic of the 1915 Panama-Pacific Exposition. From the huge colonnaded rotunda to the serene reflecting pool, the place drips with Romanesque splendor.

The Palace is especially grand under its night lighting. It's also an ideal place to take your dog while the kids go to the Exploratorium inside. Walk around the paved path that winds through the grand columns and around the pond. But keep your eyes peeled for people feeding the multitudes of pigeons, ducks, and geese. Dogs like to break up the feeding frenzy with an abrupt tug on the mandatory leash. Feathers fly and dried bread scatters everywhere.

The best place to enter for the full Roman effect is on Baker Street, between North Point and Jefferson Streets. Dogs are not allowed inside the buildings, although Joe did sneak into the Exploratorium one fine afternoon. (It's a long story.) He got as far as the tornado demonstration machine when he was nabbed and whisked away. 415/831-2700.

6 Marina Green

🐾🐾🐾 (See San Francisco County map on page 170)

The clang of halyards against masts creates a magical symphony from the nearby marinas here on windy days. Your dog's first reaction may be a puzzled 30-degree head tilt.

Most of us know the Marina Green for its high-flying kites and hard-running joggers. But it's also a decent place to take your dog, as long as he's leashed. It's too close to the rush of cars on Marina Boulevard to be comfortable off leash, anyway.

The grass is always green here, as the park's name indicates. It's a treat for eyes overdosed on dry yellow grass and paws laden with foxtails. There's also an attractive heart parcourse fitness trail and a great view of Alcatraz.

Enter on Marina Boulevard, anywhere between Scott and Buchanan Streets. 415/556-0560.

7 Fort Mason

🐾🐾🐾 (See San Francisco County map on page 170)

This park, perched high above the bay, is full of surprises. Depending on the disposition of your dog, some of the surprises are great fun. One can be downright frightening.

The best stands right in the middle of the wide-open field that constitutes the main part of the park. It's a fire hydrant, and it sticks out like a sore yellow thumb from its flat green surroundings. Joyous male dogs bound up and pay it homage time and time again.

The object that seems to take dogs aback, although people find it riveting, is a gigantic bronze statue of Phillip Burton, who helped secure the national park system, including the GGNRA. Several feet taller and broader than life (although even when alive, Burton was larger than life), with outstretched hand, it can send a dog fleeing as far as his mandatory leash will allow.

Lower Fort Mason is also interesting to investigate. You can walk alongside the piers and sniff the bay, or peer at the liberty ship *Jeremiah O'Brien.*

Enter the lower Fort Mason parking lot at Buchanan Street and take the stairs all the way up to upper Fort Mason. (Huff, puff.) Or park along Bay Street or Laguna Street and walk in. 415/556-0560.

🐾 Aquatic Park

 (See San Francisco County map on page 170)

You've got tourist friends in town and don't feel like taking them for the usual amble through Fisherman's Wharf? Here's a great plan that lets you be semi-sporting about the whole thing while you take your dog for a jaunt. Drop off your friends at Aquatic Park, point them toward the tourist attractions, and walk your dog right there.

Aquatic Park is just a few minutes from Ghirardelli Square, Fisherman's Wharf, a cable-car line, and the Hyde Street Pier. It's also a decent place for a leashed dog to romp, with its large grassy field and plenty of pine trees, benches, and flowers. But stay away from the little beach—dogs aren't allowed. If you feel like shopping for T-shirts, jewelry, or arts and crafts, you can take your dog along Beach Street, where dozens of sidewalk vendors sell their wares (see the Diversion These Stores Are for the Dogs!).

The park is on Beach Street between Hyde and Polk Streets. 415/556-8371.

🐾 Land's End/Lincoln Park

(See San Francisco County map on page 170)

This is probably the most spectacular park in San Francisco. You won't believe your eyes and your leashed dog won't believe his nose. And neither of you will believe your ears—it's so far removed from traffic that all you hear are foghorns, the calls of birds, and the wind whistling through the pines and eucalyptus.

The towering cliffs, high above the crashing tide below, overlook virtually no civilization. For miles, all you can see is ocean, cliffs, trees, wildflowers, and boats. It looks more like Mendocino did 100 years ago—at least until you round one final bend and the Golden Gate Bridge jars your senses back to semiurban reality.

If you want to venture the entire length of the dirt trail, keep two things in mind: 1) Don't wear tight pants—you'll have to do some high stepping in some spots, and you don't want your legs packed into your Levi's; and 2) don't bring a young puppy or an out-of-control dog. The cliffs here can be dangerous, especially where the trail becomes narrow.

There are many entrance points, but we like to start from the parking lot at

DIVERSION

Seize the Bay: Salty sea dogs wag their tails hard and fast when they learn that the **Blue and Gold Fleet** ferry system permits pooches on most of its runs. That means well-behaved, leashed dogs can go by ferry from San Francisco to all these destinations: Sausalito, Tiburon, Oakland, Alameda, and Vallejo. And they don't have to pay a dime! Just two places are forbidden: Angel Island and Alcatraz, both state parks that don't allow dogs.

Most dogs are enraptured when cruising on the bay. Jake the yellow Lab is a huge fan of ferrydom. He's in ecstasy when his ears flap in the chilly, fishy breeze, his eyes slightly shut as his nose greedily takes in the scents of the bay. (This is in huge contrast to poor ol' Joe, the landlubbing Airedale, who would turn green at the gills at even the sight of a boat.)

Fares range $5.25–9.50 one-way for adults, depending on your destination. Jake's favorite trip, from San Francisco to Sausalito, is $7.25 one-way. From San Francisco, the ferry leaves from Pier 41, just west of the dog-friendly tourist attraction Pier 39, in the Fisherman's Wharf area. Some routes also leave from the Ferry Building, at Market and Embarcadero Streets. Phone 415/705-8200 for schedules and more information, or 415/705-5555 for tickets; www.blueandgoldfleet.com.

---

the end of Camino del Mar. Go down the wooden steps to the wide dirt trail and turn right. As you hike, you'll come to occasional wood benches overlooking wildly beautiful seascapes. Take a moment to sit down. Your dog will appreciate the chance to contemplate the wondrous odors coming through her bulbous olfactory sensor.

As you continue, you'll pass a sign that makes its point efficiently and effectively: "Caution! Cliff and surf are extremely dangerous. People have been swept from the rocks and drowned." You'll have no problem if you proceed on the main trail and ignore the temptation to follow the dozens of tiny paths down the cliff face. (Naked men often hang out at a beach or two down there, so if your dog blushes easily, you'll have extra reason to stay on the wider paths.) A new, very long wooden stairway leads from the main path all the way down to a beautiful rock-strewn beach with great views of the Golden Gate. The trip down is worth the rather vigorous hike back up.

Leashes are now the law here, but in the future, this could change so that Lands End one day returns to its glorious leash-free self. (Please see the intro to the Parks, Beaches, and Recreation Areas section for more on this situation.)

A very convenient entry point is at the parking lot on Point Lobos (which is what Geary Street turns into toward the ocean) just above the Cliff House

DIVERSION

These Stores Are for the Dogs!: Dogs who enjoy shopping with their people love San Francisco. Following are a few of the more pooch-friendly retail spots for the leashed and well-behaved.

Beach Street: This isn't a store but a kind of outdoor tourist market where you can shop for baubles, bangles, and T-shirts with your leashed dog at any of dozens of little stands up and down this Fisherman's Wharf area street. The bulk of the stands on Beach Street are between Hyde and Polk Streets.

Neiman Marcus: Even jaded dogs can be agog when they visit this upscale store's beautiful atrium lobby. 150 Stockton Street; 415/362-3900.

Saks Fifth Avenue: Keep your dog under tight rein and she's welcome here. 384 Post Street; 415/986-4300.

Wilkes Bashford Company: Pooches of any size are welcome to peruse this upscale, Union Square store (it's to drool for), as long as they're clean and don't conduct any dog business. "I'm a nut about dogs," says Wilkes Bashford, the store's owner. "Dogs are a vital part of life." And he says all the dogs who've visited his store have been very well behaved. Bashford has been bringing his dogs to the store since 1968. Little Callie goes to work with Bashford just about every day. And even when Bashford is out of town on business, Callie makes her rounds at the store. Bashford's driver takes her there in the morning and drives her home in the afternoon. 375 Sutter Street; 415/986-4380.

and Louie's. But we like to park in the lot at the end of Camino del Mar, a little street just above that lot. You'll pass a sign for Fort Miley on your right just after you enter Camino del Mar. Leashed dogs are allowed on this large patch of trees on a hill, and the views are stunning. It's a good place to visit to get away from the weekend crowds who can descend on Land's End. 415/556-8371.

🔟 Mountain Lake Park

 (See San Francisco County map on page 170)

In this sociable park, your dog can cavort with other dogs while you shoot the breeze with other dog people. The off-leash area is between two signs on the east side of the park. You'll find a bench for humans and a pretty good safety net of trees and grass between dogs and the outside world.

The favorite game among dogs here involves a big green bush. One dog usually starts running around it for no apparent reason. Circle after circle, he'll attract more and more dogs into chasing him until almost every dog is swirling around in a dizzying loop. Watch too closely and you can get seasick.

Dogs find the rest of the park mildly entertaining, although they have to be leashed. The lake that's the park's namesake is little more than a pond. Ducks and a couple of swans live here, and the temptation may be too much for your dog. We've seen dogs drag their owners ankle-deep into the muddy pond in pursuit of a duck dinner. The park is also home to an attractive playground and a decent heart parcourse fitness trail.

To reach the dog-run area, enter on 8th Avenue at Lake Street. 415/831-2700.

11 Alta Plaza Park

🐾🐾🐾 🐕 (See San Francisco County map on page 170)

Smack in the middle of Pacific Heights, this park is where all the best breeds and most magnificent mutts gather daily. They flock to the hill on the north side of the park and conduct their dog business in the most discriminating fashion. It's not uncommon to see 25 dogs trotting around the park. Owners often address each other by their dogs' names—"Shane's mom! How are you?"

The park's off-leash run is actually on the other side of the playground and tennis courts, on the second level up from Clay Street. Bushes line the paved walkway, and it's far enough from traffic that you don't have to worry too much about cars.

The park is bordered by Jackson, Clay, Steiner, and Scott Streets. 415/831-2700.

12 Lafayette Park

🐾🐾 🐕 (See San Francisco County map on page 170)

This four-square-block park gets lots of dog traffic. The park is hilly and green and studded with palm trees, pines, and well-trimmed bushes. The official dog-run area is near Sacramento Street, between Octavia and Gough Streets. As you enter the park from the main Sacramento Street entrance, it's on your right. But most dogs gather atop the hill to the left, around two huge, smelly garbage cans.

The park is bounded by Laguna, Gough, Sacramento, and Washington Streets. 415/831-2700.

13 Washington Square

🐾🐾 (See San Francisco County map on page 170)

Grab a gelato, leash your dog, and relax in this park in the middle of North Beach. There are plenty of benches and enough trees to make your dog comfortable with his surroundings. The park is only about one block square, but it's great for a stroll when you're hitting the cafés of San Francisco's Little Italy. And if you have a child with you, so much the better. There's a small playground that's popular with local parents.

Washington Square is right across from the ornate Saints Peter and Paul Catholic Church, and the Transamerica pyramid looks close enough to reach out and touch.

Enter the park at any of its four borders: Columbus, Union, Stockton, or Filbert Streets. Try not to drive to North Beach. Even during the day, parking's a bear. 415/831-2700.

🔟 Ocean Beach

👣👣👣👣 (See San Francisco County map on page 170)

This broad, four-mile-long beach with a crashing surf isn't exactly Palm Beach. It's usually cold and windy and full of seaweed, jellyfish, jagged bits of shells, and less savory deposits from the Pacific. In other words, dogs think it's grand.

Unfortunately, this is no longer a leash-free poochy paradise. Rangers regularly patrol the beach in their trucks, so it's not easy to sneak around without a leash. But the breathtaking view and salty air still provide a good romp. (See the intro to the Parks, Beaches, and Recreation Areas section for information on potential changes to the leashes-only law.)

You can park along the ocean, between the Cliff House and Balboa Street. Walk south on the sidewalk until you hit the beach. Or park in the spaces between Fulton Street and Lincoln Way. A parking lot is also at Sloat Boulevard, but beach access is limited because of erosion. 415/556-8371.

🔟 Golden Gate Park

👣👣👣🐕 (See San Francisco County map on page 170)

This famed city park provides much dog bliss, but only in the places where dogs are supposed to be leashed. Four areas are set aside for leashless dogs (see below), but dogs in the know like to avoid those places, for good reason. The following listings are for both leash and off-leash areas, from west to east, and north to south. For information about any area in the park, call 415/831-2700.

DIVERSION

Wash That Sand Right Outta Her Hair: Soggy day at Ocean Beach? You need **Bill's Doggie Bath-O-Mat.** The beauty of Bill's is that you can bathe your dog without cleaning the waist-high tub afterward (or, worse yet, having to bathe in the tub yourself afterward!). A $12 fee includes use of shampoo, combs, brushes, towels, a doggy blow-dryer, and a cute doggy apron. Bill's a nice guy who gives good grooming advice if needed, and he gives away great puppy calendars in January. 3928 Irving Street (about 10 blocks inland); 415/661-6950.

16 Golden Gate Park (Beach Chalet)

🐾 (See San Francisco County map on page 170)

The paths in back of the Beach Chalet (near the soccer fields between the windmills near the ocean) run along the edge of the fields and can be a little unsavory at times. But to leashed dogs, they're full of good smells and interesting characters. There's also the hilly, piney area up behind the archery field. We haven't heard of any impalements up there, but be careful.

17 Golden Gate Park Dog Run

🐾🐾🦴 (See San Francisco County map on page 170)

This fenced-in dog exercise area has the dubious distinction of being right next to a field full of buffalo. Some dogs adore the location, especially when the wind is blowing in just the right direction. It's the only fenced-in dog run in the city, so it's really the only game in town for escape artists. But the park's fans aren't just dogs who walk on the wild side. All sizes and shapes of dogs come here for playtime. So many dogs use it that much of it is grassless and dusty.

The place can sometimes get a little rough around the edges when the usual dog crowd isn't around. People who like their dogs tough will occasionally drop in and hang out with something to swig while their dogs strut around. It's not usually a problem, though, especially during the normal dog rush hours (before work and after work for 9-to-5ers, and all day on weekends).

We've found more amorous dogs here than in any other park, so if your dog isn't in the mood (or you don't want her to be), this isn't the place to take her. For some reason, Jake, like dear Joe before him, gets accosted at almost every visit, so it's not one of his favorite places. He's flattered, but he's not that kind of dog.

The Dog Run is at 38th Avenue and Fulton Street. Park on Fulton Street and walk in, or take 36th Avenue into the park and go right at the first paved road. Drive all the way to the end, and there it is.

DOG-EAR YOUR CALENDAR

Pet Pride Day, sponsored by the San Francisco Department of Animal Care and Control, is a day filled with pets on parade, pets in costumes (if the event falls near Halloween, the costumes get especially interesting), pets "pawditioning" for prizes, and many pet-oriented exhibits. Donations go directly to the department's adoption and outreach programs. Pet Pride Day is held in Golden Gate Park's Sharon Meadow the last Sunday in October. For more information, call 415/554-9414.

18 Golden Gate Park (by the Polo Field)

☃ ☃ ☃ (See San Francisco County map on page 170)

Dogs who prefer playing Frisbee (on a mandatory leash) go to the meadow just east of the polo field. It's known for wide-open dells, good bushes, and plenty of gopher holes for old sports. Your best bet here is to come early in the morning.

19 Golden Gate Park (horse paths)

☃ ☃ ☃ (See San Francisco County map on page 170)

Dogs who like to promenade take to the horse paths that radiate from the now unused stables. Alas, with all the horses gone from this area (except for the police horses), there's a lot less poop to sniff out. If you don't mind walking in circles, you can simply walk along the track that circles the field. You'll pass joggers and bicyclists (or more likely, they'll pass you) and other people with happy dogs.

20 Golden Gate Park (south side)

☃ ☃ 🐾 (See San Francisco County map on page 170)

Two areas set aside for leash-free dogs are slivers along the south end of the park. One is between 2nd and 7th Avenues and bounded on the north and south by Lincoln Way and Martin Luther King Jr. Drive. It's a good length, but it's not terribly wide. The other is on the south side of the polo field, between 34th and 38th Avenues and Middle and Martin Luther King Jr. Drives. Bring your dog to these sections if he's very good off leash. They're too close to busy traffic for less disciplined dogs.

21 Golden Gate Park (Stow Lake/Strawberry Hill)

☃ ☃ ☃ (See San Francisco County map on page 170)

The summit of the man-made mountain at Stow Lake is truly a sniffer's paradise. Dogs who like to look at ducks will also enjoy the lake area. The path winds up Strawberry Hill to a breathtaking 360-degree view of the city.

Unfortunately, dogs are not supposed to be off leash. It's best to avoid this walk on weekends, when bikers and hikers and wee ones are everywhere.

Stow Lake is between 15th and 19th Avenues. From John F. Kennedy or Martin Luther King Jr. Drives, follow the Stow Lake signs.

22 Golden Gate Park (northeast corner)

😊 🐕 (See San Francisco County map on page 170)

Dogs are allowed off-leash on one of the narrow fields at the northeast corner of the park, up by the horseshoe courts. It's a strange little area with hills and dales and dirt paths. Homeless people live here, and some don't keep good house. You'll see the campfire remains, old sleeping bags, and trash of every type. It's best to avoid this place, except in the middle of the day. Enter at Stanyan and Grove Streets.

23 Golden Gate Park (The Panhandle)

😊😊😊 (See San Francisco County map on page 170)

That long, thin strip of park that extends eight blocks from the east end of the park to Baker Street is a great hangout for cool dogs. It's got a real Haight-Ashbury influence in parts, and although dogs must be leashed, they love to saunter around visiting other dogs wearing bandannas.

24 Alamo Square Park

😊😊😊 🐕 (See San Francisco County map on page 170)

A postcard comes to life in this park for you and your leashed dog. This is where the famed Painted Ladies hold court over the city. These six brightly colored Victorian homes are even better in person than they are on a postcard.

DIVERSIONS

Cruise the Castro: Your well-behaved dog is welcome to join you on a fascinating four-hour walking tour focusing on the gay and lesbian history of the **Castro district.** Tour leader Trevor Hailey will guide you and a small group to historically significant Castro settings while giving a superb narrative of how the Castro came to be what it is today. Trevor starts with the Lavender Cowboys of the 1849 Gold Rush and takes you through the impact of the 1906 earthquake, World War II, and the Summer of Love.

Dogs may not attend the brunch/lunch, included in the tour's $45 fee. Brunch is inside a restaurant, and pooches are not permitted. Trevor suggests coming with a friend and taking turns eating brunch and walking the dog. You'll miss out on a little of the history Trevor relates at mealtime, but at least you won't miss out on the tasty brunch.

All tour-takers, including dogs, get a miniature rainbow flag as part of the deal. Tours are given Tuesday–Saturday May–November; 415/550-8110; www.webcastro.com/castrotour.

Say Yippie for Hippies: The **Flower Power Haight Ashbury Walking Tour** is a delight for humans and dogs, and you don't have to be flower children/puppies to enjoy it. This riveting tour guides you through the history of the Haight, from the Victorian era to the Human Be-in, the Digger feeds, the free Grateful Dead concerts, and of course, the Summer of Love. Dogs don't dig the history much, but they revel in the smell of old hippies who sit on the sidewalks.

Humans of all ages and leashed, well-behaved dogs are welcome. A 2.5-hour tour is $15. Dogs are free. For more information or reservations, write The Flower Power Haight Ashbury Walking Tour, 520 Shrader Street, #1, San Francisco, CA 94117; 415/863-1621.

Walk up the east side of the park, near Steiner Street, to enjoy the view of the old houses with the modern city skyline in the background. (Dogs need to be leashed in this half of the park.) Even if your dog doesn't care about architecture, she'll love the grassy hills that make up this park.

Dogs who like to run around all nudey (sans leash) are joyful these days because the city has given the OK to an official leash-free area on the park's west half. Hooray! (This had been a de facto leash-free area forever. Now it has the city's seal of approval.)

The park is bordered by Fulton, Hayes, Scott, and Steiner Streets. 415/831-2700.

🐾🐾 Duboce Park

🐾 🐾 (See San Francisco County map on page 170)

If peering into people's windows is your dog's idea of fun, this urban park is his kind of place. A couple of large buildings have ground-floor windows that seem to fascinate dogs. Perhaps there's a cat colony inside.

Your dog will probably find other dogs to play with here. They're supposed to be leashed, since they're never more than a few fast steps from the nearest street. The park is grassy and has pines and a variety of smaller trees around some of its borders. A children's playground is at the west end.

The park is at Duboce Avenue between Steiner and Scott Streets. 415/831-2700.

🐾🐾 Buena Vista Park

🐾🐾🐾🐾🐕 (See San Francisco County map on page 170)

The presence of vagrants who sometimes congregate at the front of the park has scared off lots of would-be park users, but it shouldn't. They're generally a friendly lot, posing no threat to folks exploring the park's upper limits with a dog.

This park is a real find for anyone living near the Haight-Ashbury district. Hike along the myriad dirt and paved trails winding through the hills, enveloped by eucalyptus and redwood trees. Some of the gutters are lined with pieces of tombstone from a nearby cemetery. The cemetery's occupants, who died in the 1800s, were moved to the oh-so-quiet town of Colma. The gutters give the park a historical, haunted feeling.

From the top of the park, you can see the ocean, the bay, the Marin headlands, and both the Golden Gate and Bay Bridges. Birds sing everywhere, and there are lots of benches to rest on. Dogs are allowed off leash at the woodsy west side of the park, near Central Street.

A note: Sometimes people meet for assignations at the top of the park. Concealing shrubs and bushes have gotten haircuts of late, but this area is still a "hot spot," so to speak. If this bothers you or your dog, avoid this lovers' lane.

Enter at Buena Vista Avenue West and Central Street, or from Haight Street. 415/831-2700.

🐾🐾 Corona Heights Park/Red Rock Park

🐾🐾🐾🐕 (See San Francisco County map on page 170)

The rust-colored boulders atop this park cast long, surreal shadows at dawn. If you and your dog are early risers, it's worth the hike to the summit to witness this. And there's a fine view any time of day of downtown and the Castro district.

Unfortunately, dogs aren't allowed off leash on hikes up the hill. Until recently, the off-leash area was a roomy square of grass at the foot of the park.

The leash-free section has now been made smaller (about three-quarters of an acre) and is completely fenced. It was a compromise between the dog people and the folks who like to sunbathe there without getting stomped upon and sniffed at. Because of heavy use, the fenced dog park is no longer grassy, but the surrounding area—leashes mandatory—is lush. (The grass truly is greener on the other side of this fence.)

After a bit of leashless playing, you can don a leash and take your pooch up the hill. Fences keep dogs and people from falling down the steep cliffs and from treading on native habitat. Keep in mind that there's virtually no shade, so if you have a black rug of a dog, think twice about climbing the hill on hot, sunny days.

The park is at Museum Way and Roosevelt Avenue. 415/831-2700.

2.8 Mission Dolores Park

🐾🐾🐕 (See San Francisco County map on page 170)

You can get a little history lesson while walking your dog here. A statue of Miguel Hidalgo overlooks the park, and Mexico's liberty bell hangs at the Dolores Street entrance.

History may not impress your dog, but a wide-open space for running off leash will. It's behind the tennis courts.

There are two problems with this area, though: 1) It's easy for your dog to run into the road—even if she's the voice control type, she could find herself in Church Street traffic just by running a little too far to catch a ball; and 2) you have to be on the lookout that your dog doesn't run over people who live in the park. Joe once slid into a sleeping homeless woman and scared her so badly she screamed and ran away.

Enter anywhere on Dolores or Church Streets, between 18th and 20th Streets. The off-leash area is south of the tennis courts and north of the soccer field. 415/831-2700.

2.9 McKinley Square

🐾🐾🐕 (See San Francisco County map on page 170)

The view from this little patch of land is, shall we say, interesting. You can see for miles and miles, and the view includes several other leash-free parks, such as Buena Vista, Corona Heights, Mission Dolores, and Bernal Heights Parks. But you can also see such lovely sights as U.S. 101, with its cars rushing madcap-fashion just a couple of hundred feet down the hill from you. And if you ever craved a view of San Francisco General Hospital's most austere, Dickensian brick buildings, this is the place to come. If you had really long arms, you could almost reach out and touch them. Actually, depending on the direction of the wind, on some days they reach out and touch you—the steam from the hospital's huge chimneys has been known to slip right up to this hilltop park.

DOG-EAR YOUR CALENDAR

You won't strike out with your dog if you bring her to the **Dog Days of Summer** at SBC Park. In fact, you'll score a home run. If you thought hot dogs and baseball go together, you should see just plain dog dogs and baseball. It's a match made in dog heaven!

At Dog Days of Summer, your pooch gets to join you for a baseball game on a set day in August. You'll sit together in "The Dog Zone" (aka the bleachers) and watch the San Francisco Giants pound the heck out of the visiting team (we hope). But that's not all. Before the game, you and your dog can take part in a poochy parade around the field! Not many dogs (or humans) can say they've cruised around a pro ball park. There's also a dog costume contest, should your dog be feeling creative. Cost for the day is $37 for one human, and you can bring one dog. Additional humans in your party (sans dogs) are $18. Dogs have to wear ID and rabies tags. 415/972-2000; www.sfgiants.com.

Dogs are permitted off leash in the back section of the park, between the playground and the community gardens. Signs will point you in the right direction. It's nothing beautiful, just a wide path with a little running room on a hillside dotted with brush and occasional trees.

The off-leash section is on 20th Street and San Bruno Avenue, just a few blocks from the heart of the Potrero Hill business district. 415/831-2700.

30 Twin Peaks

🐾 🐾 (See San Francisco County map on page 170)

So dogs aren't allowed at the Top of the Mark. So what! The view from up here will put all those "No Dogs Allowed" establishments to shame, and it's cheaper to entertain guests up here—it's free, in fact.

The summits of the Twin Peaks are higher than 900 feet. It's usually cold up here, so bundle up. You can drive to the northern peak and park in the lot. It's very touristy, and on this peak, signs tell you what you're looking at—Tiburon, Nob Hill, Mt. Diablo, Japantown, and Mt. Tamalpais. Your dog won't get much exercise, though, since all he can do is walk around the paved viewing area on leash. And frankly, many dogs are bored by the marvelous vistas.

For your dog's sake, try exploring the other peak. It's a bare hill with wooden stairs up one side. While dogs must be on leash, it's not bad exercise. And the view—at almost 20 feet higher than the first peak—is *magnificent*. From here you can see other potential walks for you and your dog on the lower hills, where the views are almost as dynamic and the air is a little warmer. Be sure to keep him on leash, because the road is never far away.

The Twin Peaks are on Twin Peaks Boulevard, just north of Portola Drive. 415/831-2700.

31 Douglass Park

🐾🐾🐾🐾 🐕 (See San Francisco County map on page 170)

The leash-free section at Douglass Park used to be a steep hillside with fences that were falling apart. It was so bad and difficult to get to (and to stay on!) that I decided not to waste space on it in previous editions. But now the city has changed the locale, and it's a completely different animal: a big, attractive, grassy field flanked by tall trees. It's actually a barely used softball field, so your dog can make like Barry Bonds and run the bases and then go out for a fly ball (of the lobbed tennis variety) to right field. There's plenty of room for dogs to run and play, and boy do they.

Escape artist dogs are pretty safe here, although the park is not totally enclosed. The area near the entrance has no barrier. But the park is so big that you can keep your activities to a far-flung section of the field if escape is a concern.

The park has good views of downtown from the back fence area (it has some very tall fences in back from its softball days). If you want to sit and sip your coffee while your dog gallops around, you'll have to be a bump on a log: The only place to repose is a big log bordering the outfield. The leash-free part of the park is all the way at the top, on Douglass at 27th Street. 415/831-2700.

32 Glen Canyon Park

🐾🐾🐾 (See San Francisco County map on page 170)

From the cypress forests to the streams and grassy hills, this park was made for you and your dog. The nature trail in the middle of the park follows a muddy creek and is so overgrown with brush and bramble that at times you nearly have to crawl. It's as though the trail were blazed for dogs. There are so many dragonflies of all colors and sizes near the creek, and so much lush vegetation, that you may wonder if you've stepped back to the age of the dinosaurs.

Park at Bosworth Street and O'Shaughnessy Boulevard and walk down a dirt trail past a recreation center, through the redwoods and loud birds. Stay away from the paved road—it can look deserted for hours on end, and then a car suddenly whizzes by. Your dog is supposed to be leashed, but you should still be aware of the road. In a few minutes, you'll come to a long, low building. At this point, you can go left and up a hill for some secluded picnic spots or keep going and take the nature trail. When you finally emerge from the dragonflies and dense greenery, take any of several trails up the open, rolling hills and enjoy a panorama of the park.

The park is at Bosworth Street and O'Shaughnessy Boulevard. 415/831-2700.

33 Mount Davidson

(See San Francisco County map on page 170)

Hiking to the peak of this park can be a religious experience—literally. As you emerge from the tall pine and eucalyptus trees leading to the 927-foot summit, a concrete structure looms in the distance. As you get closer you'll see that it's a gigantic cross, 103 feet tall. It's so huge, and in such a prominent spot—at the end of a long, wide path surrounded by trees—that it can be a startling sight. On his first encounter, Joe backed out of his collar and collided with a tree. Since leashes are the law here, we had to quickly put him back together.

In 1934, President Franklin Delano Roosevelt became the first person to flick the switch and light the cross. It's visible for miles, especially vivid under its nighttime floodlighting. On a night hike up Mt. Davidson, you can follow the glow to the top. Recently there was lots of controversy about keeping the cross (a religious symbol) in the park (a city-run property). That church and state-mixing thing just wasn't making some folks happy. Thank God (so to speak), an Armenian group bought the property surrounding the cross. The cross, an intriguing landmark for generations—much more than a religious icon—will remain.

Since you enter the park at such a high altitude, it's only about a 10-minute pilgrimage to the peak. But you can make it a much longer walk by experimenting with different trails.

Enter at Dalewood Way and Lansdale Avenue. 415/831-2700.

34 Upper Noe Park

(See San Francisco County map on page 170)

At last sniff, the leash-free section of this park was a tiny little area of compacted dirt. It was fenced and had water and two benches but no shade and no real appeal other than being an off-leash area. At press time the city was considering redoing it and redefining its borders, so it may warrant another paw or two in the future. (To be fair, regular users say it's better than it used to be when the ground was a sandy, dusty mess.) The off-leash section is on Day and Sanchez Streets, east of the ballfield. (You can enter only on Day Street at this point.) 415/831-2700.

35 Potrero Hill Mini Park

(See San Francisco County map on page 170)

If you value your safety, don't go to the designated off-leash part of this park, even if your dog is crossing her legs in need of an off-leash romp. A friend was mugged twice at gunpoint when she used to play tennis at the courts adjacent to the dog run. (For some reason she no longer plays tennis there.) The leash-free section of this tiny park is a postage-stamp-sized lawn next to a tiny, ancient playground. A steep, uncleared patch of land that stretches from the nearby housing projects to the lawn is also supposed to be part of the dog run. The city needs to rethink this whole setup. The park is at 22nd and Arkansas Streets. 415/831-2700.

36 Pine Lake Park

(See San Francisco County map on page 170)

Adjacent to its more famous cousin, Stern Grove (below), Pine Lake Park can be even more fun for dogs because it has Laguna Puerca, a small lake at the west end of the park. Swimming isn't allowed, but there's always the muddy shore for wallowing.

The lake is in a valley at the bottom of steep slopes, so there's not much need to worry about traffic. Leashes are supposed to be on at all times, in any case. At the lake's east end, there's a big field where dogs can really cut loose—as far as leashes allow.

Enter at Crestlake Drive and Wawona Street and follow the paved path, which quickly turns into a dirt trail. 415/831-2700.

37 Stern Grove

(See San Francisco County map on page 170)

If your dog wants to hear some hot music this summer, bring her to the Stern Grove Festival concerts. Dogs can't enjoy the opera, ballet, jazz, classical, or world music performances from the meadow, but they're tolerated around the peripheral hills, on leash. Bring a picnic, a bottle of wine, a rawhide bone, and, of course, a poop bag.

Stern Grove is a treasure of trees, hills, meadows, and birds. There's even a spot where dogs are allowed off leash. Unfortunately, it's one of the least attractive areas in the park—very close to the street—although trees act as an effective barrier. And if you perch on the inner edge, the dog-run area isn't a bad place to listen to a concert. The violins get a little tinny at that distance, but your dog won't care.

City parks officials are considering allowing some of the trails here to be leash-free. But for now, the only legal leash-free area is on Stern Grove's north side, on Wawona Street between 21st and 23rd Avenues. 415/831-2700.

38 Bernal Heights Park

😸 😸 😸 🐕 (See San Francisco County map on page 170)

On one visit to this park, a dozen wolf-shepherds were the only dogs atop the amber hill. They ran and played in such pure wolf fashion that it was hard to believe they weren't the genuine item. The icy wind hit the power lines overhead and made a low, arctic whistle. The scene left an indelible impression that even in the middle of a city such as San Francisco, the wild is just beneath the surface.

The rugged hills here are fairly rigorous for bipeds, but dogs have a magnificent time bolting up and down. Humans can enjoy the view of the Golden Gate and Bay Bridges. The vista makes up for the austere look of the treeless park. Dogs are allowed off leash on the hills bordered by Bernal Heights Boulevard. It can be very windy and cold, so bundle up.

Enter at Carver Street and Bernal Heights Boulevard, or keep going on Bernal Heights Boulevard until just past Anderson Street. 415/831-2700.

39 St. Mary's Park

😸 😸 🐕 (See San Francisco County map on page 170)

If it weren't for its teeny size, St. Mary's dog park would score three paws. It's an attractive place with friendly people and well-manicured grass that somehow withstands the pounding of paws day after day. It's totally enclosed and has three picnic tables and occasional shade from trees on a steep adjacent hillside. The leash-free section of St. Mary's is very close to I-280 (and the constant drone of traffic). From the park's main entrance on Murray Street at Justin Drive, walk immediately to the right and follow a paved path downhill past a playground and to the dog park, which will be on your left. A closer entrance is a block south, on Benton Avenue at Justin Drive. 415/831-2700.

40 McLaren Park/Crocker Amazon Playground

😸 😸 🐕 (See San Francisco County map on page 170)

You and your dog can enter this large park anywhere and find a trail within seconds. The surprise is that most of McLaren's trails run through remote wooded areas and windswept hills with sweeping views. At press time, leashes were required on the trails, but the city parks department may soon be experimenting with leash-free trail access.

If you drive to the northeast part of the park, to the section bounded by John F. Shelley Drive and Mansell Street, you'll find a leash-free area far from traffic. Certain parts can be crowded with schoolchildren or company picnickers or ne'er-do-wells, so watch where you wander. There's another leash-free section in the park's south section, which is really known as Crocker Amazon Playground. You get there via the 1600 block of Geneva Avenue or the 1600 block of Sunnydale. It's in the upper part of the park. You'll have to walk through some of the park to get there, since you can't get a car too close. 415/831-2700.

41 Fort Funston

🐾🐾🐾🐾 (See San Francisco County map on page 170)

Get a hanky ready: After decades of dogs' being allowed to run around in their birthday suits (no leashes), leashes have become the law—at least temporarily. Some future decision-making offers a glimmer of hope for Fort Funston to once again be one of the world's best areas for leash-free dogs, but it may be some time before that happens again. (See the intro to the Parks, Beaches, and Recreation Areas section for more on this.) In the meantime, know that rangers do occasionally come through and issue citations to some people whose dogs aren't attached to them.

It just isn't the same here on leash, but "Fort Fun" still gets high marks for natural beauty. This scenic park set on seaside cliffs still will make your jaw drop with awe the first (and second and third) time you see it. Trails will still wind through magnificent bluffs overlooking the mighty Pacific. And dogs will still slobber with giddiness to be part of all this.

There are a few areas where you can start your walk, but the easiest access is from the main parking lot, next to the take-off cliff for hang gliders. Before you begin, walk your dog to the watering hole—actually a bowl underneath a drinking fountain—and fill her up.

Now that you're all watered and ready for adventure, turn around and take the first trail to the north of the parking lot, the Sunset Trail. You'll meander through dunes and ice plant, encountering every kind of dog imaginable. You'll soon come to the main entrance to Battery Davis, which was built in 1939 to protect San Francisco from enemy ship bombardment. It was sealed shut in recent years because of some rotten sorts who hung out there, but you can still get a good feel for the place.

Continue on trails on either side of the battery. Both eventually end up in the same place. If you take the trail at the rear of the battery, you'll quickly be able to see the Golden Gate Bridge and the Cliff House. At that point, you'll also see a trail that takes you back into a miniforest. Don't go all the way down, though, or you'll end up on a busy road.

If you visit frequently, expand your explorations. Many trails wander throughout Fort Funston, and you and your dog will want to sniff out every inch of this place that you're allowed to. (Be careful to avoid poison oak and areas marked as off-limits. A 12-acre area is now untreadable by dogs and humans because of some delicate habitat. Please heed the signs.)

To get to Fort Funston, follow the brown signs on the Great Highway. It's about one-half mile south of the turnoff to John Muir Drive. (If you get to the Daly City limits, you've gone too far south.) There's also some roadside parking near that intersection. Once on the main drive into the park, bear right (going left will take you to the interesting new Fort Funston Visitors Center, but dogs have no desire to visit, since they're not allowed). Continue past a little building with paintings of hang gliders, and drive into the main parking lot. 415/556-8371.

42 Lake Merced

🐾🐾🐕 (See San Francisco County map on page 170)

As the city's largest body of water, Lake Merced is favored by Labrador retrievers, Irish setters, and the like. An ideal spot to explore is the footbridge area near the south end of the lake. A couple of sandy beaches there are safe from traffic, but dogs are supposed to be leashed anyway. Once you cross the bridge, you'll find an inviting area with lots of little trees. This is where you'll find one of two double-decker drinking fountains for humans and their best friends. Lap up if you're going to hike around the entire lake: It's about a five-mile walk on paved trails and can be heavily used on weekends.

The off-leash section of Lake Merced is at the north lake area, at Lake Merced Boulevard and Middlefield Drive. Park on Middlefield and cross Lake Merced Boulevard at the light. You'll enter a small grassy/weedy section and come to a narrow dirt trail overlooking the lake's northeast bowl. We don't recommend letting dogs off leash until you're at least a couple of hundred feet into the park, because menacing traffic is so close by. There are birds galore and purple wildflowers in spring. The park is a tease, though, because there's no way to get to the lake from here—it's down a very formidable slope covered with impenetrable brush. 415/831-2700.

PLACES TO EAT

For a city that's known for its cool, foggy weather, San Francisco sure has a lot of sidewalk cafés. Here's just a smattering:

Angelina's Caffe: Conveniently situated one-half block from Cal's Discount Pet Supply, Angelina's is a good place for you and your dog to take a break from shopping. It's got everything from soup to pine nuts, plus a large variety of coffees. Enjoy them at one of six sidewalk tables. You can also stock on up on Italian souvenirs here, but watch out for the red, white, and green hats. 6000 California Street; 415/221-7801.

Asqew Grill: The name may be spelled all askew, but I ask you, have you ever eaten at a restaurant where almost everything is cooked and served on a skewer? Jake Dog would like to recommend any of the meat kabobs, but there are some mighty tasty veggie skewers awaiting the herbivore in your life. The restaurant serves lunch and dinner. Breakfast would be disastrous. (There's a reason you've never heard of a scrambled egg kabob or skewered pancakes.) 3348 Steiner Street; 415/931-9201.

Bella and Daisy's: If your dog has been very good, get her a canine cannoli at this fun pooch bakery and boutique. Or order some doggy donuts, cupcakes, or brownies. (All made for dogs, so no chocolate, no sugar.) If it's her birthday, let her eat cake. Bella's knows no bounds. What's unique about Bella's, compared with some other dog bakeries, is that the bakery owners provide coffee and indoor seating for dog people, so you can actually hang out here while your dog eats. Of course, a dog does not usually take very long to eat a cupcake or what have you, so the seating is really for the benefit of humans who want to meet and chat about this and that (this usually being their dog, and that being your dog). Bella's has a 1,300-square-foot party area in the back, and a small little turf area in front for dogs to sniff out. Nonbakery boutique items such as doggy cashmere and fancy bowls and carriers are big here, too. And so is the healing center, where dogs can get acupuncture, massage, and other body treatments. 1750 Union Street; 415/440-7007.

Bistro Yoffi: It seems there's always a happy dog hanging out at the sidewalk tables in front of this colorful Marina district restaurant. The international and California-style cuisine here is marvelous. Jake Dog sends a thank-you to Matt Golden and his smiling dog for the tip. 2231 Chestnut Street; 415/885-5133.

Blue Danube Coffee House: Have your cake and eat soup and sandwiches, too, at five tables outside this charming café. You can even indulge in a wide selection of beer or wine, but you'll have to drink alone if your dog is under 21. On sunny days, it may be hard to find an empty spot. 306 Clement Street; 415/221-9041.

Cafe Niebaum Coppola: Dogs are welcome to join their people at any of 12 white-cloth–covered tables outside this upscale North Beach/Financial District restaurant owned by Francis Ford Coppola. Apparently if you come here enough, you're bound to run into the famous bearded director himself. 916 Kearney Street; 415/291-1700.

Caffe Centro: The bistro dinners are so good you'll wish you could afford to come here with your dog every night to dine at the eight outdoor tables. Try the seared tuna Niçoise or the saffron fettuccine with grilled prawns. You can also get gourmet breakfasts and lunches at this South of Market café. 102 South Park; 415/882-1500.

Calzone's Pizza Cucina: You and your dog can dine on wonderful pastas, pizzas, calzones, seafood, and steak at this North Beach restaurant. It has about a trillion outdoor tables to choose from. 430 Columbus Avenue; 415/397-3600.

The Cannery: This old Del Monte packing plant is home to three delightful restaurants with courtyard tables for you and your dog, and there's often entertainment here. The restaurants usually don't have courtyard service

DOG-EAR YOUR CALENDAR

The dog's version of the famous Black and White Ball is truly a spectacle to behold. At the **Bark and Whine Ball,** well-heeled dogs and their people shine. This is definitely one of those events to see and be seen. No one even shrugs when they see someone dancing with his or her dog. The ball features good music, passed hors d'oeuvres (dogs love this, but it's really for humans), and wine (ditto). It's held in late February. Tickets are $75–125. Dogs are $20. Go to www.sfspca.org/barkandwhine for this year's date or phone 415/522-3535.

after dark because it's too cold, so call first to find out. The Cannery is at 2801 Leavenworth Street. One of its dog-friendly restaurants is **Las Margaritas Restaurant.** Seven kinds of margaritas, mesquite-grilled shark, and a great view of the courtyard below make this one of the more popular Mexican restaurants this side of the Mission district. 415/776-6996.

The Canvas Gallery: There's always a water bowl for dogs on the patio of this progressive art gallery that doubles as a very popular café and lounge. It's where the hip dogs go in the Inner Sunset district. The California cuisine is tasty, and even if you can't go inside with your dog to see the art, you can always peek in. 1200 9th Avenue (at Lincoln Way); 415/504-0060.

Cioppino's: Dogs love coming to this well-known Fisherman's Wharf seafood restaurant because they know they're more than welcome. The folks here always provide water to thirsty pooches. You can dine at any of oodles of plastic sidewalk tables here. 400 Jefferson Street; 415/775-9311.

Cool Beans: The owners of this delightful café adore dogs and keep a treat jar by the front door, near the tiny outdoor eating area. You can dine on tasty homemade soups, sandwiches, and sweets while your dog munches and crunches and drools on her biscuits. The coffee is delectable, but if you're not a coffee drinker, try the yummy chai. Thanks to Riko and her dog for the heads-up about this little gem. 4342 California Street; 415/750-1955.

Crepevine: Mmmm. MMMMMmmm. MMMMMM. That's the way Jake groans with desire when he comes here and looks at all the happy folks sitting at the outdoor tables dining on their steaming hot crepes. You can choose from a variety of delicious crepes or create your own concoction. Crepevine has a cozy, bohemian feel, even outside. 624 Irving Street; 415/681-5858.

Curbside Cafe: The servers here are very dog-friendly, and the continental cuisine is top-notch. Try not to let your dog block the sidewalk, since it's a tight squeeze here. 2417 California Street; 415/929-9030.

Curbside Too: Want to have your dog at your side while you dine on tasty

DIVERSIONS

Hop on a Bus: It's good to be a dog in San Francisco. Dogs are allowed on **Muni buses** and streetcars as long as it's not commute time (dog hours are 9 A.M.–3 P.M. and 7 P.M.–5 A.M.) Only one dog is permitted per vehicle. Dogs must be on a short leash and muzzled, no matter how little or how sweet. (There are many muzzles dogs barely notice. Shop around 'til you find one your dog doesn't despise.) Bus driver Tom Brown told us about the creative, but ineffective, ways some people muzzle their dogs. "This one man had a part pit-bull dog, and he put a little rubber band around its mouth," said Brown. "No way that dog was getting on my bus."

Dogs pay the same fare as owners. If you're an adult, you pay $1.25, and your dog does, too. Dogs of seniors pay the senior rate. Lap-sized dogs can stay on your lap, but all others are consigned to the floor. Keep your dog from getting underfoot and be sure he's well walked before he gets on. Call 415/673-MUNI (415/673-6864) for more information.

Ride Halfway to the Stars: Not many world-famous tourist attractions permit pooches. Can dogs ascend the Eiffel Tower? No. Can they visit the Vatican? No. Can they ride in a beautiful old **San Francisco cable car?** They sure can! (They can also go on the Golden Gate Bridge. See the Diversion for details.)

Jake the Dog has mixed feelings about the cable car privilege. He doesn't mind the clanging of the bells, as his predecessor Joe did. But he's not too keen on wearing a muzzle (a requirement, along with a leash; the muzzle can be a gentle nylon one that most dogs, not including Jake, barely notice), but what he really doesn't care for are the hills. On a recent descent to Fisherman's Wharf, he tried to scramble from the floor to my lap, and we both slid down the bench and smack into the open newspaper of a surprised commuter. "Welcome to the sports section," he said with a bemused grin.

Opinions vary about whether dogs should ride inside or outside. Some drivers think the outside is better because the cable noise isn't so amplified, and dogs don't get so nervous. Others say the outside is too dangerous—that a dog could panic and jump off. I opt for inside, but if you have a small dog and can hold her securely on your lap, riding outside is the best way to get the full San Francisco experience.

Only one dog is permitted per cable car. Dogs aren't allowed during peak commute times (see above for hours), and you should never take your dog on a crowded cable car. Off-season and away from touristy areas are your best bets. Dogs pay the same fare as their person. If you pay the full $3 adult rate, your dog does too. For more information, call 415/673-MUNI (415/673-6864).

French cuisine? He'll lick his lips as you down your escargot at the attractive outdoor tables here. It's casual, but high quality. Just a bone's throw from the Presidio's western entrance. 2769 Lombard Street; 415/921-4442.

Extreme Pizza: Dine on delicious gourmet pizzas and tasty salads with your happy dog at your side. The outdoor area features fun 1950s soda fountain–type stools and several tables. 1980 Union Street; 415/929-8234.

Fisherman's Pizzeria: If you and your salty mutt are sniffing around Fisherman's Wharf for pizza, you'll get a decent meal here. A sign above the entrance features a fisherman and his dog in a little boat, so you'll know you and your canine crew are welcome. Dine at the seven sidewalk tables. 2800 Leavenworth; 415/928-2998.

Ghirardelli Square: What was once a chocolate factory is now one of the classiest tourist shopping centers in the country. More important than that, it's got a lot to offer residents and their dogs. Ghirardelli Square is at 900 North Point Street. Two restaurants with outdoor cafés are: **Boudin Sourdough Bakery and Cafe:** Dine on pastries, croissants, cheesecake, or huge sandwiches as you gaze across Beach Street at the bay, 415/928-7404; and **Ghirardelli Fountain and Candy:** Here's where you can get some of that famous rich Ghirardelli ice cream with all the fixings. Just remember: The more your dog gets, the fewer sit-ups you have to do. Stay away from chocolate, though. It can be very bad for dogs, 415/474-3938.

Grove Cafe: This coffeehouse is so popular you might need a shoehorn to find room at the plentiful outdoor tables here. But if you and your dog like the Chestnut Street coffee scene, you'll enjoy sipping your joe among the Marina District masses. You can wash down your coffee with some fine sandwiches, salads, and pastries. 2250 Chestnut Street, 415/474-4843.

Horse Shoe Coffeehouse: Enjoy good coffee and pastries at a down-to-earth café with two sidewalk tables. 566 Haight Street; 415/626-8852.

Java Beach: After a morning of combing Ocean Beach, you can catch some rays and eat some lunch on one of the benches outside this mellow soup, sandwich, and salad shop. 1396 La Playa at the Great Highway; 415/665-5282.

La Mediterranée: Dog owners are lucky—there are two of these top Mideast/Greek restaurants in the city; each puts tables outside in decent weather and has a dog-loving staff. Try the vegetarian Middle-East plate. Even meat-eaters enjoy it. The restaurant at 2210 Fillmore Street, 415/921-2956, has only a couple of tiny outdoor tables. (The area inside is fairly tiny, too.) The restaurant at 288 Noe Street, 415/431-7210, has several roomy sidewalk tables, some of which are covered by an awning.

Left at Albuquerque: The Southwest comes to San Francisco at this fun Union Street eatery. For an appetizer, try the cilantro-lime shrimp quesadilla. And if you want to make your dog very happy, order the Cowboy Mix Grill, a heaping plateful of ribs, chicken, and steak, with mashed potatoes. Your drooling dog may join you at the very attractive street-side dining area. 2140 Union Street; 415/749-6700.

Liverpool Lil's: You can see two wonderful sights from this fun English pub: 1) The Golden Gate Bridge; and 2) the western end of the Presidio. Enjoy a drink and fish-and-chips with your dog at your side at the six pleasant outdoor tables. 2942 Lyon Street; 415/921-6664.

Mocca on Maiden Lane: Now your dog can dine in one of the most posh streets of the Union Square area. Just a bone's throw from the finest stores in San Francisco, Mocca is a European-style café famed for its many types of salads. Dine at the zillions of umbrella-topped tables right on the street, which is closed to traffic. 174 Maiden Lane; 415/956-1188.

Mona Lisa Restaurant: This family-owned and operated North Beach restaurant is our little secret, OK? We discovered it one day while roaming around without Joe Dog and had a most sumptuous feast inside. Everything we ordered, from salad to pasta to main dish to dessert, was wonderful. Plenty of insiders know about the Mona Lisa, but it's off the radar screen for most. We like that. But of course, after this appears, it will be on many a dog's radar. The pizza here has been called the best in North Beach by many a patron. Pooches get to join their people at four outdoor tables. 353 Columbus Avenue; 415/989-4917.

Pasta Pomodoro: San Francisco is home to eight Pasta Pomodoro restaurants, and they all have the same tasty Italian cuisine. (Don't come here for pizza, as they don't do pizza. The polenta dish is a winner, though.) Several have plenty of outdoor seating and welcome good pooches. The one we've checked out personally is in Noe Valley, at 4000 24th Street; 415/920-9904.

Pier 39: If your dog doesn't mind flocks of tourists, you'll find a wide selection of decent eateries with outdoor tables for the two of you here. Your dog gets to smell the bay and sniff at the sea lions below. Pier 39 is off the Embarcadero, near Jefferson Street. Here are a couple of the restaurants where you and your dog are allowed (and they're not allowed at all restaurants' outdoor tables, so ask before settling in with your dog): **Chowder's:** Fried seafood and several types of chowder make Pier 39 really feel like a pier, 415/391-4737; **Sal's Pizzeria:** You and your dog can get a real taste of San Francisco by biting into any of Sal's special pizzas, 415/398-1198. Sometimes it's fun to just grab a snack at one of a few walk-up windows on the pier as you stroll around. Jake highly recommends ordering a little bagful of hot and crispy-yet-gooey doughnuts from Trish's Mini Donuts, and then accidentally dropping one right in front of your dog.

Pompei's Grotto: If your dog likes the smell of seafood, he probably won't mind joining you at an outdoor table at this famous restaurant on the main drag at Fisherman's Wharf. The fish is fresh and the pasta delicious. And if your dog is thirsty, one of the friendly servers will probably offer her a cup of water. 340 Jefferson Street; 415/776-9265.

Primo Patio Cafe: If you and the pooch need sustenance before or after a good sniff around SBC Park, this casual Caribbean restaurant is a primo place to visit. It's just a block or so away from the San Francisco Giants' home, and the food is mouthwatering. Dine with your dugout dog at the two sidewalk tables here. (Sorry, no dogs in the garden section of the restaurant, since they would have to walk through the indoor section and past the kitchen.) 214 Townsend Street; 415/957-1129.

Rose's Cafe: As soon as you sit down to dine with your dog at this elegant Italian-Californian restaurant's lovely side patio, you'll know you've come to the most dog-friendly restaurant in the city. Your dog will almost immediately be greeted by someone from the staff (often the dog-loving manager, Matthew) and given a big bowl of water. Then comes the gourmet house-made dog biscuit, available for a fairly good price. Throughout the meal comes plenty of attention, often from other diners, sometimes from the folks who run Rose's.

My introduction to Rose's came a few years back, when I got a letter from reader Carol Copsey, and her dog, Bella, a flirty American Eskimo. She was a frequent patron and wanted to let Joe and me know about Bella's favorite restaurant. I phoned her, and we got together one cool summer evening for dinner at Rose's. Joe was immediately smitten by Bella's fluffy good looks, but he fell asleep somewhere between the second and third gourmet dog biscuit. Bella didn't know what to make of Joe's snoozing on their date, but she pulled through after another nibble of dog treat. We had a wonderful time dining under the cream-colored awning, heat lamps getting us warm enough to take off our wraps.

The food here is superb. The menu changes frequently, but here are a few dishes to be sure to order if you see them listed: bruschetta with fresh tomatoes, garlic and basil; peaches, kadota figs, and prosciutto; crescenza-stuffed focaccia; soft polenta with gorgonzola; sautéed sweet white corn; local albacore with tomato, fennel, romano beans, and tapenade. The desserts are every bit as delicious.

It can get pretty busy here at times, so try to come when it's less hectic, for your dog's sake as well as other patrons'. A good bet is to phone for reservations and mention that you'll be bringing your well-behaved furry friend along. There are also a few tables along the front of the restaurant, but if you have a choice, the side area is the best. 2298 Union Street; 415/775-2200.

Rustico: This eatery in Potrero Hill features pizza, pasta, panini, soup, and salads. It has lots of outside tables. 300 DeHaro Street; 415/252-0180.

Sea Breeze Café: Come here for delicious comfort food with a European twist. If you're here for weekend brunch, try the brown sugar and vanilla cream oatmeal; the weather in the Outer Sunset district is usually just right for this kind of cozy dish. But what dogs like best is that the café owners love dogs and welcome them at the sidewalk tables with a bowl of fresh water. (You can get tasty, natural dog treats at the natural food store next door.) 3940 Judah Street; 415/242-6022.

Squat and Gobble: Dogs love visiting the Castro's Squat and Gobble café and crepery. Not only are the servers really friendly, but the sidewalk alfresco dining area is spacious and there's always a bowl of water for thirsty dogs. Try the Zorba the Greek crepe. It's to drool for. (Jake urges any dogs reading this to convince their people to order the Gobble Burger instead.) 3600 16th Street (at Market and Noe); 415/552-2125.

Steps of Rome: "Of course we allow dogs!" exclaimed a manager on a recent visit. "We love dogs!" This big and bustling North Beach restaurant is a really fun place for a meal or just coffee and people-watching. The staff is friendly, and the atmosphere is very Italian, in a modern kind of way. And the food—*delicioso!* I love it here because I'm a big risotto fan, and Steps features a different risotto daily. The sidewalk tables for you and your dog are plentiful and popular. 348 Columbus Avenue; 415/397-0435.

Toy Boat Dessert Cafe: You may not be able to say it 10 times fast, but you and your dog won't feel a need to speak when you're at the outside bench eating rich and creamy desserts. 401 Clement Street; 415/751-7505.

Universal Cafe: This charming little Potrero Hill restaurant is very popular with the pooch set. The very friendly staffers here love dogs and provide them water and kind words. The restaurant features a variety of magnificent dishes with a California twist. If it's on the menu, be sure to try the caramelized onion pizza with prosciutto, fontina, and ricotta. Dine with your happy

DIVERSION

Sniff Out an Apartment with Your Dog: Looking for some digs with your dog? It's not always easy in San Francisco. But thanks to a wonderful program of the San Francisco SPCA, dog people are finding it easier to rent in the city. The **Open Door Program** helps landlords and potential tenants come together. This program has helped hundreds of canines and their people find housing since its inception a few years back. To see listings, and to get tips about how to make you and your dog more viable candidates for tenanthood, go to www.sfspca.org and click on Open Door.

dog at the five outdoor tables. (A big thank-you to Rosie Dog and her people, Melanie and Sandra, for letting us know about this gem.) 2814 19th Street; 415/821-4608.

PLACES TO STAY

The City by the Bay has some of the most wonderful dog-friendly hotels anywhere.

Campton Place: The European ambience and superb service make this a luxury hotel your dog will never forget. The rooms are magnificently comfortable, gorgeous, and filled with extra touches that really make your stay here stand out. Some of the king rooms even feature sweet window seats with roman shades. A sample photo of such a room on Campton's website shows a border collie striking a pose on the cushions of the seat. That pretty much speaks to the dog-friendly attitude: "Any size dog is welcome!" says a dog-loving hotelier. (It used to be that only dogs 25 pounds or less—no larger than a respectable Thanksgiving turkey—were allowed. The smart management here decided that just didn't make sense. We hope other hotels with size limits follow suit.)

The hotel is just a half-block away from Union Square. Rates are $335–2,000. Dogs are $35 extra per day. 340 Stockton Street 94108; 415/781-5555; www.camptonplace.com.

Castro Suites: The owners of the two gorgeous apartments in this 1890s Italianate Victorian home advertise that they cater to gay, lesbian, and straight clientele. What they don't say right off is that they also cater to dog clientele. They welcome dogs. Dogs who dig gardens (not in the literal sense of the word, please) should stay at the delectable garden suite, with its open airy feel and its beautiful garden. Urban-oriented dogs enjoy the apartment with its views of downtown and the bay. Rates are $200. Weekly rates are available. You'll get the address when you make your reservation. 415/437-1783; www.castrosuites.com.

Hotel Beresford: This Union Square–area hotel bills itself as "the friendliest hotel in San Francisco." Is it true? We don't know, as we haven't done a personality survey of the city's hotel employees. But we can say that the staff members we've encountered here have been very friendly and helpful. When asked if there's a size limit on pet guests, a chipper front desk manager replied, "No, as long as you don't bring an elephant." We like the attitude.

The family-owned hotel features attractive rooms—nothing fancy, but comfortable and clean. You'll get a decent continental breakfast with your stay. Humans get to eat at the hotel's adjacent restaurant, the White Horse Tavern. It has a real English pub feel, but the food is actually delicious—and even healthful, if you order right.

Dogs need to stay in the hotel's first-floor smoking rooms. Rates are $89–139. 635 Sutter Street 94102; 415/673-9900 or 800/533-6533; www.beresford.com.

Hotel Beresford Arms: The sister hotel of the Hotel Beresford, this one is bigger and more elegant, with a few extra amenities. The lobby, complete with pillars and a chandelier, is a bit grander. You and the pooch can stay in a standard room or a suite with a kitchen. A continental breakfast and a fun afternoon tea and wine social comes with your stay. As an added attraction, the hotel advertises that its rooms feature whirlpool baths and bidets. (We aren't sure of the lure of the latter and assume that these bidets are not of the whirlpool bath variety.)

While this hotel is the prettier of the two, it's a little tougher on dogs. Pooches need to be in the smallish range (the front desk clerk will help you decide if your dog is smallish), must stay on the third (smoking) floor, and are not allowed in the elevator. (In fairness, we really like that neither of these hotels charges an extra fee for dogs.)

On the outside, the hotel looks like any of the many decent old brick-facade apartment buildings in the slightly-off-Union-Square neighborhood. It's not the Ritz, but it is a comfy place to stay with your wee dog. Rates are $99–199. 701 Post Street 94109; 415/673-2600 or 800/533-6533; www.beresford.com.

Hotel Cosmo: Dogs love this hip hotel. The views are cool and the room are cosmopolitan yet comfy (the beds have cushy pillowtops). The hotel is artsy without being pretentious. Dogs hate pretentiousness. But what dogs like most at this hotel is that they're treated like welcome guests here. Upon arrival, every dog gets a Tails of the City Kit, which includes a pet blanket, a food and water bowl, a mat to put those on, a treat, and "Yip Yap" breath fresheners (for your dog, not you, unless of course you forgot your toothpaste). Dogs who stay here also get access to the hotel's open-air patio. Rates are $79–179. 761 Post Street 94109; 415/673-6040; www.hotel-cosmo.com.

Hotel Monaco: You and your dog will have *so* much fun at this upscale, sophisticated, whimsical hotel near Union Square. Upon entering the main lobby, you'll be wowed by the gorgeous two-story-tall French-style fireplace. (It's like the famed fireplace in *Citizen Kane*, only without the austere emotional surroundings.) Louis Armstrong hits and other sumptuous music floats around the high ceilings, which sport wonderful, light-hearted murals of the sky and hot-air balloons.

The rooms here are sumptuous, with opulent decor. You'll find a variety of furnishings, including canopied beds (with thick, rich material for the canopy), Chinese-style armoires, and cushy ottomans. If you need more room, you can stay in a gorgeous suite that comes with a big whirlpool tub and entertainment center with VCR.

The hotel's mission is to seduce and pamper, and dogs are not excluded from this noble cause. The Monaco offers something called the Bone A Petit Pet Package. It includes bottled water, clean-up bags, dog towels, quality chew toys, gourmet dog cookies, and temporary pooch ID tags. You can also ask the front desk for Lassie, Babe, or Dr. Doolittle videos. The price for all this: $0! Yes, free! But you have to mention the Pet Package when you make your reservation. In addition, so that your furry friend won't be lonely if you need to step out, dog-walking or sitting services are available for a fee.

Rates are $179–350. Don't forget to ask for the Pet Package when making your reservation. The Monaco, a Kimpton hotel (see Kimpton Hotels, below, for more on these beauties) is directly across from the Curran Theater. 501 Geary Street 94102; 415/292-0100 or 800/214-4220; www.monaco-sf.com.

Hotel Nikko: Small dogs are welcome to spend the night with you at this lovely contemporary Japanese-style hotel three blocks west of Union Square. Rates are $179–3,000. 222 Mason Street, San Francisco, CA 94102; 415/394-1111; www.nikkohotels.com.

Hotel Triton: If you're hankering for a wonderfully unique, creative, fun, intimate, whimsical, sophisticated place to stay, hanker no more, and book yourself any of the 140 rooms at the Hotel Triton. It's as if Betty Boop, Salvador Dali, Pee Wee Herman, and UB Iwerks somehow came together to create their dream lodging.

I normally consider it a sign of laziness when guidebook authors lift material straight out of a brochure, but I shall do this here with the noble purpose of letting the creative Triton folks speak for themselves: "Totally hip without the attitude, the Hotel Triton is not for your average Joe…" (I pause for a moment to say that Joe Dog tried hard not to take offense at this statement) "…but for guests with imagination and style. A tarot reading during nightly wine hour, whimsical sculptured furniture, and a twinkly-eyed staff" (I pause again to attest to the fact that their eyes do, indeed, seem to sparkle a little more than those of most other hotel staffers') "await you at this fun and funky gem. Stay in one of the celebrity suites designed by the likes of Jerry Garcia, Santana, or Graham Nash. If you're feeling environmentally correct, try an Eco-Room. For a little more yin in your yang, a Zen Den might help you attain harmony."

The hotel offers a number of special packages, but the most unusual is the "So Hip It Hurts" package: For $289, you get a deluxe guestroom and a $65 tattoo or piercing at Mom's Body Shop on Haight Street. Well, that's one way for a hotel to leave an impression on you.

Room rates are $150–389. The Triton, a Kimpton hotel (see Kimpton Hotels, below, for other dog-friendly Kimptons) is right across the street from the Dragon Gate entrance to Chinatown. 342 Grant Avenue 94108; 415/394-0500 or 800/433-6611; www.hotel-tritonsf.com.

Kimpton Hotels: There are 13 of these delightful, super-dog-friendly boutique hotels in San Francisco. Alas, there's not room to write about them all in detail. I've described three in my usual fashion in this section, but I don't want to ignore the others, so here's a synopsis of each. They charge no dog fee except when a special dog package is offered. If you want to save money, you don't have to take the package, no matter how pleading your dogs' eyes.

Union Square area

Hotel Monaco: See full listing, above.

Hotel Palomar: It's sophisticated, it's luxurious, it's South of Market, and it's got an amazing dog package called the Lap of Luxury, which includes a visit from a pet stylist to do your dog's nails and hair, a pet massage, a pet robe (it's true, it's true!), a leopard print dog bed, bottled water, treats, a Palomar signature collar and leash, doggy breath mints, and a toy. 12 4th Street 94103; 415/348-1111 or 877/294-9711; www.hotelpalomar.com.

Monticello Inn: The only thing missing in this grand colonial-style hotel is Thomas Jefferson. The hotel is housed in a landmark 1906 building. 127 Ellis Street 94102; 415/392-8800 or 866/778-6169; www.monticelloinn.com.

The Prescott Hotel: Enjoy quiet luxury at this beautiful hotel. The rich color schemes in each room are perfect for a relaxing evening with your quiet dog. 545 Post Street 94102; 415/563-0303 or 866/271-3632; www.prescotthotel.com.

The Serrano Hotel: Dogs enjoy staying at this Spanish-revival hotel not because of the interesting architecture but because of the Pet Palace Package. It includes designer mineral water, gourmet dog treats, and poopy bags. For an extra fee, dogs can get a little walk, dog food, a dog bed, or a leash. 405 Taylor Street 94102; 415/885-2500 or 866/289-6561; www.serrano hotel.com.

The Sir Francis Drake Hotel: See full listing, below.

Villa Florence Hotel: You like Italy? Stay at this lovely Italian-themed little hotel. 225 Powell Street 94102; 415/397-7700 or 866/823-4669; www.villaflorence.com.

Nob Hill

Hotel Juliana: The pillowtop beds at this contemporary, stylish hotel are great for humans, but dogs who stay here can get the Man's Best Friend package, which includes dog treats, a park map for finding a good spot for "walkies," a chew toy, and bottled water. Humans get a number of goodies in this package, including a box of chocolates and free parking. 590 Bush Street 94108; 415/392-2540 or 866/325-9457; www.julianahotel.com.

Fisherman's Wharf

Argonaut Hotel: This luxurious, historic waterfront hotel provides great views of the Golden Gate Bridge, Alcatraz, and Ghirardelli Square. 495 Jefferson Street at Hyde Street 94109; 415/563-0800 or 800/790-1415; www .argonauthotel.com.

Best Western Tuscan Inn: Yes, Kimpton runs this Best Western, and you can tell by the nice touches, including a big fireplace in the lobby. Opt for the special Wag and Stay package and you'll get dog bedding, biscuits, toys, poop bags, and a CD of music created especially for pets. (I have no idea what this sounds like.) 425 Northpoint Street 94133; 415/561-1100 or 800/648-4626; www.tuscaninn.com.

Financial District

Galleria Park Hotel: You'll find an urban oasis at this 1911 Art Nouveau–style hotel. Choose the Something to Bark About package and your dog will get a "doggy bag" filled with treats, a plush toy, bottled water, a bowl, and poop bags. 191 Sutter Street 94104; 415/781-3060 or 866/756-3036; www.galleriapark.com.

Harbor Court Hotel: The Harbor Court is homey and restful at the same time it's a happening place. Dogs who stay here can get the Pet Retreat package, which features a pet bed and pad, a rawhide bone, water and food bowls, bottled water, and poop bags. 165 Steuart Street 94105; 415/882-1300 or 866/792-6283; www.harborcourthotel.com.

Hotel Triton: See full listing, above.

Laurel Motor Inn: The owners love dogs, so many visiting dogs choose to stay here. It's conveniently situated in a lovely neighborhood just far enough from downtown to be able to get great views of it from some of the rooms. It's also just a bone's throw from the magnificent Presidio National Park (see Parks, Beaches, and Recreation Areas). Rates are $145–190. 444 Presidio Avenue 94115; 415/567-8467; www.thelaurelinn.com.

The Marina Motel: This charming 1930s motel is a few blocks from two great places to walk your dog—Crissy Field and the Presidio (see Parks, Beaches, and Recreation Areas). It has a bougainvillea and fuschia-festooned courtyard and little wrought iron balconies, which makes it feel less motelly and more Mediterranean. Some rooms have kitchens, and every room comes with free parking for one car. This alone is worth the room price in this neighborhood! Rates are $79–125. Dogs are $10 extra. 2576 Lombard Street 94123; 800/346-6118; www.marinamotel.com.

Ocean Park Motel: This art deco gem is San Francisco's very first motel. It was completed in 1937, one month before the Golden Gate Bridge. "When we took the place over (in 1977), deco was pretty much a lost art," says owner Marc Duffett. "But my wife and I put everything into this place to preserve the deco flair and at the same time make it homey."

Conveniently situated just a long block from Ocean Beach (above) and the San Francisco Zoo, this pleasant motel provides a quiet, safe atmosphere away from the hectic pace (and price) of downtown. You can hear the foghorns from the motel's relaxing hot tub. You can also hear the trolley cars, but it's not bad. And there's a special little play area for kids (the Duffetts have two and know the importance of playgrounds). Rates are $75–115. Two-room suites with three queen-sized beds and a kitchen are $160–195. Dogs are $10 extra. 2690 46th Avenue; 415/566-7020; www.oceanparkmotel.citysearch.com.

The Palace Hotel: Dogs at the Palace? I know what you're thinking: These must be those itsy-bitsy dogs you can't see until you step on them and they shriek, right? Wrong! This four-diamond luxury hotel welcomes dogs up to 80 pounds to stay here (as long as they're not pit bulls or rotties). Eighty pounds is a lot of dog, and it's thrilling to me that they're able to hunker down at this gorgeous old downtown hotel. Today the Palace, tomorrow the White House! Dogs can't have tea with you in the gorgeous tea room, but if you want a version of the infamous Tea at the Palace, you can simply order room service. Rates are $149–550. 2 New Montgomery Street 94105; 415/512-1111; www.sfpalace.com.

San Francisco Marriott Fisherman's Wharf: Stay here and you and your pooch are just two blocks from all the T-shirt and souvenir shops that have taken over Fisherman's Wharf. Actually, some fishing boats still live at the Wharf, and some local crabs still frequent the restaurants, so it's not as commercialized as it looks at first (and second) glance. The rooms are decent, and your stay includes use of the hotel's health club and sauna. Dogs need to be under 50 pounds to stay here. Rates are $159–279. 1250 Columbus Avenue 94133; 415/775-7555 or 800/228-9290.

The Sir Francis Drake Hotel: This luxurious old Union Square hotel is famous for its Beefeater doorman who helps tourists and hotel guests alike. Jake likes the Beefeater almost as much as he likes beef. So do other doggy visitors, who tend to get excited about this man in plush red and a cool hat.

This hotel has been a stylin' place since 1928, and since it's become a Kimpton hotel (see above for more on the dog-friendly Kimptons), it's also become a little more mod and super-dog-friendly. If you opt for the Bowzer Buddy Package during your stay, you can get a dog bowl with "in-room water service daily," a Sir Francis Drake Hotel chew toy, and a few other goodies. Rates for the package start at $189. You can choose a plain old stay at the hotel and it'll run you $139–429. Should you care to dance, the concierge will help you find a dog-sitter so you can cut a rug or two at the marvelous Harry Denton's Starlight Lounge, at the top of the hotel. 450 Powell Street 94102; 415/392-7755 or 800/795-7129; www.sirfrancisdrake.com.

TraveLodge by the Bay: Some rooms here have private patios. A few even have extra-length beds, should you find that you're tall. This motel is just three blocks from the part of Lombard Street that's known as "the crookedest street in the world." Rates are $65–135. Dogs are $20 extra and are relegated to the smoking rooms. 1450 Lombard Street 94123; 415/673-0691.

Westin St. Francis: The cable car stops in front of this historic landmark, so there's no excuse for not taking your dog on it. (See the Diversion Ride Halfway to the Stars for more about dogs on cable cars.) After a day of sniffing around San Francisco, your medium to small dog (40 pounds is the max allowed here) can crash on the Heavenly Pet Bed supplied by the St. Francis. It's a miniature version of the delectably comfortable Heavenly Bed that humans get to sleep on here. Dogs love this, but they're also grateful that humans get one Heavenly item dogs don't: The Heavenly Bath. Rates are $219–1,850. 335 Powell Street 94102; 415/397-7000; www.westinstfrancis.com.

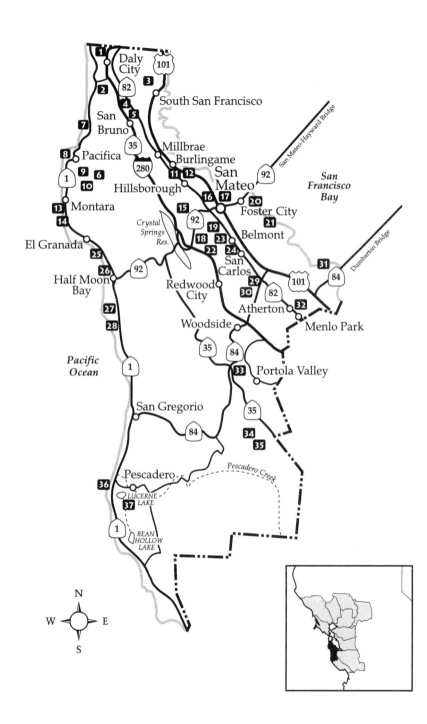

CHAPTER 8

San Mateo County

From the cool and foggy beaches of the coast to the warm and sunny inland communities, there's something for every dog's taste in San Mateo County. Sadly, the 15,000 acres of county parklands still ban dogs, and some state beaches recently followed suit. But don't let your dog cry in her kibble. A few beaches (including one off-leash beauty in Pacifica) and plenty of parks still welcome your dog. And a couple of off-leash parks were born here since the last edition.

The Midpeninsula Regional Open Space District has become one of a dog's best friends, with four preserves in San Mateo County that allow dogs. One even has a 16-acre off-leash area (see Pulgas Ridge Open Space Preserve in the San Carlos section). Be sure to follow extremely good doggy etiquette at all the district's preserves, because there are a lot of antidoggers out there who would love to get the district to take away our privileges.

The district has unique rules about poop-scooping and six-foot leashes. Scooping the poop is required in places, but because of limited trash disposal sites, if you kick the poop off the trail, that's usually considered OK. (Helpful

PICK OF THE LITTER—SAN MATEO COUNTY

BEST OFF-LEASH BEACH
Esplanade Beach, Pacifica (pages 215–216)

MOST PRIM AND TRIM DOG PARK
Foster City Dog Playground, Foster City (page 223)

BEST CHUNK OF LEASH-FREE LAND
16 acres within Pulgas Ridge Open Space Preserve, San Carlos (pages 232–233)

MOST DOG-FRIENDLY PLACES TO EAT
Beach Cafe, Pacifica (page 216)
Cameron's Inn, Half Moon Bay (page 229)
Moon Juice Cafe, Half Moon Bay (page 230)

MOST DOG-FRIENDLY PLACE TO STAY
Westin San Francisco Airport, Millbrae (pages 217–218)

BEST SEAVIEW COTTAGES
Estancia del Mar Cottages, Pescadero (pages 238–239)

FRIENDLIEST BOOKSTORE
Kepler's Books, Menlo Park (page 232)

hint: Don't wear open-toed sandals.) And retractable leashes are allowed to go beyond the six-foot mark in many instances, which is a rare thing indeed. The exceptions: when you're within 100 feet of parking lots, roads, trailheads, picnic areas, and restrooms, and when you're within 50 feet of other people or any body of water, including creeks. It's a great policy—one other park districts should implement.

The district provides excellent park brochures and a comprehensive flyer about dog rules. When we received the most recent packet, it came in an attractive translucent green vellum envelope and had everything we needed, and then some. Phone 650/691-1200 for doggy details.

Daly City

PARKS, BEACHES, AND RECREATION AREAS

Daly City isn't flush with great places to take a dog. In fact, some city parks don't even permit pooches. Here are two that do.

1 Palisades Park Dog Area

 (See San Mateo County map on page 210)

This is the smallest dog park I've ever seen. It's about 3,600 square feet—not much bigger than many backyards in the area. It's fenced and has double gates for dog safety, but it's not signed, and there's nothing in it at all except for some petrified poops scattered around the thick grass. The grass is so lush here's because it's not doggy Grand Central Station, as so many dog parks are. Without the stampeding paws, the grass will grow. If you have a dog who will chase a tennis ball, bring him here and he could get a decent workout. (Just don't throw the ball too far, or it could land in the ocean, which is just behind some tall shrubs and way down a cliff.)

The park is conveniently situated if you're on Highway 35/Skyline Boulevard and your dog starts crossing his legs. Turn west on Westridge Avenue and you'll see Palisades Park at the end of the road. Look to the right of the playground and you'll see the teeny dog park. 650/991-8006.

2 Gellert Park

 (See San Mateo County map on page 210)

The best feature of this flat, square park is that it's right behind the Serramonte Library. It's also conveniently situated if you are going to pay homage to someone at the Chinese Cemetery, right across the street. The park is made up of a few sports fields—watch out for flying baseballs, soccer balls, and softballs. The park's trees, which grow on two sides, aren't accessible—they're on top of a very steep little ridge. Your dog may become frustrated, especially since he must wear a leash through all this.

The park is on Wembley Drive at Gellert Boulevard. 650/991-8006.

South San Francisco

PARKS, BEACHES, AND RECREATION AREAS

3 Orange Memorial Park

(See San Mateo County map on page 210)

Hidden behind the park's large baseball field is a big square of land surrounded on all sides by tall trees. It's good for a quick on-leash romp. There seem to be all kinds of sniffs around the large weeping willow tree in the middle of the field. It's on Orange Avenue at Tennis Drive. 650/829-3800.

4 Westborough Park

 (See San Mateo County map on page 210)

This is a hilly little park with many picnic tables, a tennis court, and a children's playground. Your best bet is to take the narrow, paved path along the back of the park. It's lined with trees and far from the madding baseball field below. Leashes are required. It's on Westborough Avenue at Galway Drive, just west of I-280. 650/829-3800.

PLACES TO STAY

La Quinta Inn San Francisco Airport: Rates are $119–129. 20 Airport Boulevard 94080; 650/583-2223; www.laquinta.com.

San Bruno

PARKS, BEACHES, AND RECREATION AREAS

5 San Bruno Dog Exercise Area/Sandberg Field

 (See San Mateo County map on page 210)

This is a gem of a fenced-in park, where dogs can run their tails off—without a leash. The grass always seems to be green. There's plenty of water, poop bags galore, and benches for two-legged beasts. As an extra bonus, it has a great view of the bay. And for those who can't get enough of it while driving north on U.S. 101, there's an unparalleled view of that strange sign: "South San Francisco—The Industrial City."

The park opened in 1989 after local dog trainer Mal Lightfoot was fined for walking his notoriously obedient dogs off leash. "I spend all my life training dogs to be good citizens, and I was treated like a criminal," says Lightfoot, who runs the San Bruno Dog Training School. "It was the last straw." It took him and dozens of other frustrated dog owners nearly two years of working with—and against—city officials to get the park of their dreams.

Some detailed directions are necessary for finding this out-of-the-way park, even for locals. From El Camino Real, take Sneath Lane west. Just past I-280, turn right on Rollingwood Drive. Go right again at the first possible right, Crestwood Drive. Go left on Valleywood Drive and take a sharp right at Evergreen Drive. The park is in a few blocks, at Maywood and Evergreen Drives in back of the old Carl Sandburg School. Once at the school driveway, take the first road to the right and drive until you see the dog park. 650/738-7381.

6 Sweeney Ridge

🐾🐾🐾🐾 (See San Mateo County map on page 210)

If your dog appreciates breathtaking vistas of the Bay Area, with a rainbow assortment of wildflowers in the foreground, this 1,000-acre park is a rare treat. But if your canine is like most, he can take or leave such a magnificent panorama.

Still, if you like stunning views and a vigorous uphill climb, take the Sneath Lane entrance. It may be toasty when you start, but bring a couple of thick wool sweaters if you plan to hike along the ridge—it's cold and often foggy up there. The furrier your dog, the more she'll take to the invigorating conditions.

The Skyline College entrance is ideal if you want a more moderate grade, but both trailheads will take you to the same place. The leash law here can come in handy if your dog is of the pulling mentality. Just say "mush" on those steep slopes.

From different parts of the ridge, you'll be able to see the ocean (and the Farallon Islands, on a good day), as well as Mt. Tamalpais in Marin, Mt. Diablo to the east, and Montara Mountain to the south. Judging by all the canines with flaring nostrils, the scents from all four directions must be as enticing as the views.

For the Sneath Lane entrance, take San Bruno's Sneath Lane all the way to the end. There's usually plenty of parking. The Skyline College entrance, off College Drive, is in the southeast corner of campus, near Lot 2. 415/239-2366 or 415/556-8371.

Pacifica

PARKS, BEACHES, AND RECREATION AREAS

Tails are wagging fast around here these days. This coastal community now has a leash-free beach! (See Esplanade Beach.)

7 Esplanade Beach

🐾🐾🐾🐾 🐕 (See San Mateo County map on page 210)

This is the only beach between Humboldt County and Santa Cruz where dogs can legally trot around off leash these days (with the exception of two small beaches in Marin), so it's a really big deal that they're permitted to enjoy a leash-free walk if they're under voice control. The beach is fairly wide (if it's not high tide) and long enough for a very good walk. Many people who come here bring tennis-ball launchers so their dogs can really go out for a fly ball.

At the top of the long staircase that leads to the beach you'll find an attractive grassy area right in front of some long, low apartments. Leashed dogs are welcome to sniff around this area. To get to the beach, exit Highway 1 at Manor Drive and head west on Manor toward the ocean. It will dead-end at Esplanade Drive. Turn right and follow Esplanade about a third of a mile to where it makes almost a 90-degree curve to the right. (You'll see a large sign for the Land's End apartments.) The green park will be on your left, as will the staircase leading down the cliff to the beach. Park anywhere along the street. 650/738-7381.

🗲 Pacifica State Beach/Linda Mar Beach

🐾🐾🐾 (See San Mateo County map on page 210)

Even though this is a state beach, leashed dogs are welcome here. It's run by the city of Pacifica, so it doesn't have to follow the more stringent "no dogs" rules being enforced by most other state beaches in coastal San Mateo County. The setting alone warrants a visit. With green rolling hills in the distance behind you and the pounding sea before you, you and your dog won't regret stopping here. This is Surfer Heaven, so if your dog likes to see surfers doing their thing, this is the place to come. On Highway 1, park between Crespi Drive and Linda Mar Boulevard. 415/561-4700.

🗲 Milagra Ridge

🐾🐾🐾🐾 (See San Mateo County map on page 210)

Follow the trail up to the top of the tallest hill and you'll end up with both an incredible view of the Pacific and a perfect plateau for a picnic. You'll see hillsides covered with ice plant and even a few Monterey pines along the way. Visit in the spring if you want to be wowed by wildflowers.

Despite the leash law, dogs really seem to enjoy this park. Make sure to keep them on the trail, as the environment here is fragile. And keep your eyes peeled for the Mission Blue butterfly. This park is one of its last habitats. Milagra Ridge is especially magical at night. You've never seen the full moon until you've seen it from here.

Enter on Sharp Park Road in Pacifica, between Highway 1 and Skyline Boulevard. 415/239-2366 or 415/556-8371.

🔟 Sweeney Ridge

🐾🐾🐾🐾 (See San Mateo County map on page 210)

See San Bruno section.

PLACES TO EAT

Beach Cafe: After a walk on the chilly beach, there's nothing like a hot espresso and homemade croissant at the outdoor tables here. Owner Paula Thomson loves dogs, so lucky dogs who visit get a treat or two. Highway 1 at Rockaway Beach Avenue, at 4430 Highway 1; 650/355-4532.

Sam's Deli: Sam's is a refreshing spot to hit after an afternoon at Pacifica State Beach. It has good sandwiches at low prices and two outdoor tables. It's at the Linda Mar Shopping Center, just behind the beach, on the same side as Denny's and the shoe stores, about halfway down the row of shops. 1261 Linda Mar Shopping Center; 650/359-5330.

Millbrae

Now that dogs aren't allowed on trails surrounding Crystal Springs Reservoir, they are howling. But they can still grab a bite and spend the night.

PLACES TO EAT

Leonardo's Delicatessen: This truly Italian deli has plenty of outdoor tables, all comfortably far from sidewalk traffic. 540 Broadway Avenue; 650/697-9779.

PLACES TO STAY

Clarion Hotel: Rates are $89–249. Dogs are $30 extra. 401 East Millbrae Avenue 94030; 650/692-6363; www.clarionhotels.com.

Westin San Francisco Airport: If you're traveling by air and need to stay somewhere with your dog, this is about the most convenient and luxurious place you can stay. It's only two minutes from the airport. Each of the 390 rooms is well appointed and has a very comfortable bed, known as the Heavenly Bed. So that dogs don't feel left out, dogs who stay here get their own Heavenly Pet Bed. Pooches we've talked with say the beds are dreamy. For humans, there are mutt mitts (not exciting, but very handy) and better yet, there's a fitness center and a yummy Mediterranean-style bistro. Rates are $99–379. 1 Old Bayshore Highway 94030; 650/692-3500 or 800/228-3000; www.starwood.com.

Burlingame

PARKS, BEACHES, AND RECREATION AREAS

11 Burlingame Dog Exercise Park

🐾🐾🐾🐕 (See San Mateo County map on page 210)

Hooray! Burlingame's dog park is finally a reality. The half-grass, half–fine gravel park is a popular place, with a very different shape than most dog parks. It's very long, almost as long as two football fields end to end, and not extremely wide (anywhere from 30 feet to 70 feet). This lends itself very well to the park's name: It's a dog *exercise* park. With a shape like this, forward movement beckons. You and your dog can stand around and chat and sniff (as most do here), or you can really walk in this fenced park. In more typical squarish dog parks, you'd look kind of foolish taking a hike.

There are no decent-sized trees here yet. All are in the sapling stage, about waist-high at last check. But boy dogs still manage to do plenty of leg lifts on other spots they seem to find fascinating. Speaking of bodily functions, the one drawback to this park is that it's right next to a sewage treatment plant. This can make the park a little whiffy at times, depending on which way the wind is blowing, but it's usually not a problem. In fact, as far as dogs are concerned, the stinkier the better.

A nice bonus if you use this park: There's a great path you can follow. You can pick up the path behind the dog park. You have to leash up to use it, but it's a good walk. It's within Bayside Park, on the Old Bayshore Freeway between Anza Boulevard and Broadway. 650/558-7300.

12 Washington Park

🐾🐾 (See San Mateo County map on page 210)

This relatively small park has the look of an old college campus. Its trees are big and old and mostly deciduous, making autumn a particularly brilliant time. Bring a lunch and eat it on the thick, knotty old redwood picnic tables. They're something out of the Enchanted Forest. Joe Dog was always intrigued by the abundance of squirrels, but he never got too far with his pursuits, since leashes have been the law forever, and since the police station is around the corner.

The park is at 850 Burlingame Avenue below Carolan Avenue. 650/558-7300.

PLACES TO EAT

Cafe La Scala: The outdoor area at this exquisite Italian restaurant has dozens of tables, but it's still very romantic, with beautiful flowers, soft music, and pastoral murals. It's all very Florentine. Dogs need to sit at the edge of the patio area. In cooler months, the area is warmed by heat lamps. 1219 Burlingame Avenue; 650/347-3035.

PLACES TO STAY

San Francisco Airport Marriott: If you need to stay near the airport, and your dog appreciates good views of San Francisco Bay, you couldn't ask for a better hotel. Rates are $89–245. 1800 Old Bayshore Highway 94010; 650/692-9100.

Vagabond Inn: With these prices, it's a wonder they still call it Vagabond Inn. Rates are $92–120. Dogs are $10 extra. 1640 Bayshore Highway 94010; 650/692-4040.

Montara

PARKS, BEACHES, AND RECREATION AREAS

🐾 McNee Ranch State Park

🐾🐾🐾🐾 (See San Mateo County map on page 210)

State parks usually ban dogs completely, or at least from all but paved roadways. But McNee is a refreshing exception to the rule. At McNee, you can hike at the same level as the soaring gulls and watch the gem-blue ocean below. The higher you go up Montara Mountain, the more magnificent the view. Hardly a soul knows about this park, so if it's peace you want, it's peace you'll get.

And if it's a workout you want, you'll get that, too. Just strap on a day pack and bring lots of water for you and your dog. If you do the full hike, you'll ascend from sea level to 1,898 feet in a couple of hours. As you hike up and away from the ocean and the road, you lose all sounds of civilization, and Highway 1 fades into a thin ribbon and disappears below.

As soon as you go through the gate at the bottom of the park, follow the narrow trails to the left up the hills. You may be tempted to take the wide and winding paved road from the start, but to avoid any bikers, take the little trails. Besides, they lead to much better vistas.

Eventually, you'll come to a point where you have a choice of going left or right on a wider part of the trail. It's a choice between paradise and heaven. Left will lead you to a stunning view of the Golden Gate Bridge and the Farallon Islands. Right will bring you to the top of the ridge, where you see Mt. Diablo and the rest of San Francisco Bay.

This was one of Joe's favorite parks, despite the leash law. Still, he always managed to slide down several steep grassy hills on his back, wriggling and moaning in ecstasy all the way.

It's easy to miss this park since there aren't any signs and there's no official parking lot. From Highway 1 in Montara, park at the far northern end of the

Montara State Beach parking lot and walk across the road. Be careful as you walk along Highway 1, because there's hardly any room on the shoulder. You'll see a gate on a dirt road just north of you and a small state property sign. That's where you go in. A few cars can also park next to the gate on the sides of the dirt road. But don't block the gate or your car probably won't be there when you get back. 415/726-8819.

🐾 Montara State Beach

🐾🐾🐾🐾 (See San Mateo County map on page 210)

This long, wide beach has more nooks and crannies than your dog will be able to investigate. Around midbeach, you'll find several little inlets carved into the minicliffs. Take your dog back there at low tide and you'll find all sorts of water, grass, mud, and beach flotsam. It's a good place for her to get her paws wet while obeying the leash law. The water at the inlets is as calm as pond water. This is where Joe first dared to walk in water. It was only a centimeter deep, but he licked his paws in triumph all the way home.

With the recent banning of dogs at other state beaches in the area, this one has been taking a pounding of late. I know it's hard, but please keep your dog on leash, or this beach could go the way of so many others.

Off Highway 1, park in the little lot behind the Chart House restaurant. There's also a parking area on the north side of the beach, off Highway 1. 415/726-8819.

PLACES TO STAY

Farallone Bed and Breakfast Inn: Two of the nine rooms in this homey Victorian inn have a private balcony and a small whirlpool bath. Some rooms have ocean views. A basic breakfast comes with your room. Rooms are $65–130. Dogs require a $25 deposit and are charged a $25 fee for the length of their stay. 1410 Main Street 94037; 650/728-8200 or 800/818-7319; www.faralloneinn.com.

Hillsborough

PARKS, BEACHES, AND RECREATION AREAS

🐾 Vista Park

🐾 (See San Mateo County map on page 210)

You can visit this park only if you live here, unless you choose to walk miles to get to it—there's no street parking for blocks, and no parking lot. And chances are that if you live in this town, your backyard is bigger anyway. A little section in the back has several tall eucalyptus trees that leashed neighborhood dogs call their own. It's good for sniffs when you can't get to a better park.

The park is at Vista and Culebra Roads. 650/579-3800.

San Mateo

PARKS, BEACHES, AND RECREATION AREAS

16 Central Park

🐾🐾🐾 (See San Mateo County map on page 210)

Bring plenty of quarters if you want to fully experience this strange park on the edge of downtown. It costs a quarter to park in the underground lot; a quarter to put your finger in the pulse machine; a quarter to watch the chicken lay a plastic prize egg; a quarter for the Pen Vendorama; it even costs a quarter for a cup of water at the refreshment stand, although smart shoppers know there's a water fountain within 20 feet.

As you enter the park from the 5th Avenue side, you immediately encounter the concession stand and surrounding dispensers that rival any at state fairs. The stand has good ice cream and tolerable pizza.

The rest of the park is a lush, green, miniature version of Golden Gate Park. There's a Japanese garden, and although no dogs are allowed inside, the Japanese ambience spills outside. The days we've visited, there was always something going on at the outdoor stage in back of the recreation center. A couple of large meadows are bordered by big shady redwoods. There's even a pint-sized railroad that takes up part of a small field. Someone told us that dogs have been known to chase the cars as they chug along the track. Leashes are a must, a rule you'd be well advised to follow: The fine for loose dogs is not a quarter.

The park is on East 5th Avenue at El Camino Real. 650/522-7420.

17 Bayside-Joinville Park

 (See San Mateo County map on page 210)

Human olfactory senses may be mildly offended by the scents in this park, but dogs seem to thrive on them. Depending on which way the wind is blowing, the odor is bound to hit you at some point. It's a stale smell, like a dishrag that's still in the sink a week after Thanksgiving. Sometimes it's even worse. The alleged culprit is an old compost site across the street, where Shoreline Park will be built in the future. When it's potent, dogs tend to stand noses to the wind, tails slightly trembling, glued in homage.

But the park has some notable qualities. It's just across the street from San Francisco Bay, it's on Marina Lagoon (sorry, no swimming allowed), and it's well maintained.

The park has two sections. If you're the type who likes the bad news first, start at the Anchor Road entrance and take the path along the lagoon, over a guano-covered footbridge, past the big gray pump station, and onto a little dirt path on the edge of the lagoon. Then go left and take the second, cleaner footbridge over to the better half of the park. It's got a decent-sized field, young trees, and tennis courts. Or you can enter at Kehoe Avenue and Roberta Drive and reverse the path. 650/522-7420.

18 Laurelwood Park

(See San Mateo County map on page 210)

A small, clear stream winds the length of this rural park in the suburbs. Joe Dog never wanted anything to do with the water and jumped from one side to the other without getting a toenail damp. But Jake, aka Mr. Water, delights in its fresh scents and enticing sounds. Follow the bike trail—heeding the leash law, as this is a popular spot for bikers—along the stream, and enjoy tree-covered hillsides in a virtually suburb-free environment. Only a few blocks from the Laurelwood Shopping Center, this park is an ideal getaway after a quick shopping trip. The kids can use the playground at the foot of the bike trail.

The park is at Glendora and Cedarwood Drives. 650/522-7420.

19 Beresford Park

(See San Mateo County map on page 210)

The bulk of this park is made up of sports fields. But venture behind the garden center and you and your pooch can enjoy a pleasant little leashed romp on a large grassy field. Many youthful-but-shady pine trees are growing well despite dozens of daily assaults from male dogs. Several picnic tables and a large children's play area near the field make this an adequate spot for a weekend afternoon with the family. People are friendly here—we were twice offered soda and beer by locals, who wanted Joe to "hang" with them.

The park is on Parkside Way at Alameda de las Pulgas. 650/522-7420.

PLACES TO EAT

Borel's Deli: You have your choice of deli food or hot food here. "Order the baked, hot turkey. Get extra gravy. Then drop it so your dog can eat it," Joe Dog would advise. Dine with your pooch outside at two tables. 59 Bovet Road; 650/573-7710.

PLACES TO STAY

Residence Inn by Marriott: There's a walking path not far from here, so it's a good place to stay with your pooch. Besides, it's a comfy lodging—not quite home, but it tries to come close. Rates are $89–179. Dogs are $10 extra, plus a $75 fee per visit. 2000 Winward Way 94404; 650/574-4700; www.marriott.com.

Foster City

PARKS, BEACHES, AND RECREATION AREAS

20 Foster City Dog Playground

🐾🐾🐾🐕 (See San Mateo County map on page 210)

This tidy, neat, petite fenced park with artificial grass is a little like a Stepford Wife: Lovely to look at, but perfect to the point of being scary. When I visited with Jake, I spent the whole time silently praying that he'd poop on the refined gravel ground cover (formally known as decomposed granite), not on the carpetlike Field Turf. The turf is the modern version of Astroturf, and it's like a green rug that aspires to be golf-course grass. I asked a nice gent there what happens if a dog does go to the bathroom on it, and he pointed to a poop-bag dispenser (no problem), and also to a scrub brush and bucket of water near the water fountain (ah, the Cinderella routine).

In the end, Jake didn't poop anywhere. He was having too much fun playing chase games with his new friends and learning to run through an agility tire and over an agility jump. Big dogs have their own section, which is great, because the small-dog section had really tiny, breakable dogs when we visited. (The small-dog section had the air of a casual country club, with the well-dressed dog people reposing on a variety of lawn chairs.) The entire park is less than a half acre, but dogs greatly enjoy themselves. There's shade from two large green shade structures, and water, scoops, picnic tables, and benches. A couple of very cute rusted-metal dog sculptures grace one end of the park.

Exit eastbound Highway 92 at Foster City Boulevard, go left at the offramp, and then right within a block at Foster City Boulevard. Travel about .7 mile and go right on Bounty Drive, and then left almost immediately into the parking lot. 650/286-3382.

PLACES TO EAT

Dogs dig dining at Foster City's lagoon-side restaurants. Here's one that welcomes dogs. Others do, too, but don't jump at the chance to advertise it.

Plaza Gourmet: Good dogs can dine with you on the attractive woodplanked deck. If your dog is thirsty, a fresh bowl of water is hers for the asking. 929C Edgewater Boulevard; 650/638-0214.

Redwood City

PARKS, BEACHES, AND RECREATION AREAS

21 Shore Dogs Park

🐾🐾🐾🐕 (See San Mateo County map on page 210)

This park is only three-quarters of an acre, but it doesn't matter. Dogs and their people are simply overjoyed just to have some legal off-leash romping room after so many years of being banned from all city parks. (It can get might windy here, and it's quite a sight to see dogs joyously running around with their ears flapping, and then standing still only to have their ears continue to flap.)

As its name may tell you, Shore Dogs Park is near the water. And what dog doesn't dig being able to sniff the odors wafting off of San Francisco Bay? During winter and fall, the park's location gives you and your dog a front-row seat to the shorebird migration. Your dog's jaw will drop as she watches an egret flap its gigantic wings. The birds have nothing to fear, as the park is fenced, and dogs can't fly.

Speaking of fear, the park is a good place to bring a small dog who feels intimidated by big beefy canines; there's a special fenced grassy area just for the little guys. Small dogs are welcome to join their bigger cousins at the main dog run, but sometimes it can be a little intimidating if your head doesn't even reach the knee of a giant who's running full out. (I know dogs don't have knees, but you get the picture.) The park is off Redwood Shores Parkway, near the end of Radio Road, in Redwood Shores. 650/654-6538.

PLACES TO EAT

Curly, Harmony, and Brittney are Redwood City dogs with great taste in dining. Here are their tried-and-true recommendations.

City Pub: Like pub food? Dine at the outdoor tables here at this charming hangout. If your dog is thirsty, the staff will happily provide a big bowl of water. 2620 Broadway; 650/363-2620.

Milagro's: The outdoor tables at this upscale Mexican restaurant are warm and cozy year-round, thanks to some effective heat lamps. Got a thirsty dog? The friendly servers bring out bowls of water for pooch diners. "I just sat a table of dogs and people yesterday!" said a vivacious host. "They were so well behaved and fun." 1099 Middlefield Road; 650/369-4730.

Mulligan's: There are lots of tables here for you and your dog. The dining, while not fine, will make your dog put on her best begging eyes. (Hot dogs, burgers, pizza, and fries tend to do that to even the most stoic pooch.) 2650 Broadway; 650/364-5600.

Belmont

PARKS, BEACHES, AND RECREATION AREAS

22 Water Dog Lake Park

🐾🐾🐾 (See San Mateo County map on page 210)

Dogs and their people seem magically drawn to this large, wooded park with a little lake in the middle. Maybe it's the way the moss drips off the trees at the bottom of this mountainous area, or the way the lake seems to create a refreshing breeze on the hottest days.

Or maybe it's got something to do with the name. We asked several dog owners how the park came to be called Water Dog Lake Park.

"I think the lake is kind of shaped like a dog. Actually, it's more like a kangaroo, isn't it?" said the proud owner of a beagle/terrier mix.

"It would be a good place to water your dog, if that were allowed," said a woman with a black Lab.

"When dogs and people were allowed to swim here, you couldn't get the Labs and all those water dogs out of this lake," explained a man with an Irish setter.

We hate to burst the romantic fantasy that a park as alluring as this one is named after man's best friend. But after some searching through historical records, we discovered the biting truth: Water Dog Lake Park was named after salamanders. A colloquial name for a salamander is "water dog," and apparently the little critters used to wriggle all over the place around here. We still think the park is great. Too bad dogs have to be leashed.

One other thing that we discovered about this park: If people would follow their dogs, perhaps a lot fewer would stumble onto the wrong trail. The one that goes up to the top of the park never comes near the lake and leads you more than a mile away from where you started. Joe tried tugging in the other direction, but I ignored him. We got a ride back to the entrance from a teenage boy who felt sorry for us.

Upon entering the park from the Lake Road entrance, take the wide path that goes straight in front of you. It will lead you down to the lake. Neither you nor your dog can go in the water, but you can have a great picnic there, or even go fishing off the little wooden pier.

If you start off taking the smaller trail that veers to the right, you'll get good exercise and a great view of the bay, but we don't recommend it, unless you enjoy getting lost and suffering heat fatigue in the summer. A final word of warning: Watch out for bikers. They're fast here.

Enter on Lake Road, just off Carlmont Drive. Try to come back to the same place. 650/595-7441.

23 Cipriani Park Dog Exercise Area

🐾🐾🐾🐕 (See San Mateo County map on page 210)

At press time for the book's latest edition, the big trees here had just been cut down, much to the dismay of dogs and their people. And the grass and wood-chip carpet had given way to decomposed granite. But this three-quarter-acre fenced park is still a treat for leash-free pooches and their chauffeurs. That's partly because of all the social events that take place here: There are frequent potlucks, seminars on topics such as canine first aid, and even a couple of fairs a year. In addition, the park has all good dog-park amenities, including poop bags, water, picnic tables, and attractive surroundings.

The park is at 2525 Buena Vista Avenue, behind the Cipriani School. It's a little hard to find. From El Camino Real, go west on Ralston Avenue. In about 1.5 miles, you'll pass Alameda de las Pulgas. Drive about another three-quarters of a mile, and be on the lookout for Cipriani Boulevard. It's a small street you can easily miss. Turn right on Cipriani and follow it a few blocks to Buena Vista. Turn left on Buena Vista and park near the school. You won't see the dog run from the street, but if you walk west and enter through the main park entrance, you'll soon see it. Whatever you do, don't take your dog through the school's playground when kids are present. The school really frowns on this. 650/595-7441.

🐾 Twin Pines Park

🐾🐾🐾 (See San Mateo County map on page 210)

This park is a hidden treasure, nestled among eucalyptus trees just outside the business district of Belmont. You'd never guess the dog wonders that await within. Your dog may hardly notice she's leashed. The main trail is paved and winds through sweet-smelling trees and brush. A clear stream runs below. In dry seasons, it's only about two feet deep, but in good years it swells to several feet. Dogs love to go down to the stream and wet their whistles. Past the picnic area are numerous small, quiet dirt trails that can take you up the woodsy hill or alongside the stream.

It's at 1225 Ralston Avenue, behind the police department. 650/595-7441.

El Granada

PLACES TO STAY

Harbor View Inn: Each of the 17 comfortable rooms at this upscale motel features a wonderful bay window seat, where you can get a very good view of the ocean and the harbor. You'll have to look over Highway 1, since you're on the east side of the road, but it's a nice touch you don't usually find at motels. The owners, Bob and Judy, have a little Yorkie, Joey, and they're mighty dog-friendly folks. They'll point you in the direction of a couple of hush-hush dog-walking spots nearby. Rates are $85–180. 51 Avenue Alhambra 94018; 650/726-2329; www.harbor-view-inn.com.

Half Moon Bay

This is a delightful place to come for a day of sniffing around the enchanting old "downtown" and checking out the beautiful ocean views. It's a real treat on days that are scorching elsewhere: This area is air-conditioned by the god of woolly sheepdogs. No matter how steaming hot it is elsewhere, you can almost always count on cool weather here. It's often chilly and foggy in the summer, wet and windy in the winter, and moderate in the fall and spring.

PARKS, BEACHES, AND RECREATION AREAS

Dogs are no longer allowed on the sand at any of the four Half Moon Bay State Beach areas, but they're still welcome to take a stroll on the scenic blufftop paths that stretch almost from one end of Half Moon Bay to the other. (See Half Moon Bay State Beach, Bluff Top Park, and Surfer's Beach for areas of easy trail access.)

Fortunately for sand-loving hounds, two city beaches permit leashed beasts.

25 Surfer's Beach

🐾 🐾 (See San Mateo County map on page 210)

Water dogs dig being able to dip their paws in the water here. On almost any day, no matter how cold and gray it is, you'll find loads of surfers waiting for the perfect wave. The beach isn't big or wide, and it can be crowded at times, but it's a fun place to take a little stroll with your leashed dog. A trail that starts here takes you miles down the shore. It's a terrific, flat, easy, and very scenic hike. Jake highly recommends it.

Surfer's Beach is on Highway 1 and Coronado Street, just south of Pillar Point Harbor. 650/726-8297.

26 Half Moon Bay State Beach Trail

🐾 🐾 🐾 (See San Mateo County map on page 210)

This name is a misnomer. Thanks to the threatened snowy plover bird, and to people who abused the leashed-dog privilege, dogs are no longer allowed on the beach, even if they promise to wear their leashes and behave perfectly. But they are welcome on the paved blufftop trail here. The views are excellent, the sea air uplifting.

You can hook up with the trail here at several points. There's signage along different spots of Highway 1. At the very west end of Kelly Avenue you'll find Francis Beach and the entrance for the campground. (More on camping below.) At the west end of Venice Boulevard is Venice Beach (not to be confused with its radically different counterpart in Los Angeles County), and at the west end of Young Avenue you'll find both Dunes Beach and Roosevelt Beach.

This isn't the place to come for a 15-minute romp: If you park in the lots, it costs $6. You can park a little away on the street, or take your car down to the city-run Bluff Top Park, which has not only a paved trail, but a leashed-dog-friendly sandy beach—for free! (See below.)

If you can ignore all the RVs and crowds of tents, the area above Francis Beach is a stunning camping spot. Perched on ice plant–covered dunes above the Pacific, it's one of the most accessible beach camping areas in the Bay Area. All of the 52 campsites are available on a first-come, first-served basis. Sites are $20–25.

From Highway 1, follow the brown and white signs to the appropriate beach. 650/726-8820.

27 Bluff Top Park

🐾 🐾 🐾 (See San Mateo County map on page 210)

This is a splendid area to visit with a leashed dog. The beach is beautiful, long, and fairly wide, and the bluff top has a couple of fun and scenic trails. If you're hankering for a great walk, you can hoof it through other park and beach areas for several miles—almost all the way to the Half Moon Bay harbor.

From Highway 1, take Poplar Avenue west all the way to the end. A parking lot will be on your left. 650/726-8297.

28 Half Moon Bay Dog Park

🐾🐾🐕 (See San Mateo County map on page 210)

This 15,000-square-foot dog park is just temporary until the long-awaited Coastside Dog Park is up and running. (That one's been years in the planning and debating stages, so don't let your dog hold his dog breath. In fact, when I asked a former dog park coordinator about when the park might become a reality, he asked me if I was over 30. I said yes. "Not in your lifetime," he replied. Apparently there's been a lot of frustration about how the city has handled some issues.)

The park is a disheveled mass of landscaping bark and scattered dog toys surrounded by temporary and not terribly attractive fencing. In other words, dogs love it here! Jake goes kooky when he arrives at this park, running around with every dog toy in his smiling face until we have to leave. And he never wants to leave. It goes to show that a dog park doesn't have to be fancy to be a hit with the canine crowd.

From Highway 1, turn west on Wavecrest Street (the intersection is where you'll find the super-dog-friendly eatery, Cameron's; see below) and continue down the bumpy old road about .3 mile almost to the end. You'll see a brown sign that says all dogs must be on a leash. Immediately after that is a little dirt road to the right. Follow that past the horseshoe pits and you'll be there. For an update on the park situation, check out www.coastdogs.org. 650/726-8297.

PLACES TO EAT

Cameron's Inn: English pub grub and rich and creamy fountain treats are the specialty here, but burgers, pizza, and salads are big sellers, too. Dine with your pooch at the big outdoor patio. Dogs who are lucky enough to come to this funky, charming, British treasure get to sniff out a double-decker bus out front. (It makes for a very cute photo.) The folks here love dogs and provide them treats and water. Cameron's is a bone's throw from Half Moon Bay's temporary dog park. (See above.) 1410 South Cabrillo Highway/Highway 1; 650/726-5705.

Casey's Cafe: The outdoor seating here is attractive, with several umbrella-topped tables in a pretty plaza. If you like to play games other than fetch, come here on game nights, which are usually Friday and Saturday. On warmer evenings you can play your favorite board game at the outdoor tables while snacking with your dog at your side. (If he's a border collie you can even use him as your game partner.) Casey's is right next to the Zaballa House (see Places to Stay), 328 Main Street; 650/560-4880.

Half Moon Bay Brewing Company: Good beer, good food, good dog-friendly ambience, and good sniffs from the waterfront. What else could a dog want? A bowl of water? It's yours for the asking. This fun eatery and drinkery is in nearby Princeton's Pillar Point Harbor, at 390 Capistrano Road; 650/728-BREW (650/728-2739).

Moon Juice Cafe: Vicki, who owns this delightful smoothie-juicey-sandwichey café, adores dogs and welcomes them to dine with their people at the two outdoor tables in this off-street area. If she knows you have a dog with you, she'll be sure to provide a big treat and ask if your dog would like some water. If you like bacon but want to convince yourself you're being at least somewhat healthy, order the BLT wrap. It's delicious. The café is just off the north end of Main Street, at 20 Stone Pine Road; 650/712-1635.

Moonside Bakery: All the delicious treats here are baked daily, except for the soup, which generally isn't baked. (But it's still made fresh daily.) This is truly an exceptional bakery, featuring all kinds of crusty breads and delectable sweets but specializing in German baked goods. Dine with dog at the many attractive, wooden, umbrella-topped tables outside. 604 Main Street; 650/726-9070.

Pasta Moon: This restaurant offers several sidewalk tables and every type of pasta imaginable. A *San Francisco Chronicle* food critic calls the house-made pastas here "addictive." Jake Dog suggests ordering the tagliatelle bathed in cream and surrounded by sliced sausage and prosciutto. It's a big plateful that you probably can't finish yourself, so your baleful-eyed canine might get lucky. 315 Main Street; 650/726-5125.

PLACES TO STAY

Half Moon Bay State Beach: See Half Moon Bay State Beach, above, for camping information.

Holiday Inn Express: Just five blocks from Half Moon Bay State Beach, and a few blocks from downtown, this dog-friendly hotel is conveniently situated for adventure-seeking pooches and their people. Rates are $93–179. Dogs are $10 extra. 230 Cabrillo Highway 94019; 650/726-3400; www.hiexpress .com/halfmoonbay.

Zaballa House: Dogs and their human roommates get to stay in the attractive rooms and suites in back of this Victorian inn's main building—the oldest standing house in Half Moon Bay, built in 1859. Dogs don't mind the more modern digs. The rooms are spacious and very attractive, and all have fireplaces. Suites come with fireplaces, kitchenettes, whirlpool tubs, and private decks.

The owners of the inn really enjoy dog guests. "A lot of pets are nicer than their people," says one of the innkeepers. If you visit at the right time, the front-desk person might take a photo of you and your dog to put in the VIP Dog Guest photo album. The album is tucked away, and sometimes employees don't seem to know of its existence, but it's there.

The inn is right in beautiful downtown Half Moon Bay, next to some mighty dog-friendly eateries. Rates are $99–279. Dogs pay $10 extra. 324 Main Street 94019; 650/726-9123; www.zaballahouse.net.

San Carlos

PARKS, BEACHES, AND RECREATION AREAS

29 Heather Park

🐾🐾🐾 (See San Mateo County map on page 210)

This is one of the few fenced-in dog parks we've ever seen that comes complete with rolling hills, wildflowers, old gnarled trees, and singing birds. Your dog will have the time of his life here, bounding up and down hills or trotting down the winding paved path to the bottom of the park—sans leash. You may be tempted to take some of the tiny dirt trails up the steep hills, but they tend to end abruptly, leaving you and your dog teetering precariously. The only thing the park lacks is water, usually a given at dog parks.

If you have a dog who likes to wander, watch out. There are a couple of potential escape routes near the two gates at the far ends of the park. Also, some dog people have not been scooping the poop as they should be, and the city of San Carlos is trying to get them to clean up their acts. The city is

DIVERSION

Sniff Out a Good Book: Your dog doesn't have to be Mr. Peabody to appreciate fine books. In fact, even if your dog doesn't know his assonance from his alliteration, he could have fun accompanying you to **Kepler's Books.** Kepler's, one of the largest and very best independent bookstores around, permits clean, leashed, well-behaved dogs to cruise the aisles with you. In fact, dogs who visit even get a tasty treat! Common sense and good manners apply. Please, no leg lifts on the merchandise; Kepler's frowns on yellow journalism. Dogs who lean toward the literary are welcome. Those who *jump* on the literature are not. 1010 El Camino Real, Menlo Park. 650/324-4321.

publicizing the problem to increase public awareness and is also increasing enforcement. City folks sent us a fax with the poop on scooping. Please, folks, it's not a fun job, but you've gotta do it.

The park is at Melendy and Portofino Drives. 650/593-8011.

🕄 Pulgas Ridge Open Space Preserve

😾😾😾😾🐾 (See San Mateo County map on page 210)

Dogs were happy when the Midpeninsula Regional Open Space District opened this 293-acre preserve to leashed pooches a few years back. But now that 16 acres in the middle of the preserve has been designated OK for leash-free dogs, dogs are downright delirious.

The off-leash area is only for dogs under excellent voice control. That's always the case in off-leash, unenclosed areas, but it's particularly important here because of wildlife—and because of some vociferous folks who would love nothing better than to see leashes be mandatory here again. You know, those kind of people. The off-leash area is oak woodland and grassland, so dogs can explore a variety of landscapes. It's in the middle of the preserve and accessible via the Blue Oak Trail or the Cordilleras Trail.

Leashed dogs can explore the rest of this fairly flat, oak-chaparral area via three miles of trails that wind throughout. The best time to visit is in the spring, when the wildflowers come to life everywhere.

During your hike, you might see what you think looks like remnants of buildings. You'd be right. The preserve is on land that was once the site of the Hassler Health Home, a tuberculosis sanatorium owned by San Francisco. In the 1980s, the district bought the land and demolished the sanatorium, but you can still see rock retaining walls and steps here and there. Humans like this kind of trivia. Dogs could give a bark.

Exit I-280 at Edgewood Road and drive east almost a mile. Turn left at

Crestview Drive and make an immediate left onto Edmonds Road. You'll see signs for the preserve. Roadside parking is limited here, but it's usually enough. 650/691-1200.

PLACES TO EAT

Cafe La Tosca: Dogs sing the praises of this lovely Italian café. Dine on tasty pastas and a sumptuous risotto at the four outdoor tables. 777 Laurel Street; 650/592-7749.

Menlo Park

PARKS, BEACHES, AND RECREATION AREAS

🐾 Bayfront Park

🐾🐾🐾 (See San Mateo County map on page 210)

This place used to be a dump—literally. It was the regional landfill site until it reached capacity in 1984. Then the city sealed the huge mounds of garbage under a two-foot clay barrier and covered it with four feet of soil, planted grass and trees, and voilà—instant 160-acre park!

Now it's a land of rolling hills with a distinctly Native American flavor. The packed dirt trails take you up to majestic views of the bay and surrounding marshes. There's no sign of garbage anywhere, unless you look down from the top of a hill and spot the methane extraction plant. Fortunately, very few vista points include that.

Our favorite part of the park is a trail studded with large, dark rocks arranged to form symbols, which in series make up a poem. The concept was inspired by Native American pictographs—a visual language system for recording daily events. At the trailhead, you'll find a sign quoting part of the poem and giving a map of the trail, showing the meaning of each rock arrangement as it corresponds to the poem.

Although leashes are required, dogs seem really fond of this park, sniffing everywhere, their tails wagging constantly. Perhaps they can sense the park's less picturesque days deep underground. Or they may be touched by the Native American magic that imbues these hills.

The park starts at the end of Marsh Road, just on the other side of the Bayfront Expressway. To get to the beginning of the rock poem trail, continue past the entrance on Marsh Road to the second parking lot on the right. 650/858-3470.

PLACES TO EAT

Flea Street Cafe: Dogs would normally flee from a restaurant with the word "flea" in it, but not from this dog-friendly eatery. You can get upscale organic food here, including Niman Ranch meats. Drooling Jake recommends the Niman Ranch rib eye steak with wild mushroom wine au jus. The restaurant serves dinner only these days. Dine with doggy at the outdoor tables. 3607 Alameda de las Pulgas; 650/854-1226.

Iberia Restaurant: This restaurant is among the finest dog-friendly restaurants in the state. It's so elegant you can eat like a Spanish king. Dine with your dog in a stately garden under the canopy of an enormous 400-year-old oak tree. Flaming dishes are big here, so if your furry friend fears fire, try ordering something a little less dramatic. (Fans of the Garden Grill, which occupied this space until 2000, will be happy to know that the owners, Jose Luis Relinque and his wife, Jessica, are the same—and so is the impeccable service and top-notch food.) 1026 Alma Street; 650/325-8981.

Rock of Gibraltar Comestibles: If you like what you've eaten at Iberia Restaurant next door, check out the gourmet Spanish food fixin's at this store/café. *Perros* need to stay outside while you shop, but they're welcome to join you at the outdoor tables for coffee and pastries in the morning or a variety of delicious sandwiches at lunch. The Rock is owned by the Relinques, who also own the Iberia Restaurant. 1022 Alma Street; 650/327-0413.

Atherton

PARKS, BEACHES, AND RECREATION AREAS

32 Holbrook-Palmer Park

 (See San Mateo County map on page 210)

Roses. Gazebos. Bathrooms that look like saunas. Trellises. Jasmine plots. Tennis courts. Buildings that belong in a country club. People in white linen love it here; dogs are often just plain intimidated. Joe didn't lift his leg once last time we visited.

"Don't put it in your book that we allow dogs," a woman with the Atherton Parks and Recreation Department told us. "We have too many weddings and banquets going on here, and the people don't want to be disturbed."

Don't forget a leash.

Holbrook-Palmer Park is on Watkins Avenue, between El Camino Real and Middlefield Road. Leave your car at one of several lots in the park. 650/688-6534.

Woodside

PARKS, BEACHES, AND RECREATION AREAS

33 Thornewood Open Space Preserve

🐾🐾🐾 (See San Mateo County map on page 210)

This 141-acre preserve is a former estate, and the views of the valley from parts of this land are magnificent. Dogs can peruse the preserve on leash. Thornewood is the smallest of the Midpeninsula Regional Open Space District's preserves, but dogs dig the one-mile trail that runs through the oak woodland, chaparral, and redwoods here.

Dogs have to stay away from Schilling Pond because swans call it home, and dogs and swans don't mix. In fact, although the pond is almost entirely surrounded by dense vegetation, rangers have spotted dogs swimming after these beautiful birds. If this happens very much, the entire preserve could be off-limits to all dogs, so let's be careful out there.

From I-280, exit at Highway 84/Woodside Road and drive west into the hills, about five miles. The road will make several sharp turns, but keep following Highway 84. Go left at the narrow, signed driveway. It winds through the woods for a third of a mile before reaching the small parking lot on the west side of the driveway. 650/691-1200.

PLACES TO EAT

Alice's Restaurant: You can get almost anything you want at this restaurant, including a table for you and your dog on the large porch. Weekends here are packed with bikers, especially for Alice's colossal breakfasts. If your dog rides in your motorcycle sidecar, this is the place for you. It's at 17288 Skyline Boulevard, on the corner of Highways 35 and 84, just two miles north of Portola Valley's Windy Hill Open Space Preserve; 650/851-0303.

Portola Valley

PARKS, BEACHES, AND RECREATION AREAS

34 Windy Hill Open Space Preserve

🐾🐾🐾🐾 (See San Mateo County map on page 210)

You can look out from the top of the first big hill you come to and see for miles all around—and though you're on the edge of the suburbs, you'll see hardly a house. This 1,130-acre preserve of the Midpeninsula Regional Open Space District has as many different terrains as it has views, including grassland ridges and lush wooded ravines with serene creeks and drippy redwoods.

There are more than three miles of trails that allow you and your leashed canine companion. But watch out for foxtails. The park is so dry that foxtails seem to proliferate all year.

Start at the Anniversary Trail, to the left of the entrance. The hike is a vigorous three-quarters of a mile uphill, and that may be enough, especially when it's baking. But you can continue down the other side of the hill and loop right, onto the Spring Ridge Trail. Near the end of this 2.5-mile path, you'll come to a wooded area with a small, very refreshing creek. This is a good place to sit a spell before heading back. These two trails are the only ones that permit pooches, so don't try your paw at any others.

Park at the lot on Highway 35 (Skyline Boulevard), 2.3 miles south of Highway 84 and five miles north of Alpine Road. You'll see the big sign for the preserve and three picnic tables. 650/691-1200.

35 Coal Creek Open Space Preserve

🐾🐾🐾🐾 (See San Mateo County map on page 210)

Jake loves visiting this 493-acre preserve in the winter because of the little waterfalls that gurgle along a couple of creeks. In fact, year-round, this is one of the best of the Midpeninsula Regional Open Space District preserves for dogs, because it's generally cooler than most. The dense oak and madrone forests offer a real respite from the hot summer weather.

Banana slugs like this climate as much as dogs do, so don't be surprised to see a few lurking on the trails. When Joe Dog happened upon a banana slug here, at first he looked disgusted. Then he barked at it a couple of times and sat down and moaned at it when it didn't respond. I tugged hard on his leash to get him away, because I knew his next move would be to make a banana slug appetizer out of it.

If rolling meadows are more your dog's style, this preserve has those, too. The five miles of trails will take you through all kinds of landscapes. Let your dog choose his favorite, but make sure he's leashed.

The preserve has two entry points along Skyline Boulevard (Highway 35) in the southernmost part of the county (south of Portola Valley). One is about 1.2 miles north of Page Mill Road, at the Caltrans vista point, on the east side of the road. The other is at Skyline and Crazy Pete's Road, about two miles north of Page Mill Road, also on the east side of Skyline. This one has the closest access to the preserve, but there's only room for about three cars, and you'll need to walk down a fairly steep residential road to get to the trails. 650/691-1200.

Pescadero

PARKS, BEACHES, AND RECREATION AREAS

Once upon a time, long ago (OK, actually in the last edition of this book), dogs who came here were so happy their tails almost wagged off. But no more. The wonderful Pescadero State Beach no longer allows pooches, even those with leashes and shamelessly pleading eyes. And Butano State Park, which had allowed dogs on its myriad fire trails, is now just like other state parks and permits them only in the camping area and on paved roads. At least dogs still have Bean Hollow. And they've also got the magnificent Estancia del Mar Cottages, which your dog will surely want to move into after visiting. (See below.)

🐾 Bean Hollow State Beach

🐾 🐾 🐾 (See San Mateo County map on page 210)

This isn't a big sandy beach. In fact, it can be hard to find sand here at all. It's rocks, rocks everywhere, which is kind of fun. The rocky intertidal zone here is terrific for tidepooling, but only if you and your dog are surefooted. To get to the best tidepools, you must perform an amazing feat of team coordination—climbing down 70-million-year-old rock formations while attached to each other by leash. It's not that steep, just awkward. The pitted rocks can be slippery. This maneuver is not recommended for dogs like Jake, who goes deaf and senseless when the alluring ocean beckons him to swim. Besides, the surf can be treacherous in this area.

If you reach the tidepools, you're in for a real treat. But make sure your canine companion doesn't go fishing—we've seen a dog stick his entire head in a tidepool to capture a little crab. Fur and fangs aren't natural in the delicate balance of this wet habitat, so please keep dogs out of the tidepools. The mussels will thank you.

If you decide to play it safe and stay on flat land, you can still see the harbor seal rookery on the rocks below the coastal bluffs. Bring binoculars and you can really get a view of them up close and personal.

The beach is off Highway 1 at Bean Hollow Road. 415/330-6300.

37 Butano State Park

🐾 (See San Mateo County map on page 210)

This is one of the last state parks to succumb to the mandate that dogs must only be on paved roads, campgrounds, and other developed areas. It's very sad indeed, because until recently, much of this 2,200-acre state park was open to them via 11 miles of fire trails.

This park, nestled in the Santa Cruz Mountains, is resplendent with coastal scrub and redwoods. The ocean views from higher spots are breathtaking, but since tar doesn't go thar, your dog can't either.

Dogs can even camp at the 39 sites here. Sites are $20. The day-use fee is $6 if you park inside the park. Butano is five miles south of Pescadero on Cloverdale Road, and off Highway 1 from Gazos Creek Road. 650/879-2040 or 650/879-2044.

PLACES TO EAT

Arcangeli Grocery Company: There's always fresh-baked bread here—still hot—waiting for you after a cold day at the beach. We like to buy a loaf of steaming herb-garlic bread and eat it at the picnic tables on the lawn in the back of the store. 287 Stage Road; 650/879-0147.

PLACES TO STAY

Butano State Park: See Butano State Park, above, for camping information.

Estancia del Mar Cottages: The pooch-friendly cottages here are a true doggy delight. They're set on a beautiful five-acre horse farm, and that's surrounded by 30,000 acres (!) of farmland and protected open space. Dogs need to be leashed at Estancia because of the horses and the proximity to the road, but it's a small price to pay for the privilege of guesthood here.

Three of the six immaculate, cozy one-bedroom cottages welcome dogs. Two of them have great ocean views (the ocean is about 500 yards away, across Highway 1), and one looks out at the glorious Pigeon Point Lighthouse. The Lighthouse-View cottage also comes with a loft that has a queen futon, a small wood-burning stove, and a whirlpool tub. The cottage without the ocean view gets good sea scenery from its private outside yard and patio. (Many dogs prefer this one because of the yard.) All have full kitchens, which is handy if the idea of eating out for every meal turns your dog's stomach.

Rates are $125–175, and a multinight stay makes the nightly rate less expensive. Weekly rates are $650–1,100. Dogs fees are $50 for the first night, and $10 for each additional night. (The owners keep these places super-clean, doing deep cleansings and even changing the comforters after only a single night with a dog, so their cleaning expenses are high for "one-night stands.") You'll get the address once you make your reservation; 650/879-1500; www .estanciadelmar.com.

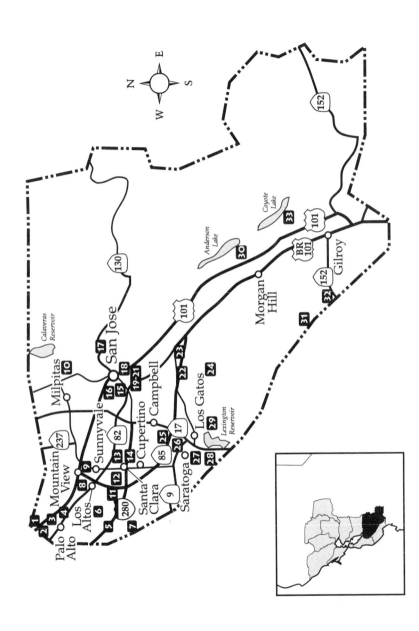

CHAPTER 9

Santa Clara County

While some parts of Santa Clara County are quite scenic, dogs have to face the facts: The place still revolves around Silicon Valley, and it's not a pretty sight. Cookie-cutter duplexes and town houses abound. So do suburban-style office buildings, strip shopping centers, and low-lying metal warehouses. Even dogs with questionable taste wince.

But if you get your dog out of the more populated areas and into the quieter county parks, you'll scarcely know you're in the middle of a megabyting, microchipping mecca. Some of the larger, wilder county parks may put your dog back in touch with the wolf inside herself. One dog we met on a trail at one park was sitting and howling every few hundred feet. Her person said she was just happy to be there. Joe Dog thought maybe the dog was just saying, "Get this leash off me!"

A few leash-free dog parks now grace the area. The newest two, San Jose's Watson Dog Park and the Milpitas Dog Park, are cause for canine celebration.

The Midpeninsula Regional Open Space District is popular with pooches of late, with three dog-friendly open-space preserves in the county. The district

PICK OF THE LITTER—SANTA CLARA COUNTY

BEST DOG PARK
Milpitas Dog Park, Milpitas (page 248)

COOLEST HIKE
Mount Madonna County Park, Gilroy (page 263)

TASTIEST DOG TREATS
Five Paw Bakery, Los Altos (page 249)

MOST DOG-FRIENDLY PLACES TO EAT
Bill's Cafe, San Jose (page 256)
Rock Bottom Restaurant and Brewery, Campbell (page 258)
Classic Burgers of Los Gatos, Los Gatos (page 261)

MOST DOG-FRIENDLY PLACE TO STAY
Cypress Hotel, Cupertino (page 252)

BEST SHOPPING
Stanford Shopping Center, Palo Alto (page 245)
Santana Row, San Jose (page 245)

FRIENDLIEST PLACE TO BUY A PLANT
Yamagami's Nursery, Cupertino (page 252)

BEST SOCIAL GATHERINGS
Society Dog (page 261)

has unique rules about poop-scooping and six-foot leashes. (See the San Mateo County chapter for more on these rules.)

Palo Alto

For dogs, this town is the county's garden spot. Here, you'll find lots of other dog lovers and well-behaved dogs, enticing city parks—all of which allow dogs—and no fewer than three leash-free dog runs. At the Baylands, you and your leashed dog can watch birds and get a good workout at the same time. And many student-oriented restaurants with outdoor seating welcome your dog. If you're lucky enough to have a Palo Alto address, or a friend with one, you may bring your dog to the glorious Foothills Park on weekdays.

PARKS, BEACHES, AND RECREATION AREAS

Unless you have a working dog (and no, this does *not* mean a dog who is working on getting the dog treats out of your coat pocket—we're talking guide dogs and their ilk), you and your pooch can no longer walk together at the Stanford Dish. We know a good many dogs who have cried into their kibble because of this pooch ban. Fortunately, other pleasant Palo Alto areas still permit pooches to paw around.

1 Palo Alto Baylands

🐾🐾🐾 (See Santa Clara County map on page 240)

This is the best-developed wetlands park in the Bay Area for adults, children, and dogs. It's laced with paved bike trails and levee trails. Along the pretty levee paths, benches face the mudflats. Don't forget your binoculars on a walk here. A cacophony of mewling gulls, mumbling pigeons, and clucking blackbirds fills the air. Small planes putt-putt into the nearby airport, and your dog will love the fishy smells coming from the marshes. This seems to be a popular spot for dog exercise. Keep your pooch leashed and on the trails.

Dogs shouldn't go near the well-marked waterfowl nesting area, but they're welcome to watch children feed the noisy ducks and Canada geese in the duck pond, as long as they don't think about snacks à l'orange.

From U.S. 101, exit at Embarcadero Road East and go all the way to the end. At the entrance, turn left for the trails, ranger station, and duck pond. A right turn takes you to a recycling center. 650/329-2423.

2 Greer Park

🐾🐾🦮 (See Santa Clara County map on page 240)

This is one of Palo Alto's parks with an off-leash dog run, but it isn't the largest (see Mitchell Park, below). The park is green and pleasant, as are all the city's parks, but it's somewhat noisy because of nearby Bayshore Road. Dogs have to be leashed outside the dog run. There are athletic fields, picnic tables, and two playground areas. The dog run, near the Bayshore side, is small and treeless, but it's entirely fenced, if that's what your dog needs.

The park is at Amarillo Street and West Bayshore Road. The parking lot is off Bayshore, conveniently near the dog run. 650/496-5928.

3 Hoover Park

🐾🐾🦮 (See Santa Clara County map on page 240)

This park may be small, but dogs don't really care. It's home to a little-known dog park that's not as popular as the run at Mitchell Park (see below), but that's part of the charm. There've been some improvements here recently, so if you haven't checked it out lately, it's worth a sniff.

The park is at Cowper Street between Colorado and Loma Verde Avenues. 650/496-5928.

4 Mitchell Park

 (See Santa Clara County map on page 240)

This generous, green park has some unusual amenities, including two human-sized chessboards and a roller-skating rink. The park is also a standout in the canine book: It has its own dog park that's completely fenced and has a row of pine trees on one side, water dishes on the other, and scrappy tennis balls everywhere. When we last visited, there were a couple of beat-up old office-style chairs just waiting to be sat upon, knocked over, or at least marked by a leg-lifting varmint.

The park has plenty of shade to delight a dog. Remember to leash outside the dog run. For kids, the playground area has sculptured bears for climbing and a water play area (sorry, no dogs). The dog park is a short walk from the parking lot.

The park is on East Meadow Drive just south of Middlefield Road. 650/496-5928.

5 Arastradero Nature Preserve

 (See Santa Clara County map on page 240)

With 613 acres of rolling savanna grassland and broadleaf evergreen forest, Arastradero Preserve is one of the more peaceful and attractive parks in the area. Dogs dig it, but they have to be leashed. It's a good rule, because mountain lions, rattlesnakes, poison oak, and coyotes can be part of the scene here. And so can bikers.

Anglers are right at home in the preserve. A hike to Arastradero Lake takes only about 20 minutes from the main parking lot, and the fishing can be very good. (Sorry, no swimming, boats, or flotation devices.)

There are 6.25 miles of hiking trails. Jake Dog enjoys the hilly 2.8-mile Acorn Trail when he's in the mood to pant. Bring plenty of water; it can get toasty here.

From I-280, exit at Page Mill Road and go south. Turn right (west) on Arastradero Road (Refuge Road on some maps) and drive into the parking lot. 650/329-2423.

6 Esther Clark Park

 (See Santa Clara County map on page 240)

This is a beautiful piece of undeveloped land with some dirt paths, right on the border of Los Altos Hills. There are no facilities but plenty of meadow and eucalyptus trees. A creek bed promises water in the wet season.

Where Old Adobe Road bends to the left and makes a cul-de-sac, the park is the undeveloped land on your right. 650/617-3156.

DIVERSION

Stop and Smell the Shopping Centers: Dogs are welcome to join you at **Stanford Shopping Center,** a 70-acre open-air mall that's disguised as a park. The grounds are home to 1,300 trees of 35 species, plus hundreds of hanging baskets and planters dripping with flowers. If a dog has to go shopping, this is one of the more pleasant places she could go. Many of the 120 stores allow dogs inside. Nordstrom and Neiman Marcus, two of the nation's most dog-friendly department stores, welcome dogs here. Rules at some of the others change frequently, so if you're interested in going inside with your dog, poke your head in and see if you can find someone to give your dog the thumbs-up. Chances are that not only will you end up sniffing out plenty of dog-friendly stores, but your dog will be offered some treats along the way. At El Camino Real and Sand Hill Road, in Palo Alto; 650/617-8200.

An intimate, slightly more trendy shopping center is the new **Santana Row** in San Jose. Charro, a San Jose pooch, wrote to tell us how much fun it is to be a dog there, and even though Jake isn't a shopping kind of dog, he enjoyed a trip there because he got so many pats from shopkeepers and fellow shoppers. (Plus there were plenty of palms and oaks to explore.) He was particularly interested in some leather shoes at Diesel (which only sometimes allows dogs), although he wasn't particular about which ones. Selecting shoes to chew is apparently a much quicker process than selecting shoes to wear. I quickly shooed him out of there and we made our way to Mutts, an amusing upscale dog boutique. Santana Row is at Winchester Boulevard and Stevens Creek Boulevard, just off I-880 in San Jose. 408/551-4600.

7 Foothills Park

🐾🐾🐾 (See Santa Clara County map on page 240)

To use this 1,400-acre park, privately owned by the city of Palo Alto, you must prove you're a resident or be the guest of one. Dogs are allowed only on weekdays (no holidays, though) and must be on leash, but they can go on all the trails.

The park has a large lake surrounded by unspoiled foothills, plus 15 miles of hiking trails of varying difficulty. At sundown, deer are plentiful. It's a beautiful sight, but be sure to keep tight hold of that leash. This park is heaven on Earth for dogs and people alike. If you don't already live in Palo Alto, it could make you consider moving.

To find Foothills Park from I-280, exit at Page Mill Road and drive about 2.5 miles south. As usual, when you're searching for a really good Santa Clara

County park, the road will become impossibly narrow and winding, and you'll think you're lost. But you aren't. Probably. 650/329-2423.

PLACES TO EAT

Downtown Palo Alto is a walker-friendly and dog-adoring kind of place. It's full of benches and plazas for sitting, and quite a few restaurants will serve both of you out on the sidewalk or patio. Here are a few snout-licking options there and elsewhere.

Fratelli Deli: Hungry for a quick salad, pasta, or sandwich? Pop over to Fratelli and grab a bite. Eat with your pooch at the two outdoor tables. 405 University Avenue; 650/323-0423.

Palo Alto Sol: The friendly staff here will bring your thirsty pooch some water while he's drooling over your tasty Mexican food. The mole sauce is a must-order. 408 California Avenue; 650/328-8840.

Taxi's Hamburger: Taxi's burgers are award-winning (yes, there apparently are awards for hamburgers) and 100 percent beef. Just passing by makes dogs drool. But you don't have to pass by. Dogs are welcome here. Many patrons of this upscale American-style grill order burgers for their dogs. Dine at the half-dozen tables outside. 403 University Avenue; 650/322-8294.

Torrefazione: All the coffees and pastries at this café are served in hand-painted Italian china. Dogs with a keen sense of aesthetics appreciate this. Coffee fans love the whole-bean coffee, but I'm not even sure what that is.

Doesn't sound like Taster's Choice to me, though. Sit outside the historic building that houses the café and dine with your dog at the two tables. Thirsty dogs get a bowl of water. 419 University Avenue; 650/325-7731.

World Wrapps: The cooks here take anything that's delicious and slightly exotic and put it in wraps. To them, the world is a burrito, just waiting to be enveloped. We had a really good Thai wrap when we visited. Jake Dog wants to know when they're going to have a dog food wrap. The smoothies are tasty, too. Dine with doggy at the 10 outdoor tables, some of which are shaded by trees. 201 University Avenue; 650/327-9777.

PLACES TO STAY

Sheraton Palo Alto: Rates are $132–329. Dogs must be under 80 pounds—a significant improvement over the former 20-pound pooch limit. 625 El Camino Real 94301; 650/328-2800; www.sheraton.com.

TraveLodge Palo Alto: Rates are $79–95. Dogs pay a $50 flat fee. 3255 El Camino Real 94306; 650/493-6340.

Mountain View

PARKS, BEACHES, AND RECREATION AREAS

8 Rengstorff Park

🐾🐾 🐕 **(with permit)** (See Santa Clara County map on page 240)

This park is typically neat, green, and interesting for people, and it has another excellent feature: A sign reads, "Dogs must be on leash (except by permit)." This means that you can get a permit from the city that allows you to train a dog off leash, with the understanding that he'll be under control. Be fore-warned, though: If you don't bring the permit along with you when training, you will be ticketed.

Rengstorff Park is at Rengstorff Avenue between California Street and Central Expressway. Call for details on getting a permit. 650/903-6331.

9 Mountain View Dog Park

🐾🐾🐾 🐕 (See Santa Clara County map on page 240)

Ahh, this fenced park has redwood trees. They're Jake's favorite arbors. Other amenities in this .75-acre park include benches and a separate area for smaller or more timid dogs. The ground cover is mostly grass, so it's easy on the paws. It's an off-leash oasis, and dogs seem mighty happy to be here.

The park is on North Shoreline Boulevard at North Road. 650/903-6392.

PLACES TO STAY

Best Western Tropicana Lodge: No Ricky Ricardo band here, but it's a decent place to stay with your pup-a-loo. Rates are $70–110. 1720 West El Camino Real 94040; 650/961-0220; www.tropicanalodge.com.

Residence Inn by Marriott: You and your dog will feel right at home at the suites at this attractive hotel. They have kitchens and lots of other extras you won't find in a regular hotel. But better than that is the very dog-friendly attitude here. "We take all pets, from snakes to rabbits. We see them as part of the family and try to accommodate the owner's needs," one manager told us. The place even has a little fenced area for exercising dogs, and the staff is happy to point you to nearby trails. Rates are $99–249. There's a $75 doggy fee per visit, so it's best to stay for a while to get the most bang for your buck. Dogs are $15 extra per night. 1854 West El Camino Real 94040; 650/940-1300.

Milpitas

PARKS, BEACHES, AND RECREATION AREAS

🔟 Milpitas Dog Park

🐾🐾🐾🐾🐾 (See Santa Clara County map on page 240)

The big-dog side of this terrific two-acre park has smallish trees. And the small-dog section has big trees. Go figure! But some of that small-dog shade leaks over to the large-dog side, so it's a win-win situation.

This is a great place to bring a dog who longs to run like the wind. It's mostly grassy, and it's a very generous size. Dogs can really work up a sweat while chasing each other or running after lobbed tennis balls. The dog park is flanked by the scenic rolling hills of the surrounding 1,539-acre Ed Levin County Park. (Dogs are allowed only on one short segment of the Bay Area Ridge Trail there, and in the picnic areas, so don't be too tempted to sniff out Ed Levin.)

The dog park has all the usual pooch amenities, from water to picnic tables to poop bags. And it has an interesting extra one: A tiny concrete-floored fenced area with a bench. No one was using it when we visited, but it looks like a decent place for a child who wants to feel protected from the pounding paws.

There's an entrance fee to get into the county park, and therefore to get into the dog park. It's a steep $5 per car. But annual passes are available for $65, should you want to make this a regular stomping ground. The dog park is at the very end of the county park. (If you're not confident you'll find it, just ask the park ranger at the fee gate.) The county park is at 3100 Calaveras Road, about 2.5 miles east of I-680. For dog-park inquiries, phone the City of Milpitas at 408/586-3210. For questions about Ed Levin, phone 408/262-6980 or 408/355-2200.

PLACES TO STAY

Best Western Brookside Inn: Rates are $79–129. Dogs are $15 extra. 400 Valley Way 95035; 408/263-5566; www.bestwestern.com.

Los Altos

Los Altos, like Saratoga and Los Gatos, is a clean town with civic pride, great for strolling. The hand-painted benches and spotless lawns look as if no dog has ever passed through, but in fact dogs are here in force. They're just mannerly.

PLACES TO EAT

Five Paw Bakery: If you want your dog to enjoy fresh, all-natural pooch pastries and treats, trot over to this terrific bakery. It's exclusively for dogs (and the occasional cat), so if you're a human with a hankering for a baked good, try the bakery next door. The cuisine at Five Paw Bakery is to drool for, and Paul, the owner, is super-friendly and truly loves what he does. The bakery also features an upscale pet boutique, should you really want to treat your best friend to something special. You can wet your dog's whistle at the ever-present water bowl outside. The bakery is conveniently situated a bone's throw from a very large, popular veterinary hospital, at 315 Main Street; 650/941-5729; www.fivepaw.com.

Italian Delicatessen: Drop by for great salami smells. Better yet, order one of the delicious specialty sandwiches and dine at the outdoor tables with your pooch. If you have a drop of Italian blood in you, the Godfather sandwich, which is loaded with mortadella, prosciutto, provolone, and lots of other great Italian ingredients, will make you drool. (But you can blame the drool on your dog.) 139 Main Street; 408/948-6745.

Santa Clara

PARKS, BEACHES, AND RECREATION AREAS

11 Santa Clara Dog Park

🐾🐾🐾🦴 (See Santa Clara County map on page 240)

It's not huge, but this 200-by-200-foot fenced dog run is the only leash-free option in Santa Clara. On the grounds of what used to be Curtis Intermediate School, it's a flat stretch of grass bordered by stands of shady trees. Inside, you'll find water, poop bags, and benches. It's your basic dog park, and Santa Clara dogs are very happy to have it.

It's at the corner of Pomeroy Avenue and Lochinvar Street, near Lawrence Expressway and Homestead Road. 408/615-2260.

DIVERSION

Go on a Pilgrimage: Mission Santa Clara, on the Santa Clara University campus, allows leashed dogs on its grounds. You might make it part of your walk if you're exploring the campus. The building, dating from 1929, is a replica of one version of the old mission, which was first built in 1777 but was destroyed five times by earthquake, flood, and fire. Preserved fragments of the original mission and the old adobe Faculty Club are the oldest college buildings standing in the western United States. The mission is on campus, off El Camino Real, Santa Clara. 408/554-4023.

🐾 Central Park

🐾 🐾 (See Santa Clara County map on page 240)

This Santa Clara city park, like most of the others, has a sign that reveals a certain slant: "No Dogs Allowed Except on Leash." If you can get past that, the park is big and has a wide assortment of trees. The creek here is large and deep, but dry in summer. A beautiful round picnic pavilion has tables fully shaded by wisteria vines, the most we've ever seen in one place.

The park is on Kiely Boulevard between Homestead Road and Benton Street. 408/615-2260.

PLACES TO STAY

Guest House Inn and Suites: Rates are $79–129. Dogs are $10 extra. 2930 El Camino Real 95051; 408/241-3010.

The Vagabond Inn: Rates are $69–99. Dogs are $10 extra. 3580 El Camino Real 95051; 408/241-0771.

Sunnyvale

PARKS, BEACHES, AND RECREATION AREAS

🐾 Las Palmas Park

 (See Santa Clara County map on page 240)

With its paved paths, green grass, and beautiful pond, this park used to be the best in town for a walk among rolling hills. Now it's really terrific, because of its recently opened dog run. The two-acre run has everything a dog could possibly desire—shade, water, poop bags, and even a fire hydrant. It's a kind of fenced-in nirvana. Dogs get deliriously happy when they visit. Some spend so much time rolling in the cool grass that they miss out on hanging with their fellow canines. But do they care? A look at their smiling snouts and flaring nostrils will answer that question.

A quick note about that fire hydrant. Enough dogs have run headlong into it that there was some thought about removing it. So far, it's still here. Doggies, keep your eyes open!

The park is at Danforth and Russet Drives. 408/730-7350.

PLACES TO STAY

Summerfield Suites: There's supposed to be a 50-pound pooch limit, but so many of the employees here have and/or love dogs that this rule is often bent. The suites are large and very livable, with kitchens and most of the amenities of home. Rates are $79–189. There's a $150 pooch fee per visit (this place is used to longish-term visitors). 900 Hamlin Court 94089; 408/745-1515 or 800/833-4353; www.wyndham.com.

The Vagabond Inn: Rates are $65–149. Dogs are $10 extra, and must be under 20 pounds. This seems a bit on the picky side for a Vagabond Inn. 816 Ahwanee Avenue 94086; 408/734-4607; www.vagabondinn.com.

Cupertino

PARKS, BEACHES, AND RECREATION AREAS

14 Fremont Older Open Space Preserve

🐾🐾🐾 (See Santa Clara County map on page 240)

This 739-acre preserve smells sweet and clean, but that doesn't disappoint dogs. Pooches have enough trees and ground-level odors to keep them happily trotting along on their mandatory leashes.

Once you park in the small lot, you'll walk several hundred feet on a paved roadway, but be sure to turn right at the first sign for hikers. Otherwise you'll find yourself in the middle of a bicycle freeway. The narrow dirt trail to the right takes you on a three-mile loop through cool woodlands and rolling open hills up to Hunters Point via the Seven Springs Loop Trail. The view of Santa Clara Valley from the top of the 900-foot hill is incomparable. More trails may be open soon, so your dog's feet will be able to explore as never before.

Signs at the entrance warn of ticks, so be sure to give your dog (and yourself) a thorough inspection after your hike.

From U.S. 101 or I-280, take Highway 85 (Saratoga-Sunnyvale Road) south to Prospect Road. Turn right and follow the road to the park entrance. 650/691-1200.

PLACES TO EAT

Bobbi's Coffee Shop: Charro the Dog told us about this eatery, where every dog gets a bowl of water upon arrival at the outdoor tables. It's a convenient

DIVERSION

Nursery Tail Wag: Dogs love visiting **Yamagami's Nursery.** Not only do they get to help you sniff out some great plants and flowers for your home, but just for setting paw inside, they get a dog treat. "We're very friendly with dogs," says a Yamagami plant doctor at this old and popular family business. 1361 South DeAnza Boulevard, Cupertino; 408/252-3347.

place to stop for a bite before or after a visit to the dog-friendly Yamagami's Nursery (see the Diversion Nursery Tail Wag), right next door. 1361 De Anza Boulevard; 408/257-4040.

PLACES TO STAY

Cypress Hotel: The word "Cypress" in a hotel name seems to confer ultra-dog-friendliness. Witness Doris Day's Cypress Inn in Carmel. The Cupertino Cypress, while larger and more hotelly than Doris Day's inn, makes dogs feel equally at home. They're not only welcome to join you at this fun boutique hotel, but they're encouraged to do so. There's even a package designed especially for pooches. It's called "See Spot at the Cypress." Included in your deluxe guestroom or executive suite is a pet area with a dog bowl, biscuits, bottled water, chew toys, and a dog bed. Your dog will also get a dog tag stating, "I was pampered at the Cypress Hotel," and some other goodies, including free valet parking—something that comes in handy when you're traveling with luggage and a dog. The rate for the package is $129–299. If you want to simply stay here without the package but with your dog, your room will run you $89–229.

For a little more money, the concierge will arrange a pet massage, a grooming session, or even some time with a doggy psychic. (If a pet psychic were to read Jake's brain, she'd be hard-pressed to get beyond his ever-present thoughts of food, food, food.) 10050 South DeAnza Boulevard 95014; 408/253-8900; www.thecypresshotel.com.

San Jose

If you think San Jose offers little for dogs, think again. Okay, it's not dog heaven, but it does permit pooches in some decent parks, and now it even has three parks where dogs can say good riddance to their leashes.

PARKS, BEACHES, AND RECREATION AREAS

San Jose's parks still have the issue of being under the shadow of the freeways (some literally) and air traffic, but some are slowly going to the dogs—in the best sense of the word. The mantra here is that each of the city's 10 districts will have at least one dog park. Now that's something to bark about.

15 Watson Dog Park

🐾🐾🐾🐾🐕 (See Santa Clara County map on page 240)

The glorious centerpiece of this grassy, 1.25-acre park is an enormous Tree of Heaven, known among more scientific dogs as an *Ailanthus altissima.* It truly is a heavenly tree. It's where people and dogs congregate, which is a refreshing change from the common crowd-near-the-park-gate syndrome. While the park looks ethereal, the sound is that of the nearby freeway. Ah well, now your dog has a great excuse not to hear you when you call her to go home. The park has all the usual amenities, from benches and picnic tables to water and poop bags. As a bonus, it has a separate section for small dogs.

The dog park is in the northeast corner of Watson Park, at Jackson and North 22nd Streets. It's just off U.S. 101. From northbound U.S. 101, exit at Julian Street/McKee Road, and turn left onto Julian Street. In a half mile, turn right onto North 21st Street, and in another half mile, make another right onto Jackson Street. The park will be within a block. 408/277-4661.

16 William Street Park

🐾🐾🐾 (See Santa Clara County map on page 240)

This park is a boy dog's dream come true. It's only about 15 acres, but it has 200 trees and 400 shrubs. The acreage-to-trees/shrubs ratio makes it easy for boy dogs to sniff out just about every arbor. The trees make it a really pleasant, attractive place to visit, even in the armpits of summer. Head for the shade and let your happy, leashed pooch loll and roll in the green grass.

The park is at 16th Street and East William Street. 408/277-4661.

17 Joseph D. Grant County Park

🐾🐾🐾 (See Santa Clara County map on page 240)

Here's another huge, gorgeous, wild park that your dog can barely set foot in. Dogs are limited to the campgrounds, picnic areas, Edwards Field Hill, and the Edwards Trail. But if you don't mind a long, winding drive for one short—albeit satisfying—trail hike, by all means try this park. Stop in at the homey old ranch house that's now the visitor center for directions to the Edwards Trail, which isn't easy to find.

Or try these directions: On Mount Hamilton Road midway between the intersection with Quimby Road and the park border is a white barn on your right as you're heading out of the park. Just past the white barn is an unmarked pedestrian gate on the left, which is the trailhead. This trail is a fine walk through a deciduous forest.

There's a $5 parking fee. The park has 22 campsites, available on a first-come, first-served basis. Sites are $9–18. To get to the park from I-680, exit at the Capitol Expressway and drive south to Quimby Road. Turn left (east) on Quimby and wind tortuously to the park entrance. It's a long six miles and the road is often a one-lane cliffhanger. Alternatively, you can get to the park from I-680 via Highway 130 (Mount Hamilton Road). It's similar, but at least it's a two-laner. 408/274-6121 or 408/355-2200.

18 Emma Prusch Park

 (See Santa Clara County map on page 240)

This park, one of San Jose's most attractive working farms, is a museum. Like a symbol of the county, it lies in the shadow of the intersection of three freeways. Yet it's a charming place and, surprisingly, it allows your leashed dog to wander around the farm with you so long as he stays out of the farm-animal areas. A smooth paved path, good for strollers and wheelchairs, winds among a Victorian farmhouse (which serves as the visitor center), a multicultural arts center, farm machinery, a barn, an orchard, and gardens. Picnic tables are on an expanse of lawn with trees.

The entrance is on South King Road, near the intersection of U.S. 101 and I-680/280. 408/277-4567.

19 Coyote Creek Multiple-Use Trail

(See Santa Clara County map on page 240)

When this trail is completely paved, it will furnish your dog with 13 miles of trail, if she doesn't mind sharing space with bicycles. You'll find poop bag dispensers along the way. You may take your dog, leashed, on any section between the Hellyer County Park end and Parkway Lakes, a private fishing concession at the south end, close to Morgan Hill. (Your only reason to go there would be to pull in some of the club's stocked trout or to enter one of its fishing derbies.)

See the directions to Coyote-Hellyer County Park (below). 408/255-0225.

20 Coyote-Hellyer County Park

(See Santa Clara County map on page 240)

This county park, which surrounds the one-acre Shadowbluff Dog Run (see below), is a generous, rustic area, popular with bicyclists. The best deal for dogs is the El Arroyo del Coyote Nature Trail, which by some miracle allows dogs. Walk to the left at the entrance kiosk and cross under Hellyer Avenue on the bike trail to find the entrance to the nature trail. Cross the creek on a pedestrian bridge to your right; once across, take the dirt path to your left. Bikes aren't allowed, making it all the better for dogs.

Willows and cottonwoods are luxuriant here, and in spring, poppies bloom. Eucalyptus groves provide occasional shade. Watch out for bees and poison oak. Otherwise, this is heavenly territory for your dog.

The park is closed Wednesdays for maintenance. Access is very easy from U.S. 101. Exit U.S. 101 at Hellyer Avenue and follow prominent signs to the

DOG-EAR YOUR CALENDAR

Bark in the Park—that's the name of a fun, incredibly popular dog day that takes place at the William Street Park in San Jose every summer. Bark in the park is also what your dog may do because he's so happy to be here. He'll be able to sniff out scads of doggy activities, such as musical dog chairs, obstacle courses, and pooch "beauty" contests. There are vendors galore, selling all the things dogs love (including *The Dog Lover's Companion to California*, plug, plug), and there's even a misting tent, complete with little wading pools, for dogs who need to cool their paws. The event is sponsored by the Beautification Committee of the Campus Community Association, a nonprofit neighborhood organization. For info about this year's event, call 408/793-5125.

park. The dog area is about 100 yards past the entry kiosk. A parking fee of $5 is charged, and that can add up fast, since there's really no good parking nearby. So if you're planning to be a regular, your best bet would be to buy a $65 park pass for the year. It's a small investment to make for your dog's happiness. 408/255-0225 or 408/355-2200.

21 Shadowbluff Dog Run

🐾🐾🐾🐾 🐕 (See Santa Clara County map on page 240)

The one-acre enclosure within the large Coyote-Hellyer County Park has just about anything a pooch could desire. You'll find shade from a few trees, water to slurp up, and lots of green grass. For humans, there are benches, poop bags, and garbage cans. (Seems the dogs get the better end of the deal.) For more information, see Coyote-Hellyer County Park, above.

22 Guadalupe Oak Grove Park

🐾🐾🐾 (See Santa Clara County map on page 240)

This park is a pleasant exception to most of the others in San Jose—it's undeveloped, beautiful, and doesn't allow bicycles—and sure enough, it may not be open to dogs forever. For years we've been hearing it may "soon" be declared an oak woodlands preserve. It hasn't been yet, so go and enjoy it.

Dirt trails wind through hills, alternately semiopen and covered with thick groves of oaks. Birds are plentiful and noisy. Be aware of high fire danger in the dry season, and don't even think of letting your dog off leash. The park ranger loves dogs, but she'll ticket you, and she's heard all the excuses—from "He just slipped out of his collar for a moment..." to "I couldn't get my dog through the gate with his leash on..."

Guadalupe Oak Grove Park is at Golden Oak Way and Vargas Drive. 408/277-2821.

23 Miyuki Dog Park

🐾 🐾 🐕 (See Santa Clara County map on page 240)

Dogs are happy to be at this tiny (three-eighths-acre) park without their leashes, even though the park isn't quite what it could be. The ground is covered with crushed granite, which can get a little dusty when everyone is running around. There's no water. The trees are small, but that will change. Meanwhile, many dogs enjoy sniffing and running around here. (Perhaps they haven't visited Watson Dog Park yet; see above.)

The park is at Miyuki Drive and Santa Theresa Boulevard. 408/277-4661.

24 Almaden Quicksilver County Park

🐾 🐾 🐾 (See Santa Clara County map on page 240)

This rustic, 3,600-acre park allows dogs on about half of its 30 miles of trails. Some of these trails are popular for horseback riding, so watch out; although leashes are the law here, they don't always stop dogs who like to chase hooves.

In the spring, the hills explode with wildlife and wildflowers. Any of the trails will take you through a wonderland of colorful flowers and butterflies who like to tease safely leashed dogs. Speaking of insects, there's a downside to this park: Ticks seem to hang out here. "We got 20 off our dog, then three more when big welts developed," a poor San Jose resident writes. Keep your pooch in the center of trails, and the bloodsucking pests will have to go elsewhere for dinner.

Dogs are allowed on the Guadalupe Trail, the Hacienda Trail, parts of the Mine Hill Trail, the Mockingbird Picnic Area, the No Name Trail, and the Senator Mine Trail. Call the park for more information about the trails and the locations of their trailheads.

You can enter the park at several points. We prefer the main park entrance, where New Almaden Road turns into Alamitos Road, near Almaden Way. 408/268-3883 or 408/355-2200.

PLACES TO EAT

Bill's Cafe: You and your favorite dog can munch on simple café cuisine at this bistro with umbrella-topped tables. Lucky dogs who visit get water and a biscuit! 1115 Willow Street; 408/294-1125.

Maggiano's Little Italy: Dogs delight in joining their people at this Southern Italian–style restaurant's large outdoor section. The portions are big, the selection is huge, and the food is delicious. Dogs get a bowl of water if they're thirsty. Maggiano's is in the Santana Row shopping center (see the Diversion Stop and Smell the Shopping Centers), 3055 Olin Avenue. (Santana Row is at Stevens Creek Boulevard and Winchester Boulevard.) 408/423-8973.

PLACES TO STAY

Doubletree Hotel: Rates are $89–179. A $100 dog deposit is required. 2050 Gateway Place 95110; 408/453-4000.

Homewood Suites: The suites here are comfy and much more like home than traditional hotels. Rates are $229. Dogs must be under 30 pounds to stay here, and they pay a $75 fee for the length of their stay, plus a deposit of $275. 10 West Trimble Road 95131; 408/428-9900.

Joseph D. Grant County Park: See Joseph D. Grant County Park, above, for camping information.

Staybridge Suites Hotel: The hotel has only suites, which makes for a comfy stay. All suites are equipped with a kitchen. It's convenient for people traveling with pooches. Rates are $89–189. Dogs have to pay a $150 fee per visit, so you'd better stay a while to make it worth that fee. 1602 Crane Court 95112; 408/436-1600.

Campbell

At press time this lovely town was in the final stages of creating its very own dog park. Check back next edition for the details.

PARKS, BEACHES, AND RECREATION AREAS

25 Los Gatos Creek County Park

🐾🐾🐾 (See Santa Clara County map on page 240)

Here your leashed dog can romp on grass, have a picnic with you in the shade of Los Gatos Creek's medium-sized trees, and watch ducks and geese in the percolation ponds of Los Gatos Creek, which are good for fishing. Jake's Labrador retriever genes make him quiver with excitement when he sees these birds, but he just watches and doesn't ruffle any feathers. The Los Gatos Creek Trail runs through here, should you care to take a jaunt.

From Highway 17, exit at Camden Avenue; go west on San Tomas Expressway, south on Winchester Boulevard, and left on Hacienda Avenue to the park. A $5 parking fee is charged in summer and on weekends and holidays. 408/356-2729 or 408/355-2200.

PLACES TO EAT

The King's Head Pub and Restaurant: Want British food and drink, with a super-dog-friendly atmosphere? Come here for some fine brews and interesting food. Your dog can join you on the shady deck, and she'll get a big bowl of water if she's thirsty. On Sunday afternoons, there's live music here. It's of the slow-jazzy-hip variety. Dogs dig it. Speaking of jazz, we owe thanks to Jaz Dog and Trevor Dog for letting us know about this eatery. (They're the

DIVERSION

You Doity Dog: Even if your dog hates a bath more than anything, he'll surely like it a bit better if it's you working him over and not some stranger. Campbell's **Shampoo Chez** (sham-POO-ches) is a wash-him-yourself dog-grooming establishment, and the current owners say they've hosted about a zillion self-service washes since they began. That's a lot of shampoo and fleas down the drain. A shampoo for any size dog is $12 for 30 minutes of wash time and an additional $1 for each five minutes after that. (There's another branch in Santa Cruz.) 523 East Campbell Avenue, Campbell; 408/379-WASH (408/379-9274).

lucky dogs of the founders of Society Dog, a social group if ever there was one. See the Diversion Drink Wine, Get Naked, Hop on a Bus.) 201 Orchard City Drive; 408/871-2499.

Orchard Valley Coffee: Enjoy coffee, snacks, and pastries, and nighttime live music, at one of five tables right on the sidewalk at this dog-friendly place. 349 East Campbell Avenue; 408/374-2115.

Rock Bottom Restaurant and Brewery: The restaurant used to have a dog menu here, but most people were just ordering things such as bunless burgers for their dogs off the human menu (even before the low-carb craze), so it went back to human menus only. If you don't want to invest in your dog's carnivorous desires, you should know that the friendly servers here provide treats and water for pooches. For people, the signature microbrews are a big draw, as are tasty salads and interesting concoctions such as alder-smoked fish-and-chips. Dine at the full-service patio with your dog (it's even heated in the chilly months). It's at 1875 South Bascom Road, in the Pruneyard Shopping Center; 408/377-0707.

PLACES TO STAY

Residence Inn by Marriott: This is a convenient, comfortable place to stay when traveling with a dog. Residence Inns have only suites and apartments, and they all come with kitchens. Rates are $129–179. Extended stays get a discounted rate. Dogs have to pay a $75 cleaning fee. 2761 South Bascom Avenue 95008; 408/559-1551.

Saratoga

PLACES TO EAT

Bella Saratoga: The slogan of this Italian date spot is, "It's Romantic," and it is, even at the front sidewalk tables next to a short stone wall right on the street. Dogs have to be tied up on the other side of the wall, but they're close enough for your handouts. Plus, the dog-friendly staff gives pooch guests a big bowl of filtered water. (None of that straight tap stuff!) If it's crowded, dogs aren't allowed, so be sure to visit during "off" times. Sit at one of the three tables by the wall. 14503 Big Basin Way; 408/741-5115.

International Coffee Exchange: This very dog-friendly café serves the best mochas around. They're made with Ghirardelli chocolate and fresh, house-made whipped cream. The café also serves pastries and sandwiches, should you want a little nosh with your pooch. Dine together at the outdoor area's umbrella-topped tables. 14471 Big Basin Way; 408/741-1185.

Vienna Woods Restaurant and Deli: If you have an appetite for Austrian food, bring your dog here. You can get bratwurst, potato pancakes, and even apple strudel. The restaurant also serves sandwiches, quiches, lasagna, and other non-Austrian items. Dine with your pooch at the sheltered outdoor tables. 14567 Big Basin Way; 408/867-2410.

Los Gatos

Dogs like Los Gatos, but they think it needs a name change. Jake suggests "Los Perros."

PARKS, BEACHES, AND RECREATION AREAS

26 Vasona Lake County Park

🐾🐾🐾 (See Santa Clara County map on page 240)

This is a perfectly manicured park, with grass like that of a golf course. Dogs find it tailor-made for rolling, although they tend to get tangled in their leashes—which the county demands they wear here.

Several pathways take you through this 151-acre park and down to the lake's edge. But no swimming is allowed. And dogs aren't allowed to visit the children's playground either. You can picnic in the shade of one of the large willows or lead your dog up to the groves of pines and firs for a relief session.

From Highway 17, take Highway 9 (Saratoga-Los Gatos Road) west to University Avenue. Go right and continue to Blossom Hill Road. The park will be on your left. Enter at Garden Hill Drive. The parking fee is $5. 408/356-2729 or 408/355-2200.

27 St. Joseph's Hill Open Space Preserve

🐾🐾🐾 (See Santa Clara County map on page 240)

Want a quick escape from urban life? Visit this scenic, 173-acre preserve with your leashed pooch. Dogs are allowed on all four miles of trails here, but beware, it can get steep. The trails wind through oak woodlands and open grassland, and at the top of the 1,250-foot St. Joseph's Hill, you'll get magnificent views of the surrounding parklands. Joe used to love to sit here and let his nostrils flare.

From Highway 17, take the Alma Bridge Road exit and go across the dam. Public parking is available at Lexington Reservoir County Park. The trail to St. Joseph's Hill starts opposite the boat-launching area at the north end of the reservoir. 650/691-1200.

28 Lexington Reservoir County Park

🐾🐾 (See Santa Clara County map on page 240)

When the reservoir is full, this park is full of life. Birds sing and the foliage is bright green. But in drought years, everything here—trees, grass, brush—is covered with silt. This death mask must frighten birds away to better nesting areas, because it's utterly silent, except for a few cars kicking up dust on a nearby road.

It can really bake during summer, too. And since there's no swimming allowed, dogs get miserable fast. (To cool himself off here, Joe would roll on the dusty ground until his entire body was coated with ash-colored silt. He looked like some kind of moving statue on a mandatory leash.)

Exit Highway 17 at Montevina Road and drive east a quarter of a mile. You can stop at any of several parking areas along the road. There is no entrance fee, except for the Miller Picnic Site, where you'll pay $5. 408/358-3741 or 408/355-2200.

29 Sierra Azul Open Space Preserve (Kennedy-Limekiln area)

🐾🐾🐾 (See Santa Clara County map on page 240)

The wildlife at this 5,000-acre preserve has it pretty good. There's so much steep, rugged terrain and dense chaparral that humans and their leashed doggy interlopers are pretty much forced to stay on the trails, out of critters' ways. Unfortunately for dogs and their people, mountain bikes seem to be everywhere on these trails, and they can go really fast. So on weekends especially, keep your eyes and ears peeled and be ready to dodge the traffic.

This is not a park for the fair of paw. A hike to the 2,000-foot ridge top can make even the most fit dog sweat. But the views from here or from the 1,700-foot Priest Rock are worth a little panting, at least on your part. Take it easy on your dog, though, and don't let him pant too much. It can get very, very hot here in the summer, and there's virtually no decent shade. The folks at the Midpeninsula Regional Open Space District beg you not to take your pooch here on summer afternoons.

DIVERSION

Drink Wine, Get Naked, Hop on a Bus: If you and your dog like to socialize, have we got a group for you: **Society Dog.** It bills itself as "a social club for dogs and their people," and boy, is it social. When we attended a doggy Easter egg hunt at a Saratoga winery, people were sipping wine and making new friends, and dogs were sniffing each others' heinies and making new friends too.

It's just one of many gatherings throughout the year for this South Bay group. It has monthly "naked" dog walks where dogs can be leash-free, and "bark in the dark" walks on Tuesday and Thursday evenings. Some get-togethers culminate in hanging out at an alfresco restaurant together. Special events include winery tours, group sojourns via bus to fabulously dog-friendly destinations such as Carmel, and a field trip to the San Francisco Giants' Dog Days of Summer event (see Dog-Ear Your Calendar in the San Francisco chapter), also via bus. A regular "Yappy Hour" was in the planning stages. Membership is free, but you pay for special events. See www .societydog.com for more info and a schedule of upcoming events.

Parking here is a real problem. More on that in the next paragraph, but if you visit on a busy day, have a contingency plan in case you don't get one of the coveted spaces. Also note that the two other sections of the Sierra Azul Preserve (Cathedral Oaks and Mt. Umunhum) don't permit pooches.

From Highway 85, exit at Los Gatos Boulevard and drive west a little more than two miles. At Kennedy Road, turn left and follow the road about two more miles to the parking spot at the trailhead. There's room for only two cars here. This is utterly inadequate, and the district is working to do something about this. In the meantime, there's room for about seven cars across Kennedy, on Top of the Hill Road. Please be considerate of the residents here, and keep noise to a minimum and don't litter. 650/691-1200.

PLACES TO EAT

Classic Burgers of Los Gatos: This dog-friendly eatery has fine burgers. Dogs drool over them at the four tables on the patio. In fact, they've drooled so much that the café's proprietors now offer dogs their very own bunless patties for $1. Dogs, even those not caught up in the low-carb trend, adore this place. They can get water if thirsty, too. 15737 Los Gatos Boulevard; 408/356-6910.

Dolce Spazio Gelato: On warm days, this is the place to come. The homemade gelato is creamy and delicious. When there's a chill in the air, try something from the café's espresso bar. The good-sized patio has heat lamps, which helps dogs and their people cozy up to a winter visit. Thirsty dogs get water on request. 221 North Santa Cruz Avenue; 408/395-1335.

Morgan Hill

PARKS, BEACHES, AND RECREATION AREAS

30 Anderson Lake County Park

 (See Santa Clara County map on page 240)

When there's enough water to keep the reservoir open to the public, dogs love to go along on fishing trips. But when it's low, dogs take solace in dipping their paws in the shady, secluded stream that runs between picnic areas. Call the rangers to find out if the reservoir is open, because if it isn't, it may not be worth a trip. You can't get anywhere near the lake if it's too low.

The only trail connects picnic areas, and it isn't even a half mile long. Plenty of picnic tables have lots of shade, but dogs tend to get bored unless hunks of hamburger happen to fall from the grills. The picnic areas can be rowdy, with lots of beer and loud music, so if your dog doesn't like rap, take him somewhere else.

From U.S. 101, follow Cochrane Road east to the park. 408/779-3634 or 408/355-2200.

31 Uvas Canyon County Park

(See Santa Clara County map on page 240)

This is a pretty, clean park of oak, madrone, and Douglas fir trees in cool canyons. The Uvas Creek Trail is a favorite trail. Dogs always appreciate a creek on a warm summer day, and this one doesn't dry up in hot weather. You might also try the wide, dirt Alec Canyon Trail, 1.5 miles long, within sight of Alec Creek, or the Nature Trail Loop, about one mile long, beside Swanson Creek. You may see some waterfalls in late winter and early spring. Dogs aren't allowed on one trail: the Knibbs Knob Trail. There's a $5 day-use fee.

Dogs are allowed in the campgrounds and picnic areas of Uvas Canyon. The park has 25 campsites, available on a first-come, first-served basis, for $9–18 a night. The campground is open daily April 15–October 31, and Friday and Saturday November–March. It's crowded on weekends during late spring and summer, so arrive early or camp during the week. Phone 408/355-2201 for reservations.

From U.S. 101, exit at Cochrane Road; go south on Business 101 to Watsonville Road, then right (west) on Watsonville to McKean-Uvas Road. Turn right on Uvas (past Uvas Reservoir) to Croy Road. Go left on Croy to the park. The last four miles on Croy are fairly tortuous. 408/779-9232 or 408/355-2200.

PLACES TO STAY

Best Western Country Inn: Rates are $78–139. Dogs are allowed in smoking rooms only and are $10 extra. 16525 Condit Road, 95037; 408/779-0447.

Uvas Canyon County Park: See Uvas Canyon County Park, above, for camping information.

Gilroy

PARKS, BEACHES, AND RECREATION AREAS

🐾 Mount Madonna County Park

🐾🐾🐾🐾 (See Santa Clara County map on page 240)

This magnificent 3,700-acre park is midway between Gilroy and Watsonville (in Santa Cruz County). No matter where you're coming from, it's worth the drive. The mountain, covered with mixed conifers, oak, madrone, and bay and sword ferns, is wonderfully quiet and cool—which is especially appreciated by San Jose dwellers, whose parks are almost never far from the roar of freeways. You may hear the screech of jays and little else.

Try driving on Valley View Road (to the right from the ranger station) to the Giant Twins Trail, where you can park in the shady campsite of the same name—at least when no one is camping there. (When we were there on a perfect Indian summer day in late September, the park was deserted.) Two huge old redwoods, green with lichen, give the trail its name. After half a mile, the trail becomes Sprig Lake Trail and continues for another two miles. Sprig Lake, really a pond, is empty in summer, but in spring it's stocked for children's fishing.

This walk isn't much of a strain. If you'd like more exercise, there are plenty of longer and steeper trails—18 miles in all, and as of this writing, your dog may enjoy every one of them. From the Redwood Trail or the Blackhawk Canyon Trail, you'll be rewarded with views of the Santa Clara Valley, the Salinas Valley, and Monterey Bay. For a walk almost completely around the park, try the Merry-Go-Round Trail.

The park's deer are only one of many reasons you should keep your dog securely leashed, tempting as it might be to let her off. "Dogs have instincts," a friendly ranger said.

Your dog might enjoy a camping vacation here. There are 113 large, private campsites. Sites are $12–20 per night. Phone 408/355-2201 for reservations. A $5 day-use fee is always charged on weekends and daily Memorial Day–Labor Day.

From U.S. 101, exit at Highway 152 west to Gilroy. Continue on 152 (Hecker Pass Highway) through part of the park. The entrance is a right (north) turn at Pole Line Road. 408/842-2341 or 408/355-2200.

🐾 Coyote Lake Park

🐾🐾🐾 (See Santa Clara County map on page 240)

This county park is full of wildlife no matter how high or low the lake. In fact, when we last visited, we saw foxes, wild turkeys, and a grazing deer—and there wasn't a drop of water in the reservoir. The reservoir had been bone dry for so long that it looked like an enormous open field. Brush and a few trees were starting to emerge from the hard, dry ground.

When it's in this drought condition, the lake bed is a favorite stomping ground for leashed canines—who are usually relegated to picnic areas, the campground, and the one-mile trail connecting them.

The campsites are roomy, and several are shaded by large oak trees. Others look out on the lake—or field, depending on the water level. We like to visit the nearby picnic areas after stopping at one of Gilroy's garlic stores for lunch supplies.

There are 74 sites here, and they're $9–18. County parks allow two dogs per site. Phone 408/355-2201 for reservations. The day-use fee is $5. From U.S. 101, exit at Leavesley Road and follow the signs to the park. 408/842-7800 or 408/355-2200.

PLACES TO STAY

Coyote Lake Park: See Coyote Lake Park, above, for camping information.

Leavesley Inn: Rates are $63–73. Dogs are charged a $20 fee per visit. 8430 Murray Avenue 95020; 408/847-5500.

Mount Madonna County Park: See Mount Madonna County Park, above, for camping information.

CHAPTER 10

Beyond the Bay

Yes, dogs, there really is life beyond the San Francisco Bay Area. And sometimes it can be most spectacular. The following dog-friendly places are excerpted from my book *The Dog Lover's Companion to California*, a 900-page scoop on where to take your dog in the Golden State.

Mendocino County

The other New England

PLACES TO STAY

MacCallum House: This is one of the most special, fun, welcoming, exquisite, first-rate places you'll ever stay with your dog. But don't let that scare you away: The prices are reasonable, and any size dog is warmly welcome—even large, drooling specimens such as Jake. "We've never, ever had any problems with dogs," says dog-loving owner Jed Ayres. "They are a joy to have around."

Just about any dog may end up drooling here: The dog-friendly attitude is so deep and firmly entrenched that even the dog-loving chef at the renowned

MacCallum House Restaurant gets in on the dog-welcoming bandwagon with his delectable doggy treats made from organic goose livers. Dogs who stay here get these treats as part as a terrific dog package, which includes a fluffy plush dog bed, a towel, a sheet, soft bedding, and dog bowls. (Everything but the treats is a loaner.)

The MacCallum House itself—a Victorian mansion built in 1882—is about the only place dogs can't stay. But there are myriad rooms, suites, cottages, and even houses on the property and on nearby MacCallum property for dogs and their people. They're tastefully appointed—some could grace the best interior design magazines—and have a warm-yet-airy ambiance.

The barn, built in the 1880s, now houses several rooms with features that include decks, ocean views, hot tubs, and sumptuous riverstone fireplaces. A handful of dog-friendly cottages dot the property. The most fabulous (and the most expensive) is the Water Tower, built in the late 1800s. It's a three-story vertical suite with to-die-for ocean views, a two-person tub, a dry sauna, and plenty of room. Water is still stored in a tank up top and you can see a real working well below the tower via glass on the first floor. The tower has been lovingly restored, and it is one of the most attractive of these old structures in the area. Slightly less expensive is the Greenhouse cottage, with a beautiful trellised back dining area next to a hot tub.

As if these choices weren't enough, every suite in the four-star luxury Mac-Callum Suites, on a hill overlooking the village, is dog-friendly and stunning. The MacCallum-run vacation homes are also hits with people and their dogs: The Oceansong house is even fenced in for extra-fun dog frolicking.

Prices for the range of accommodations are $110–395. The price includes a gourmet breakfast and a wine hour. (Dogs can join you on the wraparound porch of the main MacCallum House for these.) Dogs are $25 extra nightly. 45020 Albion Street, Mendocino 95460; 707/937-0289 or 800/609-0492; www.maccallumhouse.com.

Point Arena Lighthouse lodging: It used to take four men to keep the historic Point Arena lighthouse going, and these four men were each provided a good-sized home next to the lighthouse. Since there's no longer the need for this kind of upkeep, the homes, which have been rebuilt, are now rented out as vacation homes. And not just any vacation homes—very dog-friendly ones. Dogs who stay here get treats and lots of pats if the manager is around. A couple of cute dog photos grace the lodging's website, with the words "PET FRIENDLY!" emblazoned underneath.

"I love animals," says Jeff Gales, managing director of the nonprofit organization that now maintains the lighthouse. (Money from the house rentals is a major source of funding for the ongoing preservation of the lighthouse.) "I've never had a problem with any dog that's stayed here."

As far as I know, this is the only lighthouse in California where you can stay with your dog. Gales says it's also the only lighthouse where humans can rent a whole house, as opposed to a bed in a hostel or a room in a bed-and-breakfast.

The houses, and the lighthouse, are set toward the end of a long, thin spit of land. The spit, being a spit, is surrounded by ocean on three sides. There's nothing like being lulled to sleep by the sound of the crashing ocean. The views are to drool for, as are the tastefully furnished homes, which all have three bedrooms, two bathrooms, wood-burning fireplaces (wood is supplied), full kitchens, and satellite TV, should you want to look at something other than some of the world's most stunning ocean scenery. Leashed dogs can join you to sniff out the land near the houses.

Rates are $175–190, plus a one-time cleaning fee of $35. (This fee is for people without dogs, too.) Dog guests have to sign a pet agreement. 45500 Lighthouse Road, Point Arena 95468; 707/882-2777; www.pointarena lighthouse.com.

Tahoe Area
The great lake escape

PLACES TO STAY

Fireside Lodge: What used to be an old rundown motel is now a sparkling, fun, super-dog-friendly lodging. The rooms all sport a unique country mountain theme, with names such as the True West Room, the Angler Room, and the Bear's Den Suite (our favorite). The rooms are all cheery log-cabin style, with beautiful river-rock gas fireplaces and decor that lives up to the room's name. Each room also has a microwave and little fridge.

But wait! That's not all. Stay here and you get to go to the lodge's super-cozy Emerald Gathering Room for a wonderful cocktail hour and an expanded continental breakfast. In winter, you'll find big pots of homemade soup and bread there for your enjoyment.

But there's still more! And this is the part your dog has been waiting for: The property backs up to national forest land, and you know how joyous national forests make dogs. In addition, use of the lodge's kayaks comes free with your room, and dogs are more than welcome to ride along. It's a 15-minute walk to the lake, so either someone at the lodge will drive the kayak to the lake for you, or you can do it yourself. (The staff will also tell you about some terrific paddling spots and beaches that swimming dogs adore.) And to top it off, all dogs who visit get dog cookies. Their people get doggy sheets to put on the beds and poop bags for those less-scenic moments.

Your dog can stay in your room while you're skiing or gambling as long as she's in a crate. This dogs-allowed-alone rule is a rarity in the area. Rooms are $69–195. Dogs are $20 extra and require a $100 deposit. 515 Emerald Bay

DIVERSION

Dashing Through the Snow: While you ski at the **Tahoe Cross Country Ski Area,** your happy, leash-free dog can trot along beside you on five miles of beautifully groomed dog-friendly trails. (Leashes are required only at the trailhead and parking lot.) It's a blissful experience for most dogs. In fact, Jake is so happy when he gets to ski with us that he leaves lots of cheery yellow marks all over the place.

For obvious reasons, dogs must be under voice control. The two dog-friendly trails are open to dogs 8:30 A.M.–5 P.M. Monday–Friday and limited hours on weekends and holidays. Humans pay $19 for a day of skiing. Dogs pay $3. Season passes are available. In fact, your dog's season pass will have his photo emblazoned on it!

The ski lodge is just as welcoming as the trails. Inside the cozy lounge you'll find plenty of dog biscuits. For humans, you'll find hot chocolate and cookies.

The ski area is at 925 Country Club Drive in Tahoe City; 530/583-5475; www.tahoexc.org.

Road, South Lake Tahoe 96150; 530/544-5515 or 800/MYCABIN (800/692-2246); www.tahoefiresidelodge.com.

PLACES TO EAT

Mother Barclay's Cafe: Gorgeous golden retriever Miles and his people, Russ and Jean Glines, wrote to give us the heads-up about this wonderfully dog-friendly café. "The owners have two goldens and the walls are adorned with picture after picture of their beloved dogs (Barclay and Berger). This was a true find. They literally hovered over Miles, offering biscuits, water, and hugs," wrote Jean.

Turns out restaurant owners Jay and Pat love all dogs, not just goldens. Pooch customers really do feel welcomed by lots of attention and pats and hugs (when it's not too busy), and they also get free doggy biscuits. Even the café's logo is dog-loving—a dog (Barclay, we presume) in a chef's hat surrounded by mixing bowls and spoons. I frankly wouldn't feel comfortable with Jake the yellow Lab preparing *my* meal, but goldens are another matter all together. On the menu, in small print: "We accept Visa, MasterCard, and 50-lb. bags of Eukanuba." You've gotta love this place, whether you're a human or a dog.

The food is delicious, hearty breakfast and lunch cuisine. The menu breaks it down into cute sections such as "traditional stuff" and "not so traditional stuff." Several of the dishes have Barclay's and Berger's names on them, including Barclay's Bad Boy Burrito, Famous Barclay Burger, and Berger's Lox and Bagel. There's something for everyone here. Health-conscious folks can order the Newport Nine-Grain Cereal (served hot with brown sugar and raisins), and those in need of extra carbohydrates for the slopes can order Powder Day Potatoes. (It's such a big baked, stuffed potato that the menu exclaims that "show dogs jump over them.") The café is in Squaw Valley, USA, at 1900 Squaw Valley Road, Squaw Valley; 530/581-3251.

Yosemite
Not such a bad place for pooches after all

NATIONAL PARKS

Yosemite National Park

Ask just about everyone who's ever visited this park about what they've seen, and they'll gush about the impossibly beautiful geography, the dramatic waterfalls, the magnificent trails, the sheer cliffs, the pristine wildlife, and every other detail they can dredge up. It's not hyperbole. This fantastic park is bigger than the imagination, bigger than life. It inspires even the most jaded park-goer to sing its praises.

Then ask the same question of people who've visited with dogs. They'll be able to tell you all about the lovely car campsites here. They can even expound on the glories of the commercialization of Yosemite Village, the clever way the parking lots are set up, and how toasty the blacktop gets at 2 P.M. in August.

But it turns out that Yosemite is not really such a doggy drag. You just have to know where to go. While dogs are not allowed on any trails, in meadows, or in the backcountry of Yosemite, they are permitted to explore the beautiful Yosemite Valley area via paved roads and paths. And for better or worse, there's a lot of pavement here. That means you and your leashed dog can peruse some absolutely stunning scenery from miles of flat, easy terrain. (More silver lining: The pavement will help keep your dog's nails trimmed.)

If you want to hit the real trails, you can have your dog stay at the park's kennel Memorial Day–Labor Day. (No, not the whole time. You know what we mean.) And we're not talking luxury suites here. We're talking your basic cagelike contraptions that make you feel incredibly guilty for leaving the little guy behind. The kennel costs $8 per day, and space is limited. It's first-come, first-served, so get there early during busy times. Dogs are required to have all their shots, be more than 16 weeks old, and to be more than 10 pounds. (Sorry, teacup poodles!) The kennel phone is 209/372-8348.

Some folks think they can get away with leaving their dog tied up to their campsite for a few hours while they go exploring. But remember, if the ranger doesn't catch up with you, there's always the chance that a mountain lion or other cunning critter might catch up with your tethered dog. "We call one of these camping areas Coyote Point," a park employee told me. "You'd be a fool to leave your dog behind even for a little bit."

One clever reader wrote to us and told us how she and her husband get away with taking their smallish dogs through Yosemite. They tote them along on little doggy trailers attached to their bikes. Sometimes they strap a dog carrier to their chests and away they go. It probably isn't legal, so I won't use their names. But their truck's license plate is so wonderfully appropriate to the theme of this book that I can't help but mention it: CAB4K9S. (It sure be.)

Here are the campgrounds that permit pooches: In the valley, there's the Upper Pines Campground. Along Highway 120, you can stay at Hodgdon Meadow Campground, Crane Flat Campground (section A), White Wolf Campground (section C), Yosemite Creek Campground (front section), and the west end of the Tuolumne Meadows Campground. Along Glacier Point Road and Highway 41, you can stay at the Bridalveil Creek Campground (section A) and the Wawona Campground.

The campsites cost $14–18. Some are first-come, first-served; others are by reservation only. Call 800/436-7275 for reservation information, or 209/372-0299 for park information. Rates to enter Yosemite are $20 per car, and the pass you'll get is good for one week; www.nps.gov/yose.

PLACES TO STAY

Apple Tree Inn: Towering sugar pines surround the 18 new townhouselike cabins that make up the Apple Tree Inn. It's tree city here, which is excellent news for dogs of the male persuasion. The Sierra National Forest is right across the street, and that's wonderful for all dogs. Yosemite National Park (see above) is just two miles down the road.

This is a very peaceful place to stay, and the cabin rooms are beautifully designed. Dogs can't stay in the upstairs rooms (which are actually suites), but they're welcome at all the first-floor rooms. Surprisingly, this serene resort is home to a delightfully unserene racquetball court, and to an indoor pool and spa. Rates are $99–179. Dogs are $50 per visit. 1110 Highway 41, Fish Camp 93623; 559/683-5111 or 888/683-5111; www.appletreeinn-yosemite.com.

Narrow Gauge Inn: Stay here and you're just a bone's throw from the dog-friendly Sugar Pine Railroad and four miles from Yosemite National Park (see above). This is an old-fashioned country-style inn. Most of the 26 guest rooms are on the small side, but they sport terrific mountain views, making them feel larger. The dog rooms are on the first level of the three-story inn, and all have balcony entrances. Dogs enjoy the property's tall trees, short trail, and seasonal creek. People like taking a dip in the heated outdoor pool or soaking in the hot tub. (Dogs would too, but they have to stick to the creek.) Rates are

DIVERSION

Take a Sentimental Journey: If you're hankering to ride the old Logger Steam Train through some of Sierra National Forest's most magnificent scenery, you don't have to worry about waving good-bye to your dog. Leashed, calm dogs who can fit on your lap are welcome aboard the quaint old trains of the **Sugar Pine Railroad.** (In other words, 85-pound wiggly Jake Dog is not a good candidate.) Rates for the hour-long Logger ride are $14 for adults, $7 for kids. Dogs don't pay a cent.

If your dog is shy of loud noises, get as far back from the engine as possible, or simply take the railroad's "Model A"–powered trip. It's quieter, shorter (30 minutes), and cheaper ($10 per adult, $5 per child) than the Logger train.

For fairly obvious reasons, no dogs are allowed on the evening dinner ride. The train station is at 56001 Highway 41. It's about 12 miles past Oakhurst, two miles before the town of Fish Camp. And there's a terrific fringe benefit: It's right next to a couple of trailheads into dog-friendly Sierra National Forest. 559/683-7273; www.ymsprr.com.

$79–149. Dogs are $25 extra per visit. 48571 Highway 41, Fish Camp 93623; 559/683-7720; www.narrowgaugeinn.com.

The Redwoods in Yosemite: This group of lovely, privately owned mountain homes is by far the best thing that's ever happened to dogs in Yosemite. The Redwoods is nestled in the forest at 4,000 feet, where the air is so clean you can smell it. The homes range in size from cozy one-bedroom cottages to big five-bedroom spreads. They're all different, but they're attractive and woodsy, and most have decks and fireplaces.

General manager Pamela Kornell is a very dog-friendly person. She's trying to get as many homes as possible to open their doors to dogs. So far, 30 of the Redwoods' 125 homes say yes. Some are really magical, with wide picture windows and huge stone fireplaces.

Dogs who stay here get to peruse the surrounding area on leash. They can sniff at trees and cruise by streams. This is much more than they can do in the rest of the park. There's even a little market, the Pine Tree, where dogs can often be seen waiting for their people to finish shopping.

Homes rent for a minimum of 2–3 days. Rates are $115–650 a night. Dogs are $10 extra. P.O. Box 2085, Wawona, Yosemite National Park, CA 95389; 209/375-6666 or 888/225-6666; www.redwoodsinyosemite.com.

Carmel

The most dog-friendly place in the United States

Dogs feel more welcome in this picturesque village than almost anywhere in the world. Maybe there's an aura emanating from dog-lover Doris Day's Cypress Inn or the other gorgeous, super-dog-friendly inns here. Or perhaps it's the tantalizing dog burgers (that's burgers for dogs, lest a gruesome image flashed through your head) served at the wonderful Le Coq d'Or, or the dog burgers on pooch plates and the water served to dogs in champagne buckets at the delightful Portabella restaurant, or the biscuits offered to art-loving pooches at the Rodrigue Studio (formerly known as Galerie Blue Dog), or the dog menu offered at the Forge in the Forest, the Plaza Café and Grill, and Lenny's Deli. Of course, that welcome feeling could well come from knowing that Carmel City Beach, one of the most enticing beaches in California, lets pooches run leashless, as does the Mission Trail Park. And more well-read dogs might somehow know that the two local weekly papers have gone to the dogs—they feature regular columns about Carmel's canines.

Whatever the case, your dog can't help but be happy in Carmel, which in these busy times still shuns the idea of street addresses. You won't have a problem finding your destinations, though, because the village is small enough and the people are friendly enough that it's very hard to stay lost for long—especially with a dog at your side.

PARKS, BEACHES, AND RECREATION AREAS

Carmel City Beach

The fine white sand crunches underfoot as you and your leash-free dog explore this pristine beach. It's the only beach for many, many miles that allows dogs off their leashes, so it's a real gem for dog travelers. Bordered by cypress trees and a walking trail, the beach is also popular among humans, especially on weekends. So if your dog is the type to mark beach blankets and eat things out of other peoples' picnic baskets, you may want to leash him until you find a less crowded part of the beach.

Poop bags are available at dispensers here, but it's a good idea to bring your own just in case doggy demand is high and they run out. From Highway 1, take the Ocean Avenue exit all the way to the end, where you'll find a large parking area that's not large enough on summer weekends. 831/624-3543.

PLACES TO EAT

The Forge in the Forest: Dogs would give this wonderful restaurant five paws up if they had five paws. They get to dine with their humans at a delightful

outdoor area, which is warmed by an outdoor fireplace when a chill sets in. Better yet, lucky dogs get to order from their very own dog menu! They get to choose from several dishes, including the Quarter Hounder (a burger patty, $3.95), Hot Diggity Dog (all-beef kosher hot dog, $3.95), and the Good Dog, which the menu announces is "for the very, very good dog." The Good Dog is six ounces of grilled juicy New York steak. The cost: $12.95. Several dogs have been treated to the Good Dog, according to dog-loving co-owner Donna. It's generally bought as a birthday treat, or when the dog's person is celebrating something special.

If you don't feel like spending any money for your dog's dining, that's OK too. All dogs get dog treats here. The price: The wag of a tail. Oh, did we mention that the food for humans is delicious too? You can choose from a very wide array of seafood, pastas, gourmet pizzas, sandwiches, soups, and salads.

This heavenly eatery is on the southwest corner of 5th Avenue and Junipero Street; 831/624-2233.

Lenny's Deli: Get yourself some fine New York/California deli food (try the lox), and let your dog choose her lunch from her very own menu. Lucky dogs here can get anything from dog food to steak. If your dog can't read, just get whatever her nose points to when she sniffs her menu.

Dog menu prices are just a tad above the prices on the kid's menu. (And kids don't get to choose kibble.) Dine at the umbrella-topped courtyard tables here. Lenny's is in Carmel Plaza, at the corner of Ocean Avenue and Junipero Street; 831/624-5265.

Portabella: If you love unique French, Italian, and Spanish food, and if your dog loves being treated like the toast of the town, come to this elegant, yet casual, *ristorante*. Among the mouthwatering dishes are ravioli with pan-fried goat cheese and sun-dried tomatoes (my personal favorite). It's truly to drool for. You can get all kinds of Mediterranean-style dishes and fresh seafood here, but you can also get ye ol' basic hamburger. Dogs think that's very cool.

And they think it's even cooler that they're given water, and that the water comes not in a bowl but in a champagne bucket. It's enough to make even the most earthy mutt feel just a bit classy. Jake the Dog's first time with the champagne bucket was an embarrassingly noisy affair. The sound of his giant slurps echoed loudly off the walls of the semienclosed back patio, causing a bit of a titter among the patient diners. "Your dog was so good," said a fellow diner when we passed in the street later. "And so quiet, except when he drank."

Many dogs come here and order from the children's menu. Portabella is on Ocean Avenue between Lincoln and Monte Verde Streets; 831/624-4395.

PLACES TO STAY

Carmel River Inn: Lucky dogs who stay here get treated to some biscuits and a water bowl when they check in. And that's just the start: The 24 attractively furnished cottages here are sprinkled around 10 acres of lush, peaceful gardens. Dogs like it so much that many somehow convince their humans to keep coming here year after year. "We get lots of return guests with dogs," says an innkeeper. A few cottages are tiny; others are very generously sized. Many have fireplaces, which makes for a cozy picture if your dog likes to curl up in front of the hearth at night. (As opposed to the sprawled-out-like-he's-been-shot-in-a-bad-Western-movie position Jake assumes in front of a crackling fire.)

Rates are $125–350. Dogs are $10 extra. The inn is on Highway 1 at the Carmel River Bridge. The mailing address: P.O. Box 221609, Carmel 93922; 831/624-1575 or 800/882-8142; www.carmelriverinn.com.

Cypress Inn: Dogs get the royal treatment here, in part because actress and animal activist Doris Day owns this sumptuous hotel. The stately Moorish Mediterranean-style inn is very elegant, with fine oak floors and delicate antiques, but you never feel out of place with your dog. Day's staff makes sure your dog feels especially welcome, right down to offering pet beds and pet food for your four-legged friend. The hotel staff will help get you a pet-sitter, should you decide to venture out on your own without your dog. (We doubt your pooch will say *"que sera, sera"* to this idea. Carmel is so dog-friendly you can easily do the whole scene with him. But some very friendly, excellent pet-sitters are available through the hotel if you can stand your dog's hound-dog look when you leave.)

No two rooms are the same here, but they're all enchanting, relaxing, and first-rate. The rooms come with extras not offered by most hotels, including fresh flowers, bottled water, fresh fruit, your very own decanter of sherry, and occasional chocolates. In addition, for an extra fee you can partake in a delightful afternoon tea in the inn's gorgeous library bar. Dogs are even welcome to join you for cocktails there.

Rates are $125–500. It's $25 extra for one pooch, $40 for two. The inn is at Lincoln Street and 7th Avenue, and the mailing address is P.O. Box Y, Carmel 93921; 831/624-3871; www.cypress-inn.com.

Sunset House: It's hard to know where to start a description of this attractive, romantic, extremely dog- and people-friendly inn. The wonderful former owners, the Pikes, have moved on, but the new owners, Ray and Diane Roeder, are following in their footsteps with their hospitality and wonderful service.

First, a little about the Sunset House itself. The house was built in the 1960s to be a bed-and-breakfast inn, so all four of the rooms are large (600 square feet), with real brick wood-burning fireplaces that are match-ready, and private bathrooms. The rooms are airy, yet cozy, and are furnished beautifully with a mixture of antiques and classic contemporary furniture. The two dog-friendly rooms have private entrances. Our favorite, the Porpoise Suite, has a whirlpool tub and canopy bed. The inn is in an attractive residential neighborhood, where it's a very short, two-minute walk to leash-free Carmel City Beach and the quaint shops of Carmel.

Now a little about the service: The staff welcomes canine and human guests with gift baskets. Humans get a smallish bottle of wine, some crackers, and other tasty treats. Dogs get treats of a different ilk, toys, and towels (for après-beach). In the morning fresh fruit, juice, coffee, and yogurt are delivered to your room. In addition, you'll get a breakfast certificate to be redeemed at one of four premiere restaurants nearby. By the time you read this, there should be an evening cordials hour, too.

There's so much here that you might be tempted to stick close by. But here's something that may lure you back to the road: At press time, the Roeders were working out a system where dogs and their people could get use of one of their shiny classic cars from the '50s or early '60s. Can't you just picture driving down the beautiful Pacific Coast Highway in one of these timeless machines, top down (or up if your pooch prefers), just enjoying the sunshine and the breeze off the ocean?

Rates for the dog-friendly rooms are $210–230. Dogs pay a $25 fee for the length of their stay. The inn is on Camino Real, between Ocean and 7th Avenues, and the mailing address is P.O. Box 1925, Carmel 93921; 831/626-7100 or 877/966-9100; www.sunsethousecarmel.com.

San Simeon Area
Where a dog's hotel is his castle

PLACES TO STAY

Best Western Cavalier Oceanfront Resort: This is San Simeon's only ocean-front hotel, and it's one of the most attractive and well-run Best Westerns we've ever checked out. (But don't let its brochure get your hopes up: The picture on the cover is not of the Best Western. It's Hearst Castle.) Many of the 90 rooms have a wood-burning fireplace, a stocked minibar, close-up ocean views, and a private patio. There's even room service, so you and your dog can dine together in the comfort of your own seaside abode. The humans in your party can keep in shape in the fitness room or at the two outdoor pools here (with ocean views to drool for). And if you stay here, you and your leashed pooch will have easy access to the long beach that backs up to the lodging. This is a huge deal right now, because no other beach in the area permits pooches.

Sunny Dog, a canine reader from Dayton, Ohio, had his person, Peggy, describe what they love most about their visits here: "It is quite delightful to sit on your patio and drink in that fabulous ocean view. The firepits (surrounded by chairs) are lit at sunset and left burning through the night for those folks that want to enjoy the fire, the sound of the ocean, and the distant light from the Piedras Blancas Lighthouse." Nice writing, Sunny.

Many people are tempted to leave their dogs in their rooms when they go explore magnificent Hearst Castle, but this is a big no-no. The Cavalier makes it easy for you to do the right thing: It provides numbers for dog-sitters and for a wonderful kennel. Be forewarned, though: At busy times, you need to make dog-care reservations well ahead of your visit.

Rates are $119–279. 9415 Hearst Drive 93452; 805/927-4688 or 800/826-8168; www.cavalierresort.com.

Fogcatcher Inn: If your dog has a look of panic on his face while reading this over your shoulder, reassure him you're not taking him to the Dog-catcher Inn. (This is how I first read the sign, and I figure if I can make that mistake, dogs can too.) In fact, this is one of the most relaxing and lovely places you could stay with a dog in these parts. The inn has a lovely English country style, with vaulted ceilings and gardens that are to drool for almost all year-round. The rooms are spacious and well appointed, and each has a fireplace, microwave, and fridge. The heated outdoor pool has a decent ocean view, and a free hot breakfast buffet comes with your stay here. (No beasts at the buffet, please. We know how literally dogs take the phrase "all you can eat.")

What dogs like best is that they get a dog biscuit or two or three upon check-in. As for size limits, don't worry: "Last weekend we had a big German shepherd and a little Pekingese," says Mike, who loves doggy guests. "We take any good dog." Two rooms allow pets. Rates are $119–320. Dogs are $25 extra. 6400 Moonstone Beach Drive, Cambria 93428; 805/927-1400 or 800/425-4121; www.fogcatcherinn.com.

Santa Barbara
California's Riviera

PLACES TO STAY

Fess Parker's DoubleTree Resort: At first glance, the name "Fess Parker" and the word "luxury" make strange bedfellows. After all, Fess was the actor who brought American frontiersman Davy Crockett and Daniel Boone into millions of homes in the 1950s and '60s. But while Fess Parker's characters are synonymous with sweat and grit, the real Fess Parker, a long-time Santa Barbara County resident, is known for his good taste and good business sense. (He also owns a respected winery in the county.)

Fess, who hails from Texas, likes things big. The seaside resort has 337 luxurious guest rooms. It's set on a sprawling 24 acres. Standard rooms are a spacious 450 square feet. He also likes things first-class. The rooms are attractive and comfortable, with feather pillows (unless you're allergic), high-quality bath products, evening turndown service, and excellent views. Suites are especially spacious and attractive. The resort even has its own spa, billed as a "French sea spa."

We think Fess must also like dogs, because dogs get the royal treatment here. Fess Parker's dog guests don't have to watch hungrily as you chow down on your tasty room service meal: They can order their own. The in-room pooch dining menu includes premium ground sirloin, a quality brand wet dog food, and gourmet dog cookies. And if you really want to treat your dog, canine massages are available. For $65, your dog can get a 40-minute in-room massage from a dog-knowledgeable massage therapist from the resort's spa. The massage is supposed to be especially good for arthritic dogs.

Although the resort is across from the beach, it's a beach you can't visit with your dog friend. Try the path that runs along the beach's edge if being near the water is your wish. Otherwise, the 24-acre resort has ample room for romping with your leashed friend. Be sure to clean up after your dog.

Rates are $269–349. 633 East Cabrillo Boulevard, Santa Barbara 93103; 805/564-4333 or 800/222-8733; www.fpdtr.com.

Rancho Oso Guest Ranch and Stables: Dogs and people who enjoy the Old West love staying at Rancho Oso. It's not historic, but it looks that way. You can stay in one of five rustic one-room cabins with knotty pine walls and bunk beds. Or if you really hanker for your pooch to be a "dawgie," try one of the 10 covered wagons here. You bring the sleeping bag, the ranch provides the army cots. They're loads of fun to stay in, and they make for great photo backdrops.

The ranch is on 310 acres of hills with enough trees for decent shade in the summer. You can walk your dog on the many trails, but keep her on a leash, because a lot of horses jog on the trails too. In fact, if you want to ride a horse yourself, you can set that up back at the ranch office. Guided trail rides are offered year-round. (Lots of folks come here to camp with their horses, but that's through a members-only camping organization, and that's a horse of a different color so we won't go into detail.)

Rates are $79–89 for cabins, $54 for wagons. Dogs are $5 extra. 3750 Paradise Road, Santa Barbara 93105; 805/683-5686; www.rancho-oso.com.

San Ysidro Ranch: A word to the pooches who plan to come here: You lucky dogs! This top-notch 540-acre resort (where Laurence Olivier and Vivien Leigh wed and Jackie and John F. Kennedy honeymooned) is treat enough. But dogs who stay here get the truly royal treatment, also known as the Privileged Pet Program. The ranch has been offering the program to pooches for more than a century. Here's how it goes:

Upon registering at the Pet Register and wolfing down some tasty peanut butter biscuits, the guest dog goes to his cottage and finds his name and his accompanying human's name on a sign outside his cottage door. Inside, he'll be greeted by a basketful of VIP goodies, including a bowl filled with squeak toys, rawhides, tennis balls, cookies, and a two-liter bottle of Pawier water. His bed is soft and cedar-stuffed.

A room-service pet menu offers several dining items, including biscuits, ravioli, cheeseburgers, canned dog food, and even New York steak. If we could afford to stay here, Jake would surely check off every item on the list, vacuum it down, and wait patiently at the door for room service to deliver the next course.

Pooches who stay here can also get a luxury most people would drool for: a professional massage. A "slow and gentle" massage is said to increase circulation, help aches and pains, and soothe away fears. A half-hour massage costs $65. (Really.)

Dogs must stay in one of the ranch's 21 freestanding cottages. Rates are $399–4,100. There's a $100 fee for the length of your dog's stay. Dog menu items are extra. You must let the staff know ahead of time that you'll be coming with your pooch so appropriate arrangements can be made. 900 San Ysidro Lane 93108; 805/969-5046; www.sanysidroranch.com.

INDEXES

Accommodations Index

Camping

Restaurant Index

General Index

Keeping Current

Note to All Dog Lovers

While the information in these pages is as current as possible, changes to fees, regulations, parks, roads, and trails are often made after we go to press. Businesses can close, change their ownership, or change their rules. Earthquakes, fires, rainstorms, and other natural phenomena can radically change the condition of parks, hiking trails, and wilderness areas. Before you and your dog begin your travels, please be certain to call the phone number in each listing for updated information.

Attention, Dogs of the Bay Area

Our readers mean everything to us. We explore the Bay Area so that you and your people can spend true quality time together. Your input to this book is very important. In the last few years, we've heard from many wonderful dogs and their humans about new dog-friendly places or old dog-friendly places we didn't know about. If we've missed your favorite park, beach, outdoor restaurant, hotel, or activity, please let us know by contacting us at the address below. We'll check out the tip, and if it turns out to be a good one, we'll include it in the next edition, along with a thank-you to the dog and/or person who sent in the suggestion.

> *The Dog Lover's Companion to the Bay Area*
> Avalon Travel Publishing
> 1400 65th Street, Suite 250
> Emeryville, CA 94608, USA
> email: atpfeedback@avalonpub.com

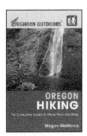